COORDINATION

OXFORD STUDIES IN COMPARATIVE SYNTAX
RICHARD KAYNE, *General Editor*

Principles and Parameters of Syntactic Saturation
GERT WEBELHUTH

*Verb Movement and the Expletive Subjects
in the Germanic Languages*
STEN VIKNER

Parameters and Functional Heads: Essays in Comparative Syntax
EDITED BY ADRIANA BELLETTI AND LUIGI RIZZI

Discourse Configurational Languages
EDITED BY KATALIN É. KISS

Clause Structure and Language Change
EDITED BY ADRIAN BATTYE AND IAN ROBERTS

*Dialect Variation and Parameter Setting:
A Study of Belfast English and Standard English*
ALISON HENRY

Parameters of Slavic Morphosyntax
STEVEN FRANKS

The Polysynthesis Parameter
MARK C. BAKER

Coordination
JANNE BONDI JOHANNESSEN

COORDINATION

Janne Bondi Johannessen

New York   Oxford

OXFORD UNIVERSITY PRESS

*This book has been printed digitally and produced in a standard specification
in order to ensure its continuing availability*

OXFORD
UNIVERSITY PRESS

Great Clarendon Street, Oxford OX2 6DP

Oxford University Press is a department of the University of Oxford.
It furthers the University's objective of excellence in research, scholarship,
and education by publishing worldwide in

Oxford New York

Auckland Cape Town Dar es Salaam Hong Kong Karachi
Kuala Lumpur Madrid Melbourne Mexico City Nairobi
New Delhi Shanghai Taipei Toronto
With offices in
Argentina Austria Brazil Chile Czech Republic France Greece
Guatemala Hungary Italy Japan South Korea Poland Portugal
Singapore Switzerland Thailand Turkey Ukraine Vietnam

Oxford is a registered trade mark of Oxford University Press
in the UK and in certain other countries

Published in the United States
by Oxford University Press Inc., New York

ISBN 978-0-19-823709-9

Preface

This book is a descendant of my Ph.D. dissertation, completed in 1993. Many of the theoretical assumptions and conclusions are the same. One major departure from the thesis is the account of "shared material," which is no longer one of "fusion" or "merging," but of deletion. The sections on multiple coordination and CoP adverbs (often called "discontinous" or "initial" conjunctions) are considerably expanded. The concept of "pseudocoordination" is also discussed. More linguistic data have been added, and the discussions of other literature and theories have been updated.

The book has benefitted from very helpful comments from two anonymous OUP referees, and from the two external members of my thesis committee—Elisabet Engdahl and Kjartan Ottósson. My two thesis supervisors were naturally very important. Helge Lødrup shared his knowledge with me, presented challenging criticisms, and was always eager to engage in fruitful discussions on various topics of the thesis. Cathrine Fabricius Hansen gave me great encouragement, offered insightful comments, and made continual and not in the end entirely fruitless efforts to make me approach coordination from a semantic perspective.

Students and staff at the Department of Linguistics, University of Oslo, have meant a lot. I would like to mention Rolf Theil Endresen, Jan Tore Lønning, Kjetil Strand, and Arnfinn Vonen, as well as Trond Kirkeby-Garstad and Kjell Johan Sæbø, for their ever willingness to take part in discussions. Several other people at the Faculty of Arts have been helpful in providing data and helping me with translations.

I spent the year of 1990 as a visitor at the Centre for Cognitive Science, University of Edinburgh. I am extremely grateful for the inspiration I received from the active research atmosphere of students and staff there, especially Elisabet Engdahl, David Adger, Guy Barry, Glyn Morrill, Martin Pickering, and Catrin Siân Rhys.

Many of the main ideas of the theory presented here were developed in May–June 1992. I must express my gratitude to David Adger, whose enthusiasm was a great motivation to pursue those ideas. Special thanks are also due to Greville Corbett, who sent me a paper on Qafar, written by himself and R. J. Hayward, which led me to see the universal tendencies presented in this work.

I have benefitted from correspondence with Richard De Armond, Bob Borsley, Annabel Cormack, Marjan Grootveld, Aaron Halpern, Eric Hoekstra, Teun Hoekstra, Dick Hudson, Paul Kershaw, David Milward, Herb Stahlke, Peter Svenonious, and Mary Tait. Some of them contacted me after I had had a posting at the electronic Linguist List, and I want also to thank several of the other participants on the List for sending me examples.

I want to thank my parents, family, and friends for having provided practical help in different ways, Jonathan for his support in discussions as well as in many other ways, and Edvard and William, whose exuberance provides a forced but very welcome relief from academic pursuits.

J.B.J.

Blindern, 6 January 1997

Conjunction junction, what's your function?
Hooking up words and phrases and clauses
Conjunction junction, how's that function?
I got three favorite cars that get most of my job done
Conjunction junction, what's their function?
I got "and," "but," and "or" for getting the job done

(From an American children's song)

Contents

1 Introduction

  1.1 General introduction   1
  1.2 Framework   4
  1.3 Data   5
  1.4 Miscellania   6

2 Unbalanced and Extraordinary Balanced Coordination

  2.1 Introduction   7
  2.2 Unbalanced coordination   7
    2.2.1 Nominal unbalanced coordination   9
      2.2.1.1 Receiving-type UC   9
      2.2.1.2 Assigning-type UC   25
    2.2.2 Verbal unbalanced coordination   34
      2.2.2.1 Receiving-type UC   34
      2.2.2.2 Assigning-type UC   38
    2.2.3 Clausal unbalanced coordination   39
  2.3 Delimiting unbalanced coordination   42
    2.3.1 Morpho-syntactic UC   42
      2.3.1.1 Affix or adposition?   43
      2.3.1.2 Coordination or subordination?   46
      2.3.1.3 "Pseudocoordination"   48
    2.3.2 Semantic-pragmatic UC   52
    2.3.3 Extraction causing UC   54
  2.4 UG and UC   54
  2.5 Extraordinary balanced coordination   60
    2.5.1 Assigning-type EBC   60
    2.5.2 Receiving-type EBC   61
  2.6 Summary   66

3 Conjunctions as Heads

  3.1 Introduction   74
  3.2 The head-status of conjunctions   74
    3.2.1 Semantic argument or functor   75
    3.2.2 Determining agreement   76
    3.2.3 Morphosyntactic locus   78

3.2.4 Subcategoriser   79
3.2.5 Distributional equivalent   81
3.2.6 Obligatoriness   82
    3.2.6.1 Overt conjunctions   82
    3.2.6.2 Empty conjunctions   84
3.2.7 Uniqueness   91
3.2.8 X^0-element   92
3.2.9 Determining word order   92
3.2.10 Projecter of features to CoP   93
3.2.11 Summary   96
3.3 Is the conjunction a functional or a lexical head?   96
3.3.1 Closed lexical class   97
3.3.2 Phonological and morphological dependence   98
3.3.3 Only one complement   98
3.3.4 Inseparable from their complement   99
3.3.5 Lack of "descriptive contents"   100
3.3.6 The head as a D-structure projection   102
3.3.7 The difference between functional and lexical
    projections   103
3.3.8 Summary   104
3.4 Summary and concluding remarks   105

4 The Conjunction Phrase

4.1 Introduction   108
4.2 The structure of the conjunction phrase   108
4.3 The role of CoP in unbalanced coordination   113
4.3.1 Nominal UC   113
    4.3.1.1 Case: assignment, licencing, default,
    overcorrection   119
        4.3.1.1.1 The conjunction—a case
        assigner?   119
        4.3.1.1.2 The conjunction—a licencer of
        default case   120
        4.3.1.1.3 Overcorrection in English   123
4.3.2 Verbal UC   127
4.3.3 Clausal UC   131
4.4 The role of CoP in balanced coordination   136
4.4.1 Extraordinary balanced coordination   136
4.4.2 Ordinary balanced coordination   139

4.5 UC, EBC, and OBC, and (parametric) variation   140
    4.5.1 Coordination in language acquisition   142
4.6 Multiple coordination   143
4.7 CoP adverbs   154
4.8 Alternative approaches to conjunction phrases
suggested in the literature   162
    4.8.1 Munn's theory   163
       4.8.1.1 Some advantages of Munn's theory   164
       4.8.1.2 Some problems in Munn's theory   164
    4.8.2 Grootveld's theory   166
       4.8.2.1 Some advantages of Grootveld's theory   166
       4.8.2.1 Some problems in Grootveld's theory   167
    4.8.3 Borsley's view   167
4.9 Summary   169

5   Coordinate-Alpha

5.1 Introduction   175
5.2 The coordinate-alpha transformation   175
5.3 Reduction   177
    5.3.1 Deletion   178
       5.3.1.1 Small conjunct coordination   180
    5.3.2 Other approaches to reduction   189
       5.3.2.1 Van Oirsouw's deletion approach   190
       5.3.2.2 Goodall's three-dimensional approach   193
       5.3.2.3 Johannessen's (1993c) approach   200
       5.3.2.4 Wesche's sharing approach   201
5.4 CoP components—full CPs or simplex categories?   204
    5.4.1 Other approaches to input categories   205
       5.4.1.1 Phrase-structure theory   206
       5.4.1.2 Categorial grammar   209
       5.4.1.3 Transformational theories   211
5.5 Summary   211

6   Extraction out of CoP

6.1. Introduction   214
6.2. The CSC–ATB principles and examples of violations   215
    6.2.1 Examples of violation of the first part of the
       CSC–ATB   215
    6.2.2 Examples of violation of the second part of the
       CSC–ATB   217

6.3. The analysis of CSC–ATB violations 218
    6.3.1 The analysis of split coordination as extraction
         of whole conjuncts 219
    6.3.2 A revised analysis of split coordination 222
    6.3.3 The analysis of extraction of part of conjuncts 228
6.4 Summary 235

7 Semantic and Thematic Issues

7.1 Introduction 237
7.2 Semantics 237
    7.2.1 Coordination and subordination 238
        7.2.1.1 Cross-linguistic variation in the
             distribution of conjunctions 239
    7.2.2 The origin of conjunctions 244
    7.2.3 Problem areas defined by semanticists 245
    7.2.4 Summary 250
7.3 Thematic properties 251
    7.3.1 Thematic roles and the lexicon 251
    7.3.2 Thematic problems 253
        7.3.2.1 Conjuncts with unacceptable different
             thematic roles 253
        7.3.2.2 Conjuncts with acceptable different
             thematic roles 256
    7.3.3 Grimshaw's argument structure 257
        7.3.3.1 The thematic dimension 258
        7.3.3.2 The aspectual dimension 261
        7.3.3.3 Problems with the aspectual dimension 262
    7.3.4 Summary 266
7.4 Summary 266

8 Conclusion 270

References 273

General index 285

1

Introduction

1.1. General introduction

In this book, a theory of coordination will be suggested in which the two most important components are the structure of the conjunction phrase (CoP) and the way the conjuncts are attached to the conjunction phrase by a generalized transformation ("coordinate-alpha"). Two kinds of coordination not previously discussed to any great extent in the literature will be presented—they strongly support the analysis put forward here.

Most theories of coordination can handle the archetypical case where two categories of the same syntactic and semantic kind are coordinated. It is not in such simple cases, however, that we can evaluate different theories. Less straightforward types of coordination include, for example, non-constituent coordination, gapping, and coordination of unlike syntactic categories. It is with respect to these and other such phenomena that theories differ. In this book, two challenging kinds of coordination are presented and discussed extensively—they are what I shall call unbalanced coordination (UC) and extraordinary balanced coordination (EBC), exemplified in the Norwegian (1) and the English (2), respectively:

(1) [Han   og meg]   var sammen om   det
    he.NOM and me.ACC were together about it
    'He and I were in it together.'
                                    (Berntsen and Larsen 1925:268)

(2) [Them and us] are going to the game together
                                    (Stahlke 1984:360)

In UC constructions, one of the conjuncts is of the expected, or normal, kind, and one is deviant. In (1), the CoP is in a subject position, which makes us expect nominative case on the conjuncts. However, only the first conjunct has nominative case, the other has the deviant accusative case. In a simplex, non-coordinated structure, accusative case would of course have been impossible on the subject constituent. The EBC construction in (2), again a CoP in subject position, is one in which both conjuncts unexpectedly have accusative case, i.e., both are deviant.

In Norwegian and English, UC and EBC constructions are not universally accepted as good data; they are most often found in colloquial speech among not so upwardly mobile persons. They have, therefore, with a few exceptions, been regarded as marginal. During the work on these constructions, I have encountered many other languages that also have UC and EBC constructions. Interestingly, in several of these languages, too, such constructions are regarded as marginal by the grammarians describing them. There is, to my knowledge, nobody who has studied UC and EBC constructions as phenomena in their own right, neither within one language nor cross-linguistically.

The lack of interest in such constructions has led to the fact that important cross-linguistic, universal generalizations have remained hidden. In this book, we shall look at examples of UC constructions from 32 languages. In at least 26 of them, it turns out that the order between conjunction and deviant conjunct is the same as that between verb and complement in each language (some of the remaining 6 languages are difficult to assess with respect to word order). Furthermore, it seems that the way the deviant conjunct differs can be predicted; for example, case-wise, it will have the default case of the language, and tense-aspect-wise, it will have the most general tense-aspect, if any. EBC constructions, too, seem to deviate in a systematic way from ordinary balanced coordination. There is, therefore, important insight to be gained from studying these constructions. UC and EBC constructions are discussed in Chapter 2.

The fact that there is a correlation in word order between the conjunction and the deviant conjunct on the one hand, and the verb and its complement on the other, justifies the question of whether the conjunction is head of a phrase. Various head properties have been discussed in the literature. We shall examine the conjunction with respect to these criteria, of which there are two types: "pretheoretic" criteria and criteria for functional head-hood. Although not all the criteria are equally applicable, the conclusion is that the conjunction is a head with respect to both types of criteria. This discussion can be found in Chapter 3.

If conjuncts are heads, then conjunction phrases must be projections of them. According to the classic X-bar theory, there will be a specifier and a complement position, which we can assume are the positions of the conjuncts. The structure of the phrase is vital for explaining why the conjuncts in specifier positions are the normal ones, while those in complement positions can be deviant. The head status of the conjunction is very important for both UC and EBC constructions; spec-head agreement leads to a projection of the specifier conjunct, but not of the complement one, resulting in UC. For some speakers/dialects/languages, CoP is a category that is interpreted as different from the categories of its conjuncts; a $CoP_{[DP]}$ (a CoP of DP conjuncts) is, in other words, a category different from a DP, and cannot get case or assign agreement features as other DPs. It therefore only gets the features available for categories not being able to receive features on their own, such as default case (resulting in EBC). UC and EBC are analyzed in Chapter 4.

The conjuncts are attached to the CoP by a generalized transformation, coordinate-alpha; it takes two full CPs as input and attaches the specifier and complement of a CoP to some category on each of the CP structures. The fact that it can only work on CPs has a number of advantages. For example, non-constituent coordination is easily accounted for: whatever is below the attachment points of the CoP is considered conjuncts, whether it is a single constituent, several constituents or part of a constituent, or some combination of these. Whatever is not coordinated is deleted. Furthermore, coordination of unlike categories is constrained by the requirement that only CPs can be input structures; such structures ensure that only subcategorized arguments are present, and it follows that not just any category can occur as a conjunct in just any CoP. Although coordinate-alpha can attach any conjuncts to a CoP, and there are no explicit constraints, there is still only a small subset of all coordinations that will be allowed. The rest are ruled out as violations of X-bar theory and deletion rules. Coordinate-alpha and deletion are accounted for in Chapter 5.

A phenomenon that has received a lot of interest in the literature is extraction out of CoP; neither whole conjuncts nor parts of conjuncts have been assumed in the literature to be extractable, unless extracted from all the conjuncts (the Coordinate Structure Constraint and Across-the-board Principle). We shall look at this phenomenon and conclude that while extraction of whole conjuncts must be considered impossible, extraction out of parts of conjuncts is always possible in principle, if there is sufficient semantic and pragmatic context for there to be a predicating link between the conjuncts. Chapter 6 discusses extraction out of CoP.

The syntactic structure of CoP is very similar to that of subordinated structures; the main difference is possibly the number of arguments. This similarity may be surprising, but it turns out that there is some semantic similarity between coordination and subordination. In a group of different constructions, where some are considered to be subordination and some coordination, languages draw the dividing line differently. Furthermore, some coordinating conjunctions have started out as subordinating ones. These, and more classical semantic problems (for example, the fact that coordination is non-compositional), as well as constraints on coordination due to thematic properties, are discussed in Chapter 7.

1.2. Framework

This book is written within the principles and parameters framework, and is to a large extent based on the same ideas as those proposed in the minimalist program (Chomsky 1995). Below, those aspects of the minimalist framework that are relevant for this book will be summarized.

The minimalist program sees language as embedded in a performance system of two general types: articulatory-perceptual and conceptual-intentional. The linguistic interface levels to these systems are phonetic form (PF) and (probably) logical form (LF). Language itself consists of two components: a lexicon and a computational system. The lexicon specifies the items which can enter into the computational system, which takes those items and computes them into pairs of interface representations. Since the computational system, the overt syntax, is assumed to be universally invariant, conditions on representations hold only at the interface levels. In the present book, there are no restrictions that are supposed to hold at the computational (syntactic) level. Coordinate-alpha may attach anywhere in any input structure (constrained only by what is given as input to the computational system, which is assumed to be propositional structures or CPs)—whether the resulting structure is acceptable depends on fundamental principles such as X-bar theory or violations of interface principles.

The computational system can only work on items of a particular kind; these are taken to be X-bar theoretic objects (Chomsky 1995:172). X-bar theory is crucial in the theory of coordination presented here, especially the terms "head," "spec-head relations," and "head-complement relations." Head-government is not a possible notion, meaning, e.g., that the way to assign case to an object is no longer done via government of a V or a P, but via spec-head agreement: the verb moves from its position to an Agr-O position, where it enters a spec-head relation with an NP sitting in [Spec, Agr-O''] (the verb afterwards moves to T and Agr-S).

The minimalist transformation is a generalized one (GT) which takes a phrase-marker K1 and inserts it into a designated empty position Ø in a phrase-marker K, forming a new phrase-marker K*, which satisifies X-bar theory (Chomsky 1995:189). If the resulting structure is not a single phrase-marker, the derivation crashes at PF. There is a slight difference between the transformation coordinate-alpha and GT; selection can happen from the lexicon at any point during the GT computation, while there is no access to the lexicon for coordinate-alpha, which is assumed to only operate on structures projected from the lexicon, i.e., CP-type structures.

Inflectional features are regarded as an intrinsic property of lexical items (Chomsky 1995:195). The features are then checked against the inflectional element in the position in which the item is inserted. If the two features match, they disappear. If they conflict, the inflectional feature remains, and the derivation will crash at PF; the features not being a legitimate PF object. For the theory of coordination in this book, assuming inflection to come from the lexicon rather than being assigned in the syntax is important. It makes it conceptually easier to understand why conjuncts may have deviant inflectional features, as they do in UC and EBC.

1.3. Data

A few words should be said about the languages under consideration and the collection of data generally. The languages from which the data are taken are not a representative sample in the ordinary sense; although they do come from all parts of the world, and they do represent many different language families, the number of languages from each varies considerably, and many families are (of course) not represented at all. The reason for this situation is the nature of the data; I have included the languages from which I have found examples, but it was difficult to find them in the first place.

Given the fact that in many languages, UC and EBC are non-standard, it is not only a problem to find informants who can give examples, but even grammar books which mention the phenomena. The way I have collected the data has therefore had to be unsystematic; looking through various grammar books in the library, asking people, etc. I have also had a general enquiry on the linguists network Linguist List, but the massive response mostly increased the amount of English data.

Another problem is the fact that coordination, including UC and EBC, can apply to any kind of category: verb, noun phrase, clause, prepositional phrase, etc. To find the interesting data in grammar books, one has to, in effect, go through all the chapters discussing the syntax of the various phrase types; sometimes only are the facts mentioned under a general heading of "coordination."

1.4. Miscellania

The present work is centred around the UC and EBC constructions, since these are for a great part new data, which should be considered for a theory of coordination. However, the theory of this book, of course, aims at being applicable to all kinds of coordination. Most of the coordinations discussed are conjunctive rather than adversative or disjunctive (coordination by "and" rather than "but" or "or"); the reason for this is due to the massive amount of conjunctive data. The theory is meant to include all kinds of coordination, and most of what is said will be equally applicable to the other types, except when otherwise stated. Furthermore, a majority of the data are examples of binary coordination, i.e., coordination with only two conjuncts. This does not mean that multiple coordination is excluded from discussion (the topic is discussed in Chapter 4), but it is done for convenience. However, it should be noted that the structure of CoP is always syntactically binary.

2

Unbalanced and Extraordinary Balanced Coordination

2.1. Introduction

There are two classes of coordinated structures which have been largely ignored in the literature. They have not been studied together, and have hardly been noted as a phenomenon at all. If they have been mentioned, it has usually been in a footnote, an appendix, or in the section on residual problems.[1] Sometimes they have been given more discussion, though; in the cases where these constructions are the norm rather than the exception.[2] The phenomena are very widespread in the languages of the world, but while they are the rule in some languages, they are non-standard in others. The two phenomena are unbalanced coordination (UC) and extraordinary balanced coordination (EBC), the first of which has one conjunct which deviates grammatically from what is expected in the position of that CoP, and the second of which both conjuncts deviate in this way.

In this chapter, we shall take a closer look at such constructions. In Section 2.2, we shall look at several examples of UC, which will give an idea of how widespread and diverse the phenomenon is. Some ways of delimiting the constructions which should be considered UC are discussed in 2.3. In Section 2.4, we shall see that the direction of unbalancedness correlates systematically with the general word-order properties in each language. In Section 2.5, we shall take a look at some instances of EBC. A summary of the chapter can be found in 2.6.

2.2. Unbalanced coordination

Unbalanced coordination is identified schematically in (1); one order of conjuncts is fine, the converse order is not.

(1) *Unbalanced coordination*:
   [X & Y] vs. *[Y & X]

The unbalancedness is due to some grammatical property lacking or being different in one conjunct compared to the other; e.g., one conjunct may have different case-marking from the other or lack number-marking. (1) is a representation of binary coordination; unbalancedness in multiple coordination also takes the form where only one conjunct has "normal" features (this will be discussed in Chapter 4).

At first glance, the phenomenon of unbalanced coordination might look diverse and arbitrary, or as if it is due to some adjacency or non-adjacency factor; when something is far away, it can be slightly deviant. However, we shall see that the unbalancedness correlates systematically with the general word-order facts of a language. Note that the description in (1) embraces more phenomena than are included in this chapter. In particular, gapping constructions (i.e., those in which a non-marginal element—usually a verb—is shared by both conjuncts) are not mentioned in this chapter.[3]

Although all UC is defined in terms of the figure in (1), we can intuitively divide it into two basic categories. One is the *receiving type*: only one conjunct has the grammatical features associated with the whole conjunction phrase (CoP).[4] This type is typically one where the CoP is in a position which is marked for case, but where only one conjunct is case-marked, or where all the conjuncts are interpreted as plural, but where only one is explicitly marked. It is exemplified in the Bergen Norwegian (2). Here, the whole CoP, being a subject, is checked for nominative case, but it is only marked on the first conjunct.

(2) Det sku'   bare mangle at   [eg   og deg]   ikkje sku'
    it should only lack   that I.NOM and you.ACC not   should
    gjere det
    do   it
    'Of course I and you would do it.'

(Larsen and Stoltz 1912:138)

The second type is the *assigning type*: one conjunct assigns features to whatever is surrounding the CoP, in spite of it possibly having conflicting features with other conjuncts. This type is typically one in which only one conjunct is responsible for agreement with elements outside the CoP. It is exemplified by the Czech (3):

(3) Půjdu   tam [já a   ty]
    will.go.1SG there I   and you
    'You and I will go there.'
                    (Trávníček 1949:433, cited in Corbett 1983:179)

Here, the conjuncts have conflicting person features, and the verb gets all
its agreement features from the first conjunct.

2.2.1. NOMINAL UNBALANCED COORDINATION

2.2.1.1. *Receiving-type UC*

A very common feature of this UC type is that only one of the conjuncts
is marked for the case which is assigned to the syntactic position in
which the CoP occurs. Most of the receiving-type UC examples below
have case as the unbalanced property, but we shall see some examples
from languages where number and person features can also occur in UC.
The latter kinds of features are not necessarily being received from another category. However, neither do they always assign features to other
categories, so they are not quite assigning features to other categories
either. Since they often co-occur with the receiving kind, they are categorized thus. The languages are presented alphabetically.

Burushaski
Burushaski is spoken by 40,000 people (Bright 1992:iv.42) in the moun-
tain areas of North Pakistan. It is not clear which linguistic family it belongs to; there are three major linguistic families represented in the same
area, viz. Indo-European, Tibeto-Burman, and Turkish (Morgenstierne
1935: p. vii, Bright 1992:iv.42).

UC with respect to case is a regular phenomenon in Burushaski; only
the last conjunct is case marked. This can be seen in the first conjunct
of the second CoP in (4). (The first CoP has pronouns in both its first
conjuncts, which makes it impossible to determine whether only the
first or both the first and the second conjuncts are exempt from case—
Burushaski does not distinguish between the relevant cases.[5]) The
Burushaski examples have been adapted and translated for presentation
by the present author.

(4) jɛ   kɛ uːŋ   kɛ miyu   oːltʌlik [iːmo
    I.NOM/ACC and thou.NOM/ACC and us.GEN.sons two   he.GEN
    wʌziːrtiŋ kɛ ʌkaːbiːrtiŋer] sɛnimi
    wazir.PL and grandee.PL.DAT he said
    'I and thou and our two sons, he said to his wazirs and grandees.'
                                                    (Lorimer 1935:381)

It frequently happens that a conjunction is dispensed with if "two nouns
are closely connected in thought and stand in the same grammatical relation to the rest of the sentence" (Lorimer 1935:105). In these cases, too,
only the last conjunct is marked with case features:

(5) [muː   muːmi.ɛ]   haːlʊm
    her.father her.mother.GEN house.from
    'from her father and mother's house'   (Lorimer 1935:105)

Dutch
Nominal unbalanced coordination may not be very widespread in Dutch,
but since there are several cases of clausal UC in Dutch (which will be
seen later in this chapter), showing that the phenomenon clearly exists in
the language, the nominal sentence below is included.

(6) ?Ik heb   niet alleen [de Kroaten in de Balkan voor ogen,
    I   have.1SG not alone the Croats in the Balkans for eyes
    maar ook zij   die elders   wonen]
    but also they.NOM who elsewhere live.PL
    'I have in mind not just the Croats who live in the Balkans, but
    also those living elsewhere.'
                          (NRC Handelsblad 21 Aug. 1992:7, quoted by
                                Jeroen Wiedenhof, Linguist List 24 Aug.)

The second conjunct in the object CoP of (6) has a nominative pronoun
zij rather than the expected *hen* or *hun*. The sentence was found by
Jeroen Wiedenhof in the monthly column of errors quoted from written
sources, in a magazine. The fact that it was printed there can be taken as
a hint that the kind of "mistake" was seen as more than a pure misprint.
Wiedenhof also finds the sentence much better, "less exceptional," than
the uncoordinated example in (7), thereby hinting to an explanation
which has to do with coordination rather than, e.g., the accompanying
relative clause.

(7) ??Ik heb   zij die elders   wonen voor ogen
    I have.1SG they who elsewhere live.PL for eyes
    'I have those living elsewhere in mind.'

Eastern Mari

In Eastern Mari,[6] a Uralic language spoken in the Volga area in Russia, unbalanced coordination is the rule rather than the exception for most morphosyntactic categories.[7] For instance, the preferred situation with respect to case-marking is one where only the final conjunct is marked (all Eastern Mari examples are provided by Trond Trosterud, p.c., unless otherwise stated):

(8) a. Məj Annan   [ydəržö   den ergəžəm]
    I   Anna.GEN daughter.3SG.POSS and son.3SG.POSS.ACC
    palem
    know.1SG
    'I know Anna's daughter and son.'

    b. *Məj Annan   [ydəržöm   den
    I   Anna.GEN daughter.3SG.POSS.ACC and
    ergəžəm]   palem
    son.3SG.POSS.ACC know.1SG
    'I know Anna's daughter and son.'

    c. Məj Annan   [ydəržö   den ergəžlan]
    I   Anna.GEN daughter.3SG.POSS and son.3SG.P.DAT
    knigam   puem
    book.ACC give.1SG
    'I give a book to Anna's daughter and son.'

    d. *Məj Annan   [ydəržəlan   den ergəžlan]
    I   Anna.GEN daughter.3SG.P.DAT and son.3SG.P.DAT
    knigam   puem
    book.ACC give.1SG
    'I give a book to Anna's daughter and son.'
                       (POSS = possessive agreement marking)

In (8a), coordination of a conjunct unmarked for case with one marked for accusative case is fine, while (8b), where both conjuncts have accusative-marking, is not accepted. Similarly, in (8c), only the final conjunct is marked for dative, which is fine, in contrast to (8d), where both conjuncts have dative-suffixes. In (9), some examples are given which show how other cases and also number are subject to the same pattern.

(9) a. Məj [agətan den kukula]   murem
       I   cock   and cuckoo.COMP sing.I SG
       'I sing like a cock and a cuckoo.'

    b. Məj [Joškar-Ola den Kazan'əšte] pašam   əštem
       I   Joškar-Ola and Kazan.INE   work.ACC do.I SG
       'I work in Joškar-Ola and in Kazan.'

    c. [Rveze den ydərvlak] modət
       boy   and girl.PL   play.3PL
       'The boy(s) and the girls are playing.'
                          (COMP = comparative case, INE = inessive case)

Notice that the example (9c) is not one in which only the last conjunct is plural, but that a likely interpretation is that both conjuncts are plural. As mentioned early in Section 2.2, number is not really a received category in the way that case is. Since, however, the features of one conjunct can clearly be representing both conjuncts, number seems to pattern with the receiving-type UC.

One may ask whether it is clear that the markings in Eastern Mari are morphological rather than syntactic. In other words, whether what looks like case suffixes in Eastern Mari are actually postpositions. If they are, the sentences above do not exemplify unbalanced coordination in which only one of the conjuncts is marked for case, but rather ordinary balanced coordination in which the conjunction phrase is a complement of a postposition, and with both conjuncts being marked the same way.

There are three reasons to maintain that the examples actually do contain case suffixes. The first one has to do with vowel reduction. In Eastern Mari, vowels are of two types: strong and weak. The latter ones are schwa and those that can take part in vowel harmony. They are reduced when followed by a suffix. In (10b), the stem-final *-e* is reduced to schwa in front of the possessive suffix, indicating that what follows is indeed a suffix. (The schwa in the possessive suffix is also reduced, as a result of the following accusative suffix *-m*.)

(10) a. erge
         son.SG.NOM

b. ergə-žə-m
    son-3SG.POSS-ACC

When, on the other hand, a full vowel is followed by something which is uncontroversially a postposition, there is no vowel reduction:

(11) erge   dene
      son.SG.NOM about

The second reason has to do with stress. In Eastern Mari, word stress is always placed on the last strong full-vowel syllable (unless the word contains no strong full vowel, in which case stress falls on the initial syllable). The stress pattern of (11) is (12a), not (12b): there are two word stresses, not one. (The very last vowel in *dene* is not considered a full vowel since it is reducible.) This can be contrasted with (10b) in which there is only one word stress (on the first syllable).

(12) a. 'erge   'dene
          son.SG.NOM   about

      b. *erge   'dene
          son.SG.NOM   about

If the postposition in (12a) had been a suffix, we would have expected two things: that the stem-final vowel in *erge* were reduced to schwa, and that word stress had fallen on the strong vowel of the suffix, leaving no stress on the stem. (When strong vowel suffixes are added to a stem, the word stress generally falls on the suffix.) Neither of these situations arises, thus showing the difference between suffixes and postpositions in this language, illustrated with the difference between (10b) and (12a).

The third reason has to do with the order of suffixes. Some case suffixes can actually occur both before and after the person suffix (which in the examples above precede the possessive suffix). Since the possessive is a morphological suffix—it triggers vowel reduction—elements that can precede it must also be suffixes. If the latter suffixes can also be shown to follow the elements we are questioning (i.e., the case-markers), these elements, too, must be suffixes and not postpositions. Consider (13–15).

(13) a. munə-žə-n   b. munə-žə-m
          egg-3SG-GEN   egg-3SG-ACC

(14) a.   muna-šta-žo   b.   muna-ška-žo
           egg-INE-3SG   egg-ILL-3SG

(15) a.   muna-ž-lan   b.   muna-lan-že
           egg-3SG-DAT   egg-DAT-3SG

(Alhoniemi 1985)

In Eastern Mari, the order of suffixes depends to some extent on the actual case and number involved. Therefore, different orders may turn up in the context of different suffixes. In (13), person-number suffixes precede the case suffixes. In (14), person-number suffixes follow the case suffixes. In (15), either order is possible (as is always the case with dative and comparative). We can conclude that case-markers are morphological suffixes.

English
Unbalanced coordination has received little attention even in English, although examples such as (16a) have been noted in the literature. There seems to be common consent that tensed clause objects of prepositions are unacceptable because an element containing a case-assigning element cannot itself receive case (Stowell 1981's Case Resistance Principle), as in (16b). When a tensed clause, in spite of this fact, is the object of a preposition, as in (16a), it must be explained by the fact that it occurs in the second conjunct, and therefore somehow avoids case-assignment (Goodall 1987:49), i.e., that only the first conjunct is case-marked.

(16) a.   Pat was annoyed by [the children's noise and that their
           parents did nothing to stop it]

      b.   *Pat was annoyed by that their parents did nothing to stop it
                                                    (Sag et al. 1985:165)

There is ample evidence that lack of case-assignment in the second conjunct in English is possible, in present-day English as well as in variants spoken several hundred years ago. In some of the examples below, only the second conjunct is a pronoun which is overtly case-marked. The first conjuncts are either lexical DPs or pronouns which happen to be ambiguous with respect to case. There is thus no way of telling whether the sentences are examples of UC or EBC. Even so, I assume that the examples below are unbalanced coordination, since substitution of any of the first conjuncts with a pronoun overtly marked by the same case as the second pronoun would yield completely unacceptable sentences.[8] Empirically, EBC constructions in English occur either in subject position (in which both conjuncts have accusative case) or as the complement of prepositions (in which case they have nominative case).

(17) a. Can someone help [my wife and I] find housing in Texas...?
(Posting on Linguist List, iii.583, 16 July 1992)

b. ... if you're tired of being heartbroken when you go home at night and you want a spring in your step and a song in your heart, you give [Al Gore and I] a chance to bring America back.
(Speech by Bill Clinton printed in the *New York Times*, 23 July 1992, quoted by D. I. Slobin in Linguist List, iii.628, 13 Aug. 1992)

c. They came to the hotel and picked [Mark and I] up.
(Letter by D. I. Slobin, 1953, quoted in Linguist List, iii.633, 18 Aug. 1992)

d. Sir T. Cascoigne. Look you, Sir, what do you know concerning the Difference between [Mr. Bolron and I]?
(State Trials XCV.17, 11 Feb. 1679, quoted by C. Ball in Linguist List, iii.633, 18 Aug. 1992)

e. All debts are cleared between [you and I]
(Shakespeare, *Merchant of Venice*, quoted in Bartlett 1972)

f. There is such a league between [my good man and he]!
(Shakespeare, *The Merry Wives of Windsor*, quoted in Bartlett 1972)

g. He says he saw [John and I] last night
(Quirk et al. 1985:338)

h. I really wanted my mother to live with [my husband, Michael and I]   (*Evening Standard*, 30 June 1992, 16)

i. For both [Steve and I], our marriage in 1979 was a second chance   (*Evening Standard*, 30 June 1992, 17)

    j. 'A Canadian soldier on leave', it ran, 'has stayed at my house and as a result both [my daughter and myself] are pregnant . . .'
       (*The Independent Magazine*, 6 June 1992, 16)

    k. [She and him] will drive to the movies (Schwartz 1985:165)

The sentences (17a–g) are examples of unbalanced coordination in which the CoP is in an object position, but where the second conjunct has nominative case. In (17j–k), the CoP is the subject of a clause; in (17j) the second conjunct is an anaphor, which is commonly thought to have non-nominative case (see Pollard and Sag 1991a:23), and in (17k), the second conjunct has accusative case.

Estonian

Estonian is a Finnic-Uralic language, and the official language of Estonia, spoken by approximately 1,100,000 people (Bright 1992:iv.207). In Estonian, only the last conjunct has to be marked by case.[9] (See also Section 2.3.1.1 for a discussion on the delimitation of affixes and adpositions applied to Estonian.)

(18) a. humanisti ja demokraadina
          humanist and democrat.ESSIVE
          'As a humanist and democrat'

      b. mehe, laste ja koeraga
          man child and dog.COMITATIVE.SG.
          'With a man, a child and a dog'

                        (Remes 1982:65)

Italian

In Italian,[10] if the second conjunct is a second person singular pronoun, the accusative rather than the nominative case is preferred, even when the CoP is a subject of a clause. This is completely regular among most speakers. The first conjunct must always have nominative case, as must other pronouns in the second conjunct.

(19) a. [tu   e io]   andremo   insieme a Roma
          you.NOM and I.NOM go.1PL.FUT together to Rome
          'You and I will go together to Rome.'

b. [*io   e   tu]   andremo insieme a Roma
   I.nom and you.NOM

c. [io   e   te]   andremo insieme a Roma
   I.NOM and you.ACC

(Renzi 1988:537)

The grammatical status of this second person pronoun is a bit unclear, since it can in fact, in colloquial speech, occur in non-object contexts even when it is not part of a CoP. The examples below are both idiomatic phrases, but *te* is not used in more neutral, declarative contexts.

(20) a. Pensaci te!
     think   you
     'That's your problem.'

    b. Te fai come vuoi
      you do as   you.like
      'Do as you like.'   (Zingarelli 1990:1967)

However, even if it is questionable to what extent *te* is a carrier of accusative case only, the relevant fact in this connection is the unbalancedness of the CoP containing the second person pronoun: *te* cannot occur in a subject CoP unless it is the second conjunct, and *tu* cannot occur in a subject CoP unless it is the first conjunct.

Japanese
In Japanese, the obligatory object-marker *o* is usually situated inside a quantified DP, i.e., between the determiner and the noun.[11] This is the normal case, and is seen in (21a). However, it is possible for only one of the conjuncts to be marked thus; in (21b), only the second conjunct contains the object-marker. The fact that the object-marker is inside the DP shows that it is inside a conjunct and does not sit in a position outside the conjunction phrase (which is also a possibility in Japanese). Since the conjuncts cannot change positions, as in (21c), this is a case of true unbalanced coordination.

(21) a. [Hon o   issatsu to pen o   nihon] kau
      book OBJ one   and pen OBJ two   buy
      'I will buy one book and two pens.'

b. [Hon issatsu to pen o nihon] kau
   book one   and pen OBJ two   buy
   'I will buy one book and two pens.'

(Martin 1975:159)

c. *[Hon o   issatsu to pen nihon] kau
   book OBJ one   and pen two   buy
   'I will buy one book and two pens.'

(Reiko Auestad, p.c.)

Norwegian

Unbalanced coordination in Norwegian is attested in at least three different town-dialects; those of Bergen (22), Stavanger (23), and Tromsø (24) (it does not seem to have been discussed in descriptions of rural dialects). In all three dialects, the construction is found in pronominal conjuncts with respect to case; the second conjunct in a subject position is marked by accusative case as opposed to the nominative case of the first conjunct. The opposite does not occur.[12]

(22) Det sku'   bare mangle at [eg   og deg]   ikkje sku'
    it   should only lack   that I.NOM and you.ACC not   should
    gjere det
    do   it
    'Of course I and you would do it.'

(Larsen and Stoltz 1912:138)

(23) [Han   og meg]   var sammen om   det
    he.NOM and me.ACC were together about it
    'He and I were in it together.'

(Berntsen and Larsen 1925:268)

(24) Ska [æ   og dæ]   gå?
    shall I.NOM and you.ACC go
    'Shall you and I go?'   (Iversen 1918:8)

Old Hebrew

In Samaritan Hebrew and Biblical Hebrew, the non-nominative marker ʔɛθ regularly marks the second conjunct of coordinated DPs, even in subject position.[13]

(25) *Samaritan Hebrew*:
Wayyirḥọṣu [yohošuaʕ wɛ ʔɛθ kɔl ʔɔšɛr
and.washed.3PL Joshua and NON-NOM. all that
ʕimmo] ʔɛθ kɔl bśɔrɔm
with.him NON-NOM. all their.flesh
'And Joshua and all who accompanied him washed the whole
of their body.'
(The Samaritan Chronicles, quoted in Gil 1982:128)

(26) *Biblical Hebrew*:
Uvɔʔ [hɔʔari wɛ ʔɛθ haddov]
and.came.3SG.M the.lion and NON-NOM. the.bear
wanɔśɔʔ śɛh mɛhɔʕeðɛr
and.bore.3SG.M lamb from.the.flock
'And there came a lion, and a bear, and took a lamb out of the
flock.' (Samuel I 17:34, quoted in Gil 1982:128)

Notice that although the non-nominative marker could indicate subordination in (26), this would be a less likely analysis of (25), since there, the
verb agrees with all the conjuncts, not just the first one. Notice also that
even in (26), the fact that the verb agrees only with the first conjunct is
not evidence that the subject is not a CoP, since it is quite regular in Old
Hebrew, as well as in Arabic (see the Palestinian Arabic example further
below) and some other languages, that a preposed verb agrees only with
the first conjunct.

Old Irish
In Old Irish poetry, the conjuncts of a CoP requiring accusative or dative
case may have nominative case as long as the first conjunct is marked
with the required case, (27). Also, in Old Irish prose,[14] the same phenomenon can occur when a prepositional pronoun and a noun phrase are
coordinated. (28) is a Middle Irish version.

(27) rí do.rigni (-gne MS) [aéar n-úar ocus tene réil
king has.made air cold.ACC and fire clear
rorúad ocus talam bladmar brass]
very.red.NOM and earth glorious great.NOM
'The King made the cold air, and the clear red fire, and the
glorious great earth.'
(Kiparsky 1968:54)

(28) Forrumai nonbor díib [thorom-sa ocus Conchobar]
comes nine of.them past-me.ACC and Conchobar.NOM
'Nine of them came past me and Conchobar.'

(Best and Bergin 1929:154)

Qafar
In the Cushitic language Qafar, spoken by approximately 250,000 people in northeastern Ethiopia and in Djibouti, UC can be found in nonstandard varieties: it is possible for the final conjunct of a subject CoP to have nominative case while the first conjunct has absolutive case. (The example is taken from Hayward and Corbett (1988), and the terminology is theirs.) It is impossible for any of the other, non-final conjuncts to have nominative case. (The verb in the example agrees only with the second conjunct. An alternative is for it to agree by semantic number resolution, thus yielding plural agreement marking on the verb.)

(29) [lubàk-kee yangulì] yumbulle
lion.ABS-and hyena.NOM were.seen.M.SG
'A lion and a hyena were seen.'

(Hayward and Corbett 1988:271)

Tamil
In Tamil,[15] there are two ways of expressing coordination: either all the conjuncts have the conjunction -*um* cliticized onto them, and the conjuncts have the normal and expected case-marking (30a), or only the last conjunct is marked by the conjunction (30b). In the latter case, only the last conjunct has the required case-marking, the other conjuncts being invariably in the base form, a typical example of UC.

(30) a. [viittaiyum toottattaiyum kutiraikalaiyum] kotuttaaN
house.ACC.CO garden.ACC.CO horses.ACC.CO he.gave
'He gave a house, a garden and some horses.'

b. [viitu toottankutiraikalaiyum] kotuttaaN
house garden.horses.CO.ACC he.gave
'He gave a house, a garden and some horses.'

(Arden 1954:128)

Tokelauan
In Tokelauan, a Polynesian language spoken by 4,500 people (Bright

1992:iii.251), UC regularly occurs in coordination of (verbal) adjectives. The article is invariably singular in the second conjunct, even if the interpretation is plural. In (31a), an example of balanced coordination is shown; both conjuncts are singular (which can be seen in the singular form of the adjectives agreeing with the noun). In (31b), however, the conjuncts are both plural, as seen in the plural form of the adjectives. In spite of this, the article of the second conjunct is singular; a plural article would be unacceptable (31c).

(31) a. toku   tuagāne pele   ma te   alofa.
        my.SG brother dear.SG and the.SG love.SG
        'my darling and loving brother'

                                            (Arnfinn Vonen, p.c.)

     b. oku   tuagāne p[e]pele ma te   ālolofa.[16]
        my.PL brother dear.PL and the.SG love.PL
        'my darling and loving brothers'
               (Hoem, Hovdhaugen, and Vonen 1992:114)

     c. *oku   tuagāne p[e]pele ma naa   ālolofa.
        my.PL brother dear.PL and the.PL love.PL
        'my darling and loving brothers'
                                              (Arnfinn Vonen, p.c.)

One could argue that the conjunction is not *ma*, but *mate*. However, in the closely related language Samoan (see the previous footnote), the article is *le*, and the conjunction + article in cases like (31b) is *ma le*, supporting the analysis of *male* as a sequence of morphemes rather than an unanalyzable unit.

Turkic

In old Turkic, here represented by Old Uighur, coordination is usually expressed without a conjunction. However, the fact that coordination can be unbalanced indicates that the constructions should be analyzed as coordination rather than simple juxtaposition. (For a discussion of empty conjunctions, see Chapter 3.)

    Grønbeck (1979) makes the generalization that while the rule is that all conjuncts are inflected, in certain cases where one would like to see the conjunct as a whole ("group formation" rather than "enumeration") only the last member is inflected. This difference is illustrated in (32) and (33).

(32) *Dative*:
    a. [ögiŋä   qaŋyŋa]
       mother.POSS.3SG.DAT father.POSS.3SG.DAT
       'to his mother and father'

    b. [ög   qaŋyŋa]
       mother father.POSS.3SG.DAT
       'to his parents'   (Grønbeck 1979:124)

(33) *Locative*:
    a. [äwdä   barqta]
       house.LOC home.LOC
       'house and home'

    b. [äv   barqta]
       house home.LOC
       'house and home'   (Grønbeck 1979:125)

Other examples where only one conjunct is inflected are given below. In (34a), only the second conjunct has dative case-marking; in (34b), accusative case; in (34c), locative case, in (34d), dative case, in (34e), plural and dative case, and in (34f), plural. (The comments above for unbalanced plural in Eastern Mari are relevant here, too.) Notice that (34c,d) have explicit coordinating suffixes (marked as CO) in each conjunct, a fact which does not change the interpretation or the extent of the UC phenomenon. Notice also that a natural interpretation of (34e,f) is one where both conjuncts are plural, not only the one where it is explicitly marked as such.

(34) a. [körumči jultuzčyya]   ajytmaz
        seer   astrologer.DAT ask.NEG.3P
        'They do not ask the seer and astrologer.'

    b. [jalaŋuqlar tynlyɣlaryɣ]
       man.PL   animal.PL.ACC
       'men and creatures'

    c. [täŋrili   jirlida]
       godly.CO earthly.CO.LOC
       'in heaven and earth'

d. [qyzly   küdaguligä]   törü   toqu
   daughter.co groom.co.dat ceremonies.nom rites.nom
   qylmys bolɣai
   done   be.fut.3p
   'The rites will be completed for the daughter and for the son-in-law.'

e. [bušyčy qoltuɣučylarqa]
   beggar petitioner.pl.dat
   'for the beggars and petitioners'

f. [bäg   qunčujlar]
   prince princess.pl
   'princes and princesses'   (Grønbeck 1979:124–7)

One might ask whether the data above is coordination rather than compounding. If the latter were the case, one would expect only one noun to be inflected. Since the data above are from Old Turkish, phonological arguments are hard to find. Similarly, looking for syntactic evidence in either direction is not easy. However, the same phenomenon exists in Modern Turkish (an overt conjunction is necessary in Modern Turkish, but this, if anything, strengthens the point):

(35) a. [annesine   ve babasına]
        mother.poss.3sg.dat and father.poss.3sg.dat
        'to his mother and father'

     b. [anne   ve babasına]
        mother and father.poss.3sg.dat
        'to his mother and father'   (Emel Türker, p.c.)

It would be surprising for a compound to appear with a conjunction. Also, there is no phonological support for assuming that (35b) is a compound. Furthermore, it is possible to have different adjectives for each conjunct, something which would hardly be possible for a compound:

(36) güzel   anne ve çirkin babasına]
     beautiful mother and ugly father.poss.3sg.dat
     'to his beautiful mother and ugly father'

                                        (Emel Türker, p.c.)

The unbalancedness of the conjuncts also shows up in the interrogative
(37), which contains the conjunction *veya* 'or (inclusive),' where the
conjuncts are treated as a group, in that the interrogative sentence requires a yes/no type answer.[17] Again, a compound would not be expected
to contain a conjunction.

> (37) [elma   veya armutları]   yediniz   mi
>   the.apple or   the.pear.PL.ACC eat.PAST.2PL Q
>   'Did you eat the apples or the pears?'
>
>   (Bernt Brendemoen, p.c.)

Vedic

Vedic coordination is expressed by a conjunction *ca* enclitic to the second conjunct. There are several examples from the Rig Veda where the
first conjunct has vocative case and the second has nominative case.[18]

> (38) [vāyav indraś ca]
>   VOC NOM and
>   'Vāyu and Indra'   (Kiparsky 1968:54)

Welsh

Not only morphosyntactic features, but also phonological ones, may be
distributed unevenly in a CoP. In Welsh, as in many other Celtic languages, phonological changes are triggered by grammatical categories.
"Soft mutation" is a phenomenon where some words get a different
initial consonant when preceded by certain categories, than they would
otherwise. An account of soft mutation given by Zwicky (1984) explains
the phenomenon as a realization of accusative case, while Harlow (1989)
gives an explanation where a preposed phrasal category, such as the subject DP in the example below, triggers it. The important point here is that
the phonological change is not triggered by phonological features of the
preceding element. When a CoP is preceded by a soft-mutation-triggering
element, we should therefore expect all conjuncts to be mutated, and not
only the one that happens to be closest to it. However, it turns out that
only the first conjunct is subject to soft mutation:

> (39) Bwytais i [fara, menyn a   chaws]
>   ate   I bread butter and cheese
>   'I ate bread, butter and cheese.'   (Harlow 1989:314–15)

In (39), *fara* is a mutated form of *bara*, while the noun *menyn* occurs in its citation form rather than being mutated to *fenyn*.[19] We have to conclude that unbalanced coordination occurs in Welsh. This is also attested later in this section, where we shall see that verbal CoPs, too, can be unbalanced.

2.2.1.2. *Assigning-type UC*

This kind of UC is a type where the conjuncts may have conflicting features, and where one of the conjuncts determines the features of the whole conjunction phrase. Typical features in this kind of UC are various agreement features such as person, number, and gender.

While it is not a matter of course that a language has receiving-type UC, as above, most languages have a way of dealing with situations in which conjuncts have conflicting features. It seems to me that there are three ways in which conflicts can be solved. The first way is to avoid conflicts altogether: e.g., many Bantu languages, such as Zulu and Xhosa, do not allow coordination where the conjuncts have different gender (unless the conjuncts are [+human]) (Givón 1970); alternative constructions with comitative are used instead. Similarly, Norwegian avoids feature conflicts between conjuncts:

(40) a. *[huset   og hytta]   vår
      the.house.N.SG and the.hut.F.SG our.F.SG
      'our house and hut'

    b. *[huset   og hytta]   vårt
      the.house.N.SG and the.hut.F.SG our.N.SG
      'our house and hut'

    c. [huset   vårt   og hytta   vår]
      the.house.N.SG our.N.SG and the.hut.F.SG our.F.SG
      'our house and our hut'

Above, a coordinated structure, in which the conjuncts are N' categories with different gender, should agree with a determiner marked for either of the relevant genders, (40a,b). Both are unacceptable, in contrast to (40c), where the determiner does not agree with the whole CoP$_{[N']}$, but where there is now one determiner per conjunct, agreeing with each individually.[20]

A second way of avoiding feature conflicts is by resolution rules, of which there are a host of different versions in different languages around the world. Resolution rules can be taken to imply that "computation" is involved (Corbett 1991:265). They can be semantically or syntactically based. Semantically based resolution rules are those which refer to the meaning denoted by the conjuncts rather than to their gender. This kind is found in Tamil, according to Corbett (1991:269): conjuncts denoting rationals (masculine and feminine) trigger a rational (plural) agreement form (41a), while those denoting non-rationals (neuter) trigger a non-rational (plural) agreement form, (42b). Some speakers, in addition, allow a rational and a non-rational to be conjoined, in which case the agreement form is rational (42c). (The percentage sign suggests that the construction is used by some, not all, of the population.)

(41) a. [akkaa-vum   aɳɳan-um]   neettu
          elder.sister-and elder.brother-and yesterday
          va-nt-aaŋka
          came.3PL.RATIONAL
          'Elder sister and elder brother came yesterday.'

     b. [naay-um puune-yum] va-nt-atuŋka
          dog-and cat-and   came.3PL.NEUTER
          'The dog and the cat came.'

     c. %[Raaman-um naay-um] va-nt-aaŋka
          Raman-and dog-and   came.3PL.RATIONAL
          'Raman and the dog came.'
                                            (Corbett 1991:269–70)

Syntactically based resolution rules are those where it is not what the conjuncts denote which determines the agreement triggering basis, but rather the grammatical features themselves. For instance, in French, while conjuncts with masculine and feminine gender trigger agreeing constituents with masculine and feminine features, respectively, a coordinated structure which has conjuncts of both genders invariably triggers masculine agreement (see, e.g., Corbett 1991:279). In Old Norse, the situation is parallel, except that when masculine and feminine genders are coordinated, the whole phrase triggers neuter agreement:[21]

(42) [Gunnhildr ok synir þeira] váru   farin   til Danmerkr
     Gunnhild.F and sons.M their   were.PL gone.N to Denmark
     suðr
     South
     'Gunnhild and their sons had gone South to Denmark.'
                                           (Nygaard 1966:71)

It is the third way of dealing with feature conflicts which we shall look at in this section; i.e., the assigning-type UC. While resolution rules take both conjuncts into account when determining the kind of agreement they trigger, conjuncts in assigning-type UC-structures have only got a role to play in determining agreement if they happen to be in the right position: in some languages, the first conjunct is the privileged conjunct; in others it is the last one. The other conjuncts in the CoP are completely ignored.

Languages do not always use only one of the three ways of conflict resolution above. It is not uncommon that some constructions trigger one way, while another triggers another way (see, e.g., Old Norse further below). In other languages, the choice seems to be freer. In Burushaski, e.g., either both conjuncts, or the last one, may determine the agreement features of the verb (Lorimer 1935:105). Below, both verbs have jointly determined the last conjunct, but it is equally possible for only the last conjunct to do so (the latter is not illustrated by Lorimer).

(43) muː   kɛ   muː miˑɛ   muyɛtsʊmʌn
     her.father and her.mother.TRANS-NOM.AG 3SG.F.saw.PL
     'Her father and mother saw her.'   (Lorimer 1935:105)

What we shall see in this section are examples of languages in which it is syntactic position alone which determines which conjunct assigns agreement features onto another category.

Afrikaans
Afrikaans generally has doubly marked negation, so that the negative *nie* 'not' or other negators agree with a sentence-final negative marker *nie*. If the negator is some (other) negative adverb or adjective, "the nie comes at the end of the negative extension or phrase, which may or may not conclude the sentence" (Burgers 1963:159–60).

Neither of the grammars that I have consulted (Burgers 1963; Botha et al. 1989) mentions the behaviour of *nie* when it agrees with a negator which is part of a conjunct, like (44).

(44) a. dat daar [baie studente en geen professors] is nie
         that there many students and no professors are NEG
         'that there are many students and no professors'

   b. *dat daar [geen professors en baie studente] is nie
         that there no professors and many students are NEG
         'that there are no professors and many students'

   c. dat daar [geen professors nie en baie studente] is
         that there no professors NEG and many students are
         'that there are no professors and many students'

(Karin Robbers, p.c.)

(44a) is fine, since no non-negated phrase intervenes between *nie* and its agreeing phrase (the second conjunct). (44b) is out, since a non-negated DP interferes between the marker and its agreeing negated phrase. (44c) is fine, since the negative marker is now next to its agreeing phrase. It is the first conjunct which is deviant for the following two reasons: (i) in (44a), with the negative marker sitting outside the CoP, we expect both conjuncts to be negative, i.e., to share the negative marker *nie*, since only the last conjunct is negative, the first conjunct is deviant; (ii) in (44c), the verb is alone outside the CoP. Since it has no *nie* following it (the marker usually being the last word in the clause), we expect the conjuncts to have positive polarity. Since only the second conjunct is positive, the first conjunct is deviant. This makes Afrikaans a language with UC constructions, however marginal, since to my knowledge, no other UC can be found.

Czech

In Czech, the first conjunct regularly determines the agreement features of the verb when the predicate precedes the subject. No resolution has taken place; the second conjunct is simply ignored for the purpose of agreement.

(45) Půjdu   tam [já a   ty]
     will.go-1SG there I and you
     'You and I will go there.'

(Trávníček 1949:433, cited in Corbett 1983:179)

Gã

In Gã, a Kwa language of the Niger–Congo family, spoken by 1,020,000 people (Bright: 1992:ii.296), only the first subject regularly determines the agreement features of the verb, according to Mithun. (The example she gives does not show which of the conjuncts has determined agreement.)

(46) [mì kè lè] tà   / *trà
     I   and he sit.SG / sit.PL
     'I and he sit.'   (Mithun 1988:340)

German
German normally follows semantic resolution rules, where two singular DPs as subject conjuncts trigger plural agreement. (There is a difference between DPs denoting objects and people and those denoting more abstract properties, according to Findreng 1976.) However, when the verb is preposed, there is a tendency for the verb to agree with only the first conjunct, even though it is singular and the second one is plural:

(47) Aber links war   [die Binnenalster   und die weissen
     but left was.SG the inner.Alster.SG and the white.PL
     Lichtreklamen]
     light.advert.PL
     'But to the left were the inner Alster (lake) and the white light-
     adverts.'   (Duden, quoted in Findreng 1976:65)

Hopi
UC regularly occurs in Hopi, a Shoshonean language of the Uto–Aztecan family, spoken by 5,000 people in northeastern Arizona (Bright 1992:iv. 212). Only the last conjunct in a coordinated DP subject determines verb agreement. In (48a), the second conjunct is plural, thus triggering plural marking on the verb. In (48b), the second conjunct is in the singular, and thereby triggers singular agreement on the verb, which is unmarked and not expressed overtly.

(48) a. ['Itana   niq 'ima totimho 'yam] taatapiy
        our father.SG and these boy.PL   cottontail.PL.ACC
        qöqya
        killed.PL.PL-OBJ
        'Our father and these boys killed cottontails.'

b. ['ima totimho 'yam niq 'itana] taatapiy
these boy.PL and our father.SG cottontail.PL.ACC
qöya
killed.SG.PL-OBJ
'These boys and our father killed cottontails.'

(Van Oirsouw 1987:232)

Latin

In Latin, agreement in the predicate can be determined by the last conjunct. Below, a masculine and a feminine conjunct together agree with a feminine participle, because the feminine conjunct is closest.

(49) [Populi   provinciaeque] liberatae   sunt
people.M.PL province.F.PL.and liberated.F.PL are
'The people and the provinces are liberated.'

(Eitrem 1966:63)

Old Norse

The rules for solving agreement conflicts in Old Norse vary according to construction. When a verb or participle precedes a coordinated subject, only the first conjunct determines agreement features, as in (50a–d). (This is parallel to Czech, above, Old Hebrew, Section 2.2.1.1 on receiving-type UC, and other languages, as we shall see.) When the verbal element follows the subject, on the other hand, resolution rules are used. The way of resolving feature conflicts, then, depends on the construction.[22]

(50) a. hefi   [ek ok mínir menn] haft alla þessa stund þat
have.1SG I and my men had all this time that
einu oss   til framflutningar
only we.DAT to maintenance
'All this time have I and my men had only this for maintenance.'

b. samþyktist [Finnr] því   [ok Árni]
agreed.3SG F. that.DAT and A.
'Finn and Arne agreed to that.'

c. sat [konungr ok dróttning] í hásæti ok
sat.3SG king and queen in high-seat and
drukku bæði samt um kveldit
drank.3PL both together in the.evening
'The king and queen sat in the high-seat and both drank
together in the evening.'

d. þá var tekinn [borðbúnaðrinn ok
then was.SG taken.SG the.table-ware.SG and
dúkarnir]
the.tablecloths.PL
'Then the table-ware and the table-cloth were taken.'
(Nygaard 1966:69–71)

Palestinian Arabic

In Palestinian Arabic, as well as in Classical Arabic and other varieties
of Arabic (see Aoun, Benmamoun, and Sportiche 1994; Johannessen
1996), the rules for subject-verb agreement differ depending on the word
order of the clause in which the coordinated structure occurs (like Old
Hebrew, Czech, and Old Norse, above, and Serbo-Croat, below). There
is nothing special in SVO clauses, where semantic criteria are used to
resolve agreement conflicts (see Old Norse above and the introduction to
the section). However, in VSO clauses, the first conjunct is the one which
determines agreement. In (51a,b), the word order is SVO, and verb
agreement is solved semantically, by masculine dominating feminine,
and plural being the natural choice where the conjuncts are at least two
individuals altogether. In (51c, d), however, the verb is preposed, which
triggers agreement only by the first conjunct.

(51) a. [ʔel-walad we-l-banaat] gataluu ʔel-bisse
the-boy and-the-girls killed-3PL.M the-cat
'The boy and the girls killed the cat.'

b. [ʔel-banaat we-l-walad] gataluu ʔel-bisse
the-girls and-the-boy killed-3PL.M the-cat
'The girls and the boy killed the cat.'

c. Gatalen [ʔel-banaat we-l-walad] ʔel-bisse
killed-3PL.F the-girls and-the-boy the-cat
'The girls and the boy killed the cat.'

d. Gatal   [ʔelwalad we-l-banaat] ʔel-bisse
    killed-3SG.M the-boy   and-the-girls the-cat
    'The boy and the girls killed the cat.'

                                        (van Oirsouw 1987:232)

Qafar

The example from Qafar below (also partly used previously) shows that
in a coordinated subject, the second conjunct can be nominative. When
it is, verb agreement can result from assigning-type UC: a nominative
second conjunct is able to assign agreement features to the verb. Below,
the second conjunct is masculine singular, which are also possible features for the verb. It is also possible for there to be conflict solving by
semantic resolution rules. Then the verb gets plural features. It is never
possible for the verb to agree with the first conjunct alone.

(52) [lubàk-kee   yangulì]   yumbulle   / yumbullen
      lion.ABS-and hyena.NOM.M.SG were.seen.M.SG / PL
      'A lion and a hyena were seen.'

                                        (Hayward and Corbett 1988:271)

Serbo-Croat

In Serbo-Croat, as in Czech, the first conjunct determines verbal agreement when the predicate precedes the subject. In (53a), a feminine and
a neuter DP are coordinated, but since the first conjunct is feminine, the
participle gets feminine agreement features. In (53b), the situation is converse; there a neuter conjunct is first, and it is that one which determines
the participle agreement features (despite the distance between them).

(53) a. toj sluzbi   su bil-e   posvecen-e   [njene
          this job.DAT are been-FEM.PL devoted-FEM.PL her
          misli   I   njena osecanja] . . .
          thoughts.FEM.PL and her feelings.NEUT.PL
          'To this job were devoted her thoughts and her feelings.'
          (Andrić, Travnička hronika, quoted by Corbett 1991:266)

b. [Ona   stalna   duboko urezana svijetla   i
   Those constant deeply   cut   lights.NEUT.PL and
   sjene   koje je   naslikao umjetnikov kist]
   shades.FEM.PL which has painted the artist's brush
   bila   su jaca   od realne svijetlosti
   were.NEUT.PL stronger.NEUT.PL than real   light
   'Those constant, deeply cut lights and shades which the
   artist's brush painted were stronger than real light.'
                     (Desnica, quoted by Corbett 1983:180)

Slovene
In Slovene, too, UC constructions can be found in which the number and
gender agreement features of the first conjunct determine the participle
agreement. Unlike the other Slavic examples above, however, here the
predicate may follow the coordinated subject. Below, a feminine DP is
the first conjunct, thereby determining the participle to be feminine; the
second (and closest) conjunct, which is masculine, plays no role.

(54) [groza   in   strah]   je prevzel-a   vso
     horror.FEM.SG and fear.MASC.SG is seized-FEM.SG whole
     vas
     village
     'Horror and fear seized the whole village.'
                     (Toporičič 1972:187, quoted by Corbett 1991:266)

Swahili
In Swahili, the gender of the second conjunct is the one which determines
agreement on the verb; in (55a), the second conjunct has the third gender,
therefore the verb is marked with third-gender agreement features. In
(56b), the second conjunct has the seventh gender, which triggers those
features on the agreeing verb.

(55) a. [ki-ti   na m-guu wa meza] u-mevunjika
        7-chair and 3-leg of table 3-be broken
        'The chair and the leg of the table are broken.'

     b. [m-guu wa meza na ki-ti]   ki-mevunjika
        3-leg of table and 7-chair 7-be broken
        'The leg of the table and the chair are broken.'
                     (Bokamba 1985:45, quoted in Corbett 1991:266)

2.2.2. VERBAL UNBALANCED COORDINATION

Just like nominal coordination, non-nominal UC can also be divided into two types, where one can be considered a receiving type, and one an assigning type. Included in this section are verbal conjuncts, i.e., verbs and verb phrases, and also clausal conjuncts in which the unbalancedness is manifested on the verbs.

2.2.2.1. *Receiving-type UC*

In verbal receiving-type UC, there is typically one verb which is inflected in the ordinary way; by tense, aspect, and mood, and various agreement features such as person and number. The other conjunct(s) either occur(s) in their base form, or in some or other infinite form. We can include so-called serial verb constructions in this group, too: in such constructions, there is typically only one finite verb, the other verbs can be morphologically unmarked, or they can occur in a form unique for this construction.

"Serial verb" as used in the literature usually means one of the following two possibilities, according to Zwicky (1990:2): "1) a serial is any combination of two or more verbal constituents which is problematic because it exhibits some properties of subordination and some of coordination . . ., possibly exhibiting as well both the independence of parts characteristic of syntactic phrases and the 'intimate combination' characteristic of syntactic words. 2) a serial is an intimate multi-V combination . . . [with] a single DP serving as direct object of one verb and as subject . . . or as direct object . . . of the other verb." (An extensive outline of serial verb constructions in various languages can be found in Sebba 1987.)

Amharic

Amharic, a Semitic language, is the official language of Ethiopia, spoken by 1,410,000 people (Bright 1992:i.51). It has two ways of expressing coordination of actions. One is by ordinary coordination; i.e., by a conjunction surrounded by the conjuncts, (56). The other way is by serial verbs; i.e., without a conjunction, but with a serial suffix, (57a,b).[23] In both cases, however, the result is unbalanced coordination; in ordinary coordination as well as in serial constructions, the first conjunct lacks a tense suffix.

(56) [yɨ-rrammɛd-ɨnna yɨ-rɔt'-al]
    3SG.M-walk-and 3SG.M-run-3SG.M.NON-PAST
    'He walks and (then) runs / will run.'

(57) a. t'ɛm-tɔ-t   bira t'ɛt't'a
          be.thirsty-3SG.M.SER-to.him beer drink.3SG.M.PAST
          'He was thirsty and drank beer. /
          He drank beer because he was thirsty.'

      b. t'ɛm-tɔ-t   bira yɨ-t'ɛt't'a-l
          be.thirsty-3SG.M.SER-to.him beer 3SG.M-drink-NON-
          PAST
          i. 'He will be thirsty and drink beer.'
          ii. 'When he gets thirsty, he'll drink beer.'
          iii. 'Because he will be thirsty, he'll drink beer.'
                                    (Kjell Magne Yri, p.c.)

Fulfulde
Fulfulde belongs to the West-Atlantic branch of the Niger–Kordofanian
languages. In Fulfulde, coordination of VPs can be expressed by serial
verb forms. It is possible for all the verbs to be represented by a serial
verb form (58a), but it is also possible for the first conjunct (no subsequent ones) to have the ordinary form which also occurs in non-coordinated structures, (58b):

(58) a. Baaba nyaami, haari,   looti   juude
          father eat.SP become.full.SG.SP wash.SG.SP hands
          muudum, wi'i . . .
          his,   say.SP
          'The father ate, became full, washed his hands, and said . . .'

      b. Janngo   mi yahay,   mi foonda   ki, mi
          Tomorrow I go.SG.HAB I investigate.SG.SI it I
          ndaara . . .
          see.SI
          'Tomorrow I shall go and investigate it and see . . .'
          (SP = serial perfective, SI = serial imperfective,
          HAB = Habitual)
                    (Arnott 1970, quoted in Endresen 1992a:51–7)

Homeric Greek
In Homeric Greek, there is a phenomenon called "the infinitive of command": the second VP might contain an uninflected infinitive instead of
an expected imperative, aorist imperative, or optative (Kiparsky 1968:

appendix I). (59a) is an example of ordinary imperative coordinated with infinitive; (59b) has optative and infinitive.[24]

(59) a. pánta tád' aggeîlai mēdè pseudoággelos eînai
        all   this tell.IMP not   false.messenger be.INF
        'Tell him all this and do not be a false messenger.'
    b. paîda   d'emoì   lúsaite   phílēn tàd'apoina
        daughter 1SG.DAT release.OPT dear   ransom
        dékhesthai
        take.INF
        'May you release my own daughter and take the ransom.'

                                                              (Kiparsky 1968:53)

Japanese

Verbal coordination in Japanese cannot take place with an overt conjunction (Bleiler 1978:97). There are two ways of expressing coordination instead. One is exemplified below; the verb of the first conjunct is in a participle form, which is, then, an example of UC. The other way is not relevant here; it is by the use of subordinating conjunctions such as *to* 'if, then' or *kara* 'because'.

(60) Ginza e itte   miyagemono o   okaimasho
    Ginza to going souvenirs   OBJ let.us.buy
    'Let's go to the Ginza and buy some souvenirs.'

                                                             (Bleiler 1978:97)

Modern Turkish

Verbal coordination in Modern Turkish usually occurs without an overt conjunction, so that coordination is expressed by juxtaposition. The first conjunct may lack markers for past tense and person and number, and may instead get a dependent marker *-ip*, cf. the difference between (61a) and (61b).

(61) a. Kalk-ti-k git-ti-k
        we.rose we.went
        'We rose and we went.'

    b. Kalk-ip gittik
        rise.   we.went
        'We rose and we went.'

                  (Lewis 1967:178, quoted in Payne 1985:27)

A dependent marker is not necessary, but it is still only the last verb which is inflected for tense, person, and number features:

(62) pastahaneye   gid-er   dondurma   ye-r-di-k
     patisserie.DAT go.HAB icecream.NOM eat.HAB.PAST.1PL
     'We used to go to the patisserie and have ice cream.'
                                         (Bernt Brendemoen, p.c.)

Sidaamu Afo
Sidaamu Afo is a Cushitic language spoken by 1,400,000 people (Bright 1992:i.328) in South Ethiopia. In this language, in multiple VP coordination ("serial verbs"), only the last verb is finite and has a tense suffix. The other verbs are infinite; having a tenseless suffix agreeing with the subject. In the example below, in which a woman describes how she prepares the dough for a traditional meal, the "serial" suffix is *-te* ('3SG.F. having.done').

(63) kakkad-te-nna   'anga-te sei-se
     tread-3SG.F.having.done-and hand-for it.was.ready-for.her
     -ha   'ikki-kki-ro k'ol-te
     -NOMINALISER-OBJ it.was-not-if turn-3SG.F.having.done
     ka'-te   galagalch-te
     (empty.verb)-3SG.F.having.done do.again-3SG.F.having.done
     k'ish-te   la'-tanno.[25]
     squeeze-3SG.F.having.done look-she.NON.PAST.
     'If it is not ready for her hands (= feels good to knead) after she
     has trodden on it, she turns it and squeezes it again, and then
     looks at it (= investigates it again).'   (Kjell Magne Yri, p.c.)

Welsh
Rouveret (1990:73) says about Welsh: "It happens frequently that in a sequence of coordinate clauses, only the verbal head contained in the first one is morphologically specified for tense, person and number, the following ones containing a verbal noun instead of an inflected form." This is a typical instance of unbalanced coordination.

(64) Aethant   i 'r ty   ac eistedd a   bwyta
     go.PAST.3PL to the house and sit   and eat
     'They went to the house, sat and ate.'
                                         (Rouveret 1990:73)

Yagnobi
Yagnobi is an Iranian language spoken by 2,000 people in Tajikistan (Bright 1992:ii.233). In past tenses, the first verb in the CoP is the only one to be marked by person and number:

(65) a. Man [a-šáw-im   a-tiraš]
        I   PAST-go-1SG PAST-fall
        'I went and fell.'

    b. A-tiraš-ór   a-únxoy
        PAST-fall-1PL PAST-break
        'They fell and broke.'

                              (Xromov 1972, quoted in Payne 1985:27)

2.2.2.2. *Assigning-type UC*

Typical assigning-type verbal UC is the kind where the verbs in each conjunct have different subcategorization properties; they assign, e.g., different case to their complements.

German
In German, it is the last conjunct which determines the case of the object complement. This can be seen in the verbs of (66):

(66) a. Maria [begrüsste und half]   dem   / *den   Mann
        Maria greeted   and helped] the.DAT / the.ACC man
        'Maria greeted and helped the man.'

    b. Maria [half   und begrüsste] *dem   / den   Mann
        Maria helped and greeted   the.DAT / the.ACC man
        'Maria helped and greeted the man.'

                                              (Rolf Thieroff, p.c.)

The verb *begrüssen* assigns accusative case, and *helfen* dative case; when *begrüssen* is the first conjunct and *helfen* the last conjunct, *begrüssen* plays no case-assigning role, as seen in (66a), where the object has dative case. The converse is true when *begrüssen* is the last conjunct, and *helfen* the first conjunct, in which case the object has accusative case (66b).[26] It should be noted that the facts are more complicated, however. Consider (67).

(67) a.   dass Maria *ihm   /*ihn   [begrüsst und geholfen]
          that Maria him.DAT /him.ACC [greeted and helped
          hat
          has
          'that Maria has greeted and helped him'

b.   Maria hat *ihm   / *ihn   [begrüsst und geholfen]
     Maria has him.DAT / him.ACC [greeted and helped
     'Maria has greeted and helped him.'

(Rolf Thieroff, p.c.)

When the object is preposed, no matter whether the reason is that it occurs in a subordinate clause, as in (67a), or that there are auxiliary verbs
in the clause (67b), unbalanced coordination is impossible. Neither verb
is in a position to win the case-assignment competition. Since there are
no resolution rules for these situations, the only possibility is for such
situations to be avoided.

2.2.3. CLAUSAL UNBALANCED COORDINATION

Clausal UC is taken to mean coordination where clausal conjuncts belong
to different clause-types word-order-wise, but not interpretation-wise.
Cases where one conjunct has a complementizer which the other conjunct
lacks (and where the interpretation is constant), i.e., *[COMP + IP &
Ø + IP]*, do not count as unbalanced coordination here, rather, they must
be seen as cases of complementizer-sharing, i.e., *[COMP [IP & IP]]*, just
as when two DPs are coordinated, they must be seen as sharing the rest
of the sentence. What does count are cases where both conjuncts have the
same function and the same meaning, but where the conjuncts surprisingly seem to be of different types. A typical example is German, where,
as we shall see, for many speakers, two coordinated subordinate clauses
do not have the same word order; one has the verb-final word order expected in that position, and one has main clause word order.

Dutch
In Dutch, main clauses are taken to be verb-second (verb-first if imperative), while subordinate clauses are verb-final. The complementizer *als*
is usually taken to block V2-order, and trigger subordinate order. The
examples in (68) are therefore of an interesting type: the first and the
second conjunct belong to different types; the second conjunct actually
has main clause word order, in spite of it being coordinated with another

clause which is governed by *als*, and which has the expected verb-final order. (The reason it is clear that the second conjunct of (68c), too, has main clause word order is based on agreement facts: the verb-form *gaat* is only used when the subject precedes the verb.)

(68) a. [Als je te laat thuiskomt en je hebt geen sleutel bij
      if you too late home.come and you have no key by
      je] . . .
      you
      'If you come home too late, and you don't have a key with
      you, (then . . .)'   (E. Hoekstra 1992)

    b. [Als je gepakt wordt en je bent al veroordeeld
      if you caught are and you have already convicted
      geweest]
      been . . .
      'If you are being caught and you have already been con-
      victed before, (then . . .)'
          (van Zonneveld 1992, cited by Joop Houtman, p.c.)

    c. Als je niet verder kunt, dan [keer je je om
      if you not further can then turn you yourself around
      en gaat dezelfde weg terug]
      and go the.same way back
      'If you can't go further, then turn round and go back the
      way you came.'
         (Zwart 1991, quoted in Heycock and Kroch 1992:11)

German

The same comments can be made for German as were made for Dutch above. The complementizer *wenn* blocks the V2-effect, and yet, the second conjunct has the verb in the second position (69a). This is not possible for the first conjunct (69b).

(69) a. wenn [jemand nach Hause kommt und da steht$_i$ der
      when someone to house comes and there stands the
      Gerichtsvollzieher vor der Tür t$_i$]
      bailiff in front of the door
      'when someone comes home and there stands the bailiff in
      front of the door'

b. *wenn [da   steht$_i$ der Gerichtsvollzieher vor   der
   when there stands the bailiff   in front of the
Tür t$_i$ und jemand   nach Hause kommt]
door a and someone to   house comes
'when there stands the bailiff in front of the door and someone comes home'   (Höhle 1989)

Norwegian

In Norwegian, a conditional clause can be realized in two ways; by a complementizer triggering subordinate word order, or by a clause with verb-first main clause word order (the same type that is used in yes/no questions) (70a,b). The subordinate word order in (70a) can be recognized by the sentence adverb *ikke* 'not' sitting in front of the finite verb —in (70b), *ikke* follows the finite verb, which is the main clause word order.

(70) a. Hvis jeg ikke har   penger, går   jeg
     if   I   not have money walk I
     'If I don't have money, I walk.'

    b. Har jeg ikke penger, går   jeg
     have I   not money walk I
     'If I don't have money, I walk.'

If two conditional clauses of the same kind are coordinated, they both retain the same word order. However, if the two different types are coordinated with each other, in the order [question & complementized clause], the result is surprising: there is no complementizer present, and yet, the second conjunct has subordinate word order (71a). It is not obligatory, since (71b), with main clause word order is also fine.

(71) a. [Har jeg penger, og ikke gidder å gå] tar   jeg toget
     have I   money and not bother to walk take I   the.train
     'If I have money, and can't be bothered to walk, I take the train.'

    b. [Har jeg penger, og gidder ikke å gå,] tar   jeg toget
     have I   money and bother not to walk take I   the.train
     'If I have money, and can't be bothered to walk, I take the train.'

The fact that it is (71a), and not (71b), which is unbalanced can be seen in (72). The subordinate clause word order is never allowed in the first conjunct if it lacks a complementizer.

(72) a. *[Jeg ikke gidder å gå   og har   penger,] tar jeg toget
         I   not bother to walk and have money   take I   the.train
         'If I cannot be bothered to walk, and have money, I take the
         train.'

     b. [Gidder jeg ikke å gå   og har   penger,] tar jeg toget
        bother I   not to walk and have money   take I   the.train
        'If I cannot be bothered to walk, and have money, I take the
        train.'

2.3. Delimiting unbalanced coordination

2.3.1. MORPHO-SYNTACTIC UC

Although unbalanced coordination clearly is a real phenomenon, it is important to be critical to the data. Sometimes something looks like UC which in the end turns out to be something different. One such case might be Breton. Consider (73).

(73) An dud   ne lavarent netra met a chome   sioul
     the people PCL said.3PL nothing but PCL stayed.3SG quiet
     'The people said nothing but stayed quiet.'
                                   (Borsley and Stephens 1989:§6)

In (73), the verb of the second conjunct lacks agreement. It thus looks as if unbalanced coordination w.r.t. agreement is an alternative to ordinary balanced coordination with agreement on every conjunct. However, Fredrik Otto Lindeman (p.c.) has informed me that the lack of agreement in the second conjunct is the normal case; in Breton, the verb in an affirmative clause is always inflected for third person singular, regardless of whether it occurs in a coordinated structure or not. However, in negated clauses, the verb agrees with the subject. In Breton, therefore, the lack of agreement has nothing to do with coordination.

Consider also the West Greenlandic (74).[27]

(74) Paliitsit 276-inik   ammassattortoq
Paliitsit 276–INST.PL sardine-eat-NOM.PART.3SG
nipisallu   ilivitsut   marluk
lumpfish.ABS.PL.CONJ whole.PL two
'. . . that P. ate 276 sardines and two whole lumpfish.'

(Sadock 1986:28)

Here, the first conjunct has been incorporated into the verb, while the second conjunct stays in situ (West Greenlandic is an OV language, see Sadock 1985:394–5). Since the incorporated conjunct lacks morphosyntactic features such as case and number it is tempting to suggest that it is a case of UC. However, this would not be quite right. In UC, the deviant conjunct is most often one which would not be allowed to stay in the same syntactic position if simplex. In West Greenlandic, this is clearly not the case, since object-incorporation is extremely common, and incorporated objects are never morphosyntactically inflected, the reason being, of course, that as part of a compound, it lacks an independent syntactic status. The lack of morphosyntactic features in the first conjunct, therefore, has nothing to do with the fact that it is part of a CoP, but that it is incorporated.[28] It would be wrong, then, to assume that the case difference between the first and the second conjunct is evidence for UC in West Greenlandic.

2.3.1.1. *Affix or adposition?*

Adpositions and case-marking often have overlapping semantics, and one might therefore be mistaken in the analysis. For instance (75a) may look like a case of UC, something like (75b), given the impossibility of reversing the conjuncts as in (75c):

(75) a.   Mary looked at Peter and Fred

      b. *Mary looked [CoP [at Peter] and [Fred]]

      c. *Mary looked [CoP [Fred] and [at Peter]]

However, the literature on coordination agrees that coordination can only take place for categories of the same type, i.e., which can have the same syntactic context. They must therefore be syntactically of the same category. The analysis suggested in (75b,c) must be wrong, since it involves coordination of a constituent PP and a DP. (The input clauses prior to coordination would have had to be *Mary looked at Peter* and *Mary looked Fred*.) Since, for independent reasons, we know that *at* is a syntactic word, there is instead a balanced analysis available, in which *at* is shared by both conjuncts:

(76) Mary looked at [CoP Fred and Peter]

In principle, then, we will not include as UC coordination which involves independent words that can be unproblematically shared syntactically by both conjuncts. UC will usually involve morphology or independent words that are in such a position within the conjunct that it is impossible for them to be shared in a straightforward way syntactically (such as the Japanese example (21)).[29]

Estonian may serve as an example of how we can determine whether or not a phenomenon must be considered to be UC.[30] In this language, there are only four cases, the so-called CATE suffixes (comitative, abessive, terminative, and essive), out of fourteen that can take part in what could be regarded as UC constructions; i.e., where only one conjunct is case-marked (for examples, see above, Section 2.2.1, on nominal UC). Since these four case suffixes are also among the few that are syllabic a relevant question might be if these four morphemes are perhaps cliticized postpositions rather than case suffixes. If this were the case, then obviously the constructions above would not be examples of UC.

One test which is often used to distinguish a clitic from an affix is the relative position of the element; only clitics can follow other clitics (see, e.g., Johannessen 1989, for an overview). In Estonian, the elements under consideration cannot follow other clitics (77). Ordinary postpositions can, on the other hand, stay on either side of the clitic (78).

(77) a. linnagagi
town.COM.too

b. *linnagiga
town.too.COM.

(78) a. linnagi   taga
town.too behind

b. linna tagagi
town behind.too

In Estonian, a further test is the shape of the stem to which the element has attached; while clitics can attach to both nominative and genitive stems, typical case suffixes only attach to genitive stems. Again, the CATE suffixes behave like other case suffixes rather than like clitics:[31]

(79) a. linngi
      town.too

   b. linnagi
      town.GEN.too

   c. *linnga
      town.COM.

   b. linnaga
      town.GEN.COM.

Furthermore, while most prepositions require partitive case of their complement, some actually require one of the CATE cases. This, again, supports a view in which these elements are not postpositions.

(80) a. koos   linnaga
      together town.COM.
      'with the town'

   b. ilma   linnata
      without town.ABE.
      'without the town'

   c. kuni linnani
      to   town.TERM.
      'to the town'

We can deduce, after having applied the various tests, that the Estonian data actually do contain case suffixes rather than cliticized postpositions, and that the data therefore exemplify UC.

To conclude, the burden of evidence for UC lies in the general analysis of a language, and the usual criteria for determining whether something is a word (syntactic unit) or a bound affix (sub-syntactic unit) can be applied. Such criteria include, e.g., the possibility for the unit to be stressed; of participating in otherwise word internal morphophonological processes; of having intervening elements between it and what would be the stem; or of determining other grammatical features (e.g., an adposition often assigns a particular case, while an affix does not). In addition, some considerations on symmetry can also be included; e.g., in Turkic languages, if the case affixes had been analyzed as postpositions, we would still wonder what to do with the unbalanced number-marking, which would not lend itself so easily to an adpositional analysis.

I have not made additional investigation of the languages from which the UC examples in this chapter are drawn. However, some of the examples are from languages of which I have a fair knowledge. Most of the others have been provided by linguists who, in many cases, must be counted as particularly professional, given that they have noticed (and included in a published grammar or paper) UC examples which from their point of view may be marginal and unexpected. I have trusted these linguists to have applied the ordinary criteria when determining whether something is a word or an affix.

2.3.1.2. *Coordination or subordination?*

There is a potential problem in distinguishing unbalanced coordination from subordination. After all, while unbalancedness is not expected in coordination, there is no reason not to expect that the object of, for instance, a comitative adposition has different properties from that of the head DP, e.g., case-wise. In other words, when do we know that we have (81a) (a comitative construction), and when (81b) (coordination)? In this section, comitative constructions will be used as an example of subordination, but most of the points can probably be carried over to other subordinate constructions, too.

(81) a.   [Mary with Peter] went to town

     b.   [Mary and Peter] went to town

Some ideal criteria for determining whether a construction is a co-ordinated or a comitative construction are listed below. Not all criteria require to be fulfilled simultanously.

Agreement. If the assumed conjuncts together agree with an element outside the assumed CoP (82a), such as when two singular DPs constituting a subject agree with a plural-marked verb, this is a strong indication that the phrase is best analyzed as a CoP.

(82) a. [Mary and Peter] are going to town

    b. [Mary with Peter] is going to town

Movability. If part of the construction can move, it is more comitative-like than if there are restrictions on movement, (83a) vs. (83b). If the construction-marker can also move, it is more likely a subordinate construction, (83c) vs. (83d).

(83) a. Who did you see [Mary with t]?

    b. *Who did you see [Mary and t]?

    c. With who(m) did you see [Mary t]?

    d. *And who did you see [Mary t]?

Like categories. There are stronger restrictions against the use of different syntactic categories in coordinated structures (84b), than in comitative structures (84a).

(84) a. [Green with black stripes] is my favourite pattern

    b. ?[Green and black stripes] is / are my favourite pattern

Semantics. If each conjunct adds semantically to the totality (85a), rather than to just the adjacent member (85b), it is most likely a CoP.

(85) a. Mary and Peter and Paul and Polly . . . (= a group)

    b. Mary with Peter with Paul with Polly . . .
                                           (= nested couples)

However, it must be stressed that these criteria are neither necessary nor sufficient, at least not taken independently. For instance, Modern Greek usually has a clear distinction between coordination and comitative constructions (Joseph and Philippaki-Warburton 1987:60); first, the elements on either side of the conjunction have the same case, while those on either side of a comitative preposition do not. Second, two DP conjuncts require plural agreement, while in comitative constructions, this is not the case. The distinction is shown in (86).

(86) a. [o   Janis   ke i   Maria] horepsan /
ART.NOM Janis.NOM and ART.NOM Maria danced.PL /
*horepse
danced.SG
'Janis and Maria danced.'

b. o   Janis   horepse   / *horepsan me
ART.NOM Janis.NOM danced.SG / danced.PL with
ti   Maria
ART.ACC Maria
'Janis danced with Maria.'
                        (Joseph and Philippaki-Warburton 1987:61)

However, sentences like (87) are also possible; where a comitative construction actually triggers plural agreement, but where the elements have
different case (viz., the one expected in each of the positions):

(87) o   Janis   me ti   Maria horepsan
ART.NOM Janis.NOM with ART.ACC Maria danced.PL
'Janis danced with Maria'
                        (Joseph and Philippaki-Warburton 1987:61)

Joseph and Philippaki-Warburton (1987:61) attribute this possibility to
a reanalysis of *me* to have become a conjunction in this context. They
may be right, but it does not explain why 'the conjunction' *me* allows
split coordination, while the ordinary conjunction *ke* usually does not.
    The Greek example shows that there is not always a clear distinction
between what must be counted as coordination and what must be counted
as subordination. This topic will be further discussed in Chapter 7, where
it will also be shown that conjunctions often originate from subordinating
elements.

2.3.1.3. *"Pseudocoordination"*

One construction that can be found in Mainland Scandinavian (Norwegian, Swedish, and Danish) is the so-called pseudocoordination (also
called subcoordination).[32] The phenomenon has been discussed to some
extent in the literature (more recently by Johnsen 1988, Josefsson 1991,
Wiklund 1996), and there is some controversy regarding its status as
subordination or coordination. Structurally, it looks like VP coordination
in which the first conjunct contains one of a limited number of verbs of

(mostly) location or direction. Semantically, however, it clearly differs from other types of coordination in that the conjuncts do not simply create a group of any kind, but they create an aspectual interpretation determined to some extent by the meaning of the verb in the first conjunct. The original meaning of that verb is often reduced in these constructions.

(88) a. Per [kommer og spiser middag i dag].   (Norwegian)
         Per comes   and eats   dinner today
         'Per is coming for dinner today.'

     b. Lars [sitter och läser en bok].   (Swedish)
         Lars sits   and reads a book
         'Lars is reading a book (while sitting).'   (Wiklund 1996)

     c. Jens [sidder og fisker nede ved åen].   (Danish)
         Jens sits   and fishes down by the.river
         'Jens is fishing down by the river (while sitting).'
                                            (Josefsson 1991:130)

Since verbs in the Scandinavian languages are not morphologically marked for aspect pseudocoordination is one way of expressing aspect syntactically. However, the question remains as to whether it should be regarded as coordination or not. Josefsson (1991) suggests that it should, while Johnsen (1988) and Wiklund (1996) takes the opposite view, suggesting instead that the conjunction is to be regarded as a non-finite head of a TP. There are a number of ways in which pseudocoordination (PC) differs from ordinary coordination. (The examples sentences below are all from Norwegian; the (a) sentences are examples of PC and the (b) sentences of ordinary coordination; the asterisks in the (a) sentences are for the PC interpretation—they may be grammatical in an ordinary coordination interpretation.)

(89) *Extraction is possible in PC* (Johnsen 1988:196)
     a.   Middag kommer Per og spiser i dag
           dinner   comes Per and eats   today
           'Dinner is what Peter is coming for today.'

     b. *?Middag leser Per og spiser i dag
           dinner   reads Per and eats   today
           'Dinner is what Peter reads and eats today.'

(90) *Both conjuncts must have the same tense in PC*
(Josefsson 1991:139)
   a. *Per [kom og spiser middag i dag].
     Per came and eats   dinner today
     'Per was coming and has dinner today.'

   b. Mia [hadde boka   igår   og gir   den tilbake i dag].
     Mia had   the.book yesterday and gives it   back   today
     'Mia had the book yesterday and gives it back today.'

(91) *No overt subject can appear in PC* (Johnsen 1988:196)
   a. *Mona sitter og hun fisker
     Mona sits   and she fishes
     'Mona is fishing (while sitting).'

   b. Mona lager   middag og hun fisker.
     Mona makes dinner and she fishes
     'Mona cooks the dinner and she fishes.'

(92) *The order of conjuncts in PC cannot be changed without*
semantic distortion (Josefsson 1991:148)
   a. Mona [sitter og fisker] / [fisker og sitter].
     Mona sits   and fishes / fishes and sits
     'Mona is fishing / Mona fishes and sits'

   b. Mona [lager middag og fisker] / [fisker og lager
     Mona makes dinner and fishes / fishes and makes
     middag].
     dinner
     'Mona cooks the dinner and fishes / fishes and cooks the
     dinner.'

The above points show that pseudocoordination is different from ordinary coordination in a variety of ways. As a sidestep, we can note that the last of the above arguments is interesting from the point of view of unbalanced coordination. It is taken from Diderichsen (1968:154) in a list of conditions for ideal paratagms. This particular condition says that changing the order of the conjuncts should not disturb the semantical or logical contents of the construction. It does not mention purely formal results of changing the order of conjuncts, which is what unbalanced coordination deals with. Going back to pseudocoordination, there is one argument that to my mind is most important when determining the status of the construction. This is the fact that there is only one conjunction that can be used—viz. the equivalent of 'and' (*og, och*):

(93) *There is only one conjunction that is possible in PC*
    (Johnsen 1988:197)
    a. Mona [sitter og fisker].
        Mona sits   and fishes
        'Mona is fishing (while sitting).'

    b. *Mona [sitter eller/men fisker].
        Mona sits   or/but   fishes
        'Mona is fishing (while sitting).'

These points all show that pseudocoordination is a construction that has little resemblance to coordination, be it syntactically or semantically. The only common feature seems to be the conjunction *og* (No., Da.), *och* (Sw.) 'and'. But this is poor evidence, since this conjunction is homophonous with other function words such as the infinitival marker *å* (No.), *at* (Da.), and *att* (Sw.) 'to' and the adverb *og(så)* (No., Da.) 'too' —they are all pronounced /o/ (Endresen 1992a). If pseudocoordination is not coordination, we predict that it cannot be modified by a word such as *både* 'both', which can only be used with conjunction phrases. This is indeed the case:

(94) *PC cannot be modified by* både *'both'*
    a. *Mona både [sitter og fisker].
        Mona both sits and fishes
        'Mona is fishing (while sitting).'

    b. Mona både [lager middag og fisker].
        Mona both makes dinner and fishes
        'Mona both cooks the dinner and fishes.'

I therefore conclude that pseudocoordination as found in the Mainland Scandinavian languages is not coordination, but probably subordination, as suggested in Johnsen (1988) and Wiklund (1996).

2.3.2. SEMANTIC-PRAGMATIC UC

All the examples in this chapter have been unbalanced with respect to morphological or syntactic features—either on the conjuncts or on some element that agrees with one of them. There is, however, a very common type of unbalancedness which I have not discussed in this chapter, and which will remain untouched in the whole book: semantic-pragmatic unbalanced coordination, of which some examples follow below.

In (95), the idiom *opp og ned* 'up and down', a metaphor meaning that things are sometimes good and sometimes bad, is used in a metaphoric sense, but the journalist has attached metaphoric meaning to each of the conjuncts, and, crucially, in such a way that the order is significant. The skater Johan Olav Koss started out badly, but got better; the converse was true for the skater Ådne Søndrål.

(95) For Johan Olav Koss gikk det [ned og opp].
for Johan Olav Koss went it down and up
'Things went down and up for J. O. K.'

For Ådne Søndrål gikk det derimot [opp og ned].
for Ådne Søndrål went it on.the.other.hand up and down
'Things went up and down, on the other hand, for Å. S.'
(Arbeiderbladet, Jan. 1993)

In (96a), the order of the verbs is interpreted as the order of the events described by the verbs, so that it contrasts with (96b). Similarly, (96c) and (96d) mean different things.

(96) a. John [drank the poison and died]

b. John [died and drank the poison]

c. Mary was [poor but honest]

d. Mary was [honest but poor]   (Goodall 1987:31)

In Irish, there is a preferred order of DP conjuncts which depends on the grammatical person of the DP. A conjunct with first person comes before second person, which comes before third person, etc.[33] (In English, the converse is the norm, which is also a good illustration of this point.)

(97) a. mise agus an rí
     I   and the king
     'I and the king'

    b. eadar   mise agus tusa
       between I   and you.2SG
       'between me and you'

    c. an   libhse   nó leosan   é?
       Q.is with.you.2PL or with.them it
       'is it yours or theirs?'

    d. an   agatsa   nó aigesean atá   sé?
       Q.is at.you.2PL or at.him   that.is it
       'is it you or he who has it?'
                         (New Irish Grammar 1988:88)

A very special kind of semantic-pragmatic UC is what is often called *zeugma*, described thus: "solche koordinierte Strukturen, deren gemeinsames Prädikat zwei syntaktisch oder semantisch ungleichartige Satzglieder verknüpft" ('such coordinated structures, whose common predicate binds together two syntactically or semantically different parts of speech') (Bussman 1990:866). The actual cases to be categorized as zeugma of course depend on the definition of the various terms "syntactic," "semantic," "different," etc. Some examples (collected and kindly provided by Sue Blackwell) are given below:

(98) a. In the midst of all this is Mr. Stuart Weir, who took over
     editorship of the Statesman last November and has taken
     responsibility for cutting [staff, corners and the teeth of the
     new magazine].   (The Guardian, 1 June 1988)

    b. Our neighbour grows [his own vegetables and restless
     whenever he mentions his nightly exploits].
                            (van Oirsouw 1980)

    c. Working class people die [younger and more frequently]
     than the rich   (Letter to the Socialist Worker)

The reason this type of example is not included in this book is that they must have a different explanation from the morpho-syntactic UC above, not the least because the phenomenon is different: semantic-pragmatic UC is not strictly unacceptable syntactically: a conjunct order which involves even the strangest and most unlikely interpretation is possible with some stretching of imagination, politeness criteria, or allowance for lying about actual events. Morpho-syntactic UC, on the other hand, involves a conjunct order which is unacceptable; stretching the imagination does not help.

2.3.3. EXTRACTION CAUSING UC

Two special cases of unbalanced coordination are those that at first glance may look like extraction of a whole conjunct or part of a conjunct. The first case is one where the CoP seems to be split, with one conjunct having moved away from the rest of the CoP, and the other case is one where part of a CoP has moved out. Two examples are given below.

(99) a.   All the heaviness had gone, and the height

(Morrison 1988:148)

b.   How many courses can you take for credit and still remain
sane?   (Lakoff 1986)

Although there is reason to include them as UC constructions, they are rather special, since in each case, the unbalancedness consists not only of different features in the different conjuncts, but also of the existence of empty conjuncts, in some sense. Such constructions will be discussed in Chapter 6.

2.4. UG and UC

Having shown that UC is a phenomenon that must be accounted for, and divided it into categories according to locus of unbalancedness (nominal, verbal, etc.) and way (receiving or assigning), we are still left with one generalization that needs to be pointed out. We have seen that languages vary as to whether the deviant conjunct (i.e., the one not having or assigning the features expected in that position in the clause) is initial or final in the CoP. We have also seen that normally the order seems to be constant within a language, as in, e.g., Turkish and Eastern Mari, where the deviant conjunct is initial in the CoP in all the examples.

The fact that languages seem to be fairly constant with respect to the direction in which the unbalancedness occurs makes it a relevant question to ask whether this is accidental or not. Obviously, from a UG point of view, such variation ought not to be accidental, since that would mean an additional burden on the learning process, in addition to the mystery: how would children learn that unbalanced coordination always goes in one direction in the particular language, with lack of evidence for the contrary?

It is worth investigating, then, whether the direction of unbalancedness correlates with the general word order of other elements in the language. Below is a table (100) where the unbalanced coordination data from this chapter are compared with the direction of verb and object (often taken to define the general word order in a language—we could have chosen some other head-complement pair such as adposition + complement, too, nothing hinges on this) in the same language. The results are remarkable. There is a very strong correlation between, on the one hand, the order of verb + object, and on the other, that of normal conjunct + deviant conjunct (usually the same as that between conjunction + deviant conjunct).

(100)

| Language | General word order[34] | | | Deviant conjunct in UC | |
	OV	VO	Mixed, unclear	1.conj.	2.conj.
Amharic	X			X	
Burushaski	X			X	
Eastern Mari	X			X	
Hopi	X			X	
Japanese	X			X	
Latin	X			X	
Qafar	X			X	
Sidaamu Afo	X			X	
Swahili	X			X	
Tamil	X			X	
Turkic	X			X	
Yagnobi	X				X
Czech		X			X
English		X			X
Fulfulde		X			X

Language	General word order			Deviant conjunct in UC	
	OV	VO	Mixed, unclear	1.conj.	2.conj.
Gã	X				X
Italian	X				X
Norwegian	X				X
Old Hebrew	X				X
Old Irish	X				X
Old Norse	X				X
Palestinian Arabic	X				X
Serbo-Croat	X				X
Slovene	X				X
Tokelauan	X				X
Welsh	X				X
Afrikaans		X		X	
Dutch		X			X
Estonian		X		X	
German		X		X	X
Homeric Greek		X			X
Vedic		X		X	X

The table (100) shows that the correlation between general word-order facts and UC facts is significant. In most languages, a language which is head-final has a normal final conjunct and a deviant first conjunct; similarly, a head-initial language has a normal initial conjunct and a deviant final conjunct. This suggests that the direction of unbalancedness is regular and predictable. Interestingly, Ross (1970) suggested that gapping is predictable in the same way: an SVO language like English is predicted to have forward gapping, while an SOV language like Japanese has backward gapping. (Ross also included a third category for languages with free word order, like Russian; they could gap either way.) Some examples are given in (101), for English, and (102), for Japanese:

(101) a. I ate fish, Bill rice, and Harry roast beef

    b. Tom has a pistol, and Dick a sword   (Ross 1970:250)

(102) watakusi wa sakana o, Biru wa gohan o   tabeta
      I   PRT fish   PRT Bill PRT rice   PRT ate
      'I ate fish, and Bill rice.'   (Ross 1970:251)

Since gapping is a kind of UC according to the description in (1), it is relevant that gapping and the UC constructions considered in this chapter follow the same generalizations with respect to the general word-order facts of the language.

However, there are some cases in which the correlation in the table is not obvious. The third group in the table consists of languages that have a less clear status word order wise. Let us consider the three Germanic languages in the mixed group: Dutch, German, and Afrikaans. Afrikaans is usually taken to be a dialect of Dutch (see, e.g., Bright 1992:i.379). We are then left with the two languages Dutch and German, which are usually regarded as mixed languages word-order-wise, the reason for which is that the finite verb occupies different positions in main and subordinate clauses. For instance, in Bright (1992:i.381), it is stated that while main clause word order in Dutch is verb-second, in subordinate clauses, "constituents are ordered from right to left, with the main verb as the focal point":

(103) als   Jan morgen   met den auto naar Amsterdam gaat
      when Jan tomorrow with the car   to   Amsterdam goes
      'When Jan goes to Amsterdam tomorrow with the car.'
                          (Bright 1992:i.381)

The German word order has the same characteristics: "In subordinate clauses containing a finite verb, all verb forms (finite and non-finite) are final" (Bright 1992:ii.66).

(104) Ich glaube dass mein Vater vor   einigen Tagen nach
      I   think   that my   father before several days   to
      London gefahren ist
      London gone   has
      'I think that my father went to London several days ago.'
                          (Bright 1992:ii.66)

From these considerations in isolation, it seems that German and Dutch word order could be taken to be as much OV as VO; indeed, the VO order is usually taken to follow from the two requirements of (1) having a verb in a tense-agreement position, and (2) having a verb in C when this position is not filled by a complementizer. This is accepted by most linguists (see, e.g., Holmberg 1986), but it makes the unbalanced coordination seem more arbitrary. However, over the last few years these word-order claims have been refuted. Zwart (1992), inspired by Kayne's (1994) hypothesis that all languages are underlyingly SVO, argues that not even subordinate clauses in Dutch and German are head-final. Although his point is ultimately to show the underlying word order, he gives a number of interesting data of surface order, which are relevant here.

The Dutch data below show that complement clauses must appear in a VO order, (105a) vs. (105b), even in subordinate clauses; that other lexical projections are head-initial, (106a) vs. (106b); and that complement clauses are not islands, which indicates that they are in an L-marked position, (107a) vs. (107b).

(105) a.   . . . dat Jan zei dat hij Marie gekust had
                    that Jan said that he Marie kissed had
              '. . . that Jan said that he had kissed Marie.'

       b. *. . . dat Jan dat hij Marie gekust had zei
                    that Jan that he Marie kissed had said
              '. . . that Jan said that he had kissed Marie.'

(106) a.   de verwoesting van de stad
              the destruction of   the city

       b. *de van de stad verwoesting
              the of   the city destruction

(107) a.   Wie denk je   dat Jan mij vertelde dat hij gekust had?
              who think you that Jan me told   that he kissed had
              'Who do you think John told me he had kissed?'

       b. *Wie denk je   dat Jan mij het verhaal vertelde dat hij
              who think you that Jan me the story   told   that he
              gekust had
              kissed had
              'Who do you think John told me the story that he had
              kissed?'   (Zwart 1992)

Furthermore, other heads than verbs also have variable word order in the same languages. Nowadays, most adpositions are head-initial (prepositions), but there still exist some postpositions, although those that still exist are relics or extremely bookish:

(108) a. meinet*wegen*
           me.GEN because.of
           'because of me'

      b. seiner Meinung *nach*
          his   opinion after
          'in his opinion'

      c. den Vorschriften *gemäss*
          the rules   according.to
          'according to the rules'

      d. Der Bach   entlang wuchs Grass
          the stream along   grew grass
          'Along the stream grew grass.'

                                         (Kjell Johan Sæbø, p.c.)

It is reasonable to conclude, then, that there is, and has been, a fair amount of variation in general in the order of head and complement in these languages, and that this may also influence the order of head and complement in CoP.

The word-order facts of many of the other languages in this group are unclear as well. In Estonian, there are no strict rules with respect to verb-complement order (Haman 1962:13). Furthermore, there are both postpositions and prepositions in the language. The same comment can be made about Vedic and Homeric Greek; it is difficult to assess what the general word order is in these languages. In Dover (1960:25–31), the general tendency of Ancient Greek word order is that of OV. However, there is great variance between different texts, and each of the analyzed texts also points in more than one direction, so nothing certain can be said. Vedic, too, has a tendency towards OV order (Bright 1992: iii.371), but here, unbalanced examples of both types can be found, too. It therefore seems wise to leave the discussion about these languages, without a much more thorough investigation of empirical material and grammar.

This section has shown that, where there is a strict general word order between heads and complements in general, this order extends to that between conjuncts, and between a conjunction and one of the conjuncts (the deviant one). Whether the problem cases can be attributed to competing word-order patterns is not clear without a thorough investigation of the individual languages.

2.5. Extraordinary balanced coordination

In the previous sections, we have seen examples of unbalanced coordination, which is a phenomenon rarely mentioned in the literature. In addition, however, there is another phenomenon to be found, which is, in some contexts, quite surprising, and which we can call "extraordinary balanced coordination" (EBC). EBC is the case where a coordinated structure has different grammatical features from a simplex structure in the same surroundings. It is schematically represented below. (109a,b) suggest that a simplex category X or Y with feature(s) ϕ is not grammatical in a context Z. (109c,d) show that a coordination of X and Y (in any order) with the same features as before is acceptable in the same context as before.

(109) a. $*X_{[\phi]} / Z$

　　　 b. $*Y_{[\phi]} / Z$

　　　 c. $[X_{[\phi]} \& Y_{[\phi]}] / Z$

　　　 d. $[Y_{[\phi]} \& X_{[\phi]}] / Z$

2.5.1. ASSIGNING-TYPE EBC

In its simplest form, EBC is a very common and actually unsurprising type of coordination, if we interpret the ϕ-features in (109) as number-features: two singular conjuncts together make up a plural coordinated structure.

(110) a. Mary$_{[sg]}$ is happy

　　　 b. Peter$_{[sg]}$ is happy

c. [Mary and Peter]$_{[pl]}$ are happy

Number-EBC does not have a simple analysis, even though it is almost ubiquitous: it is far from clear whether these features are actually part of the syntactic representation, or whether they are semantic. If they are syntactic, it is unclear how the features have been inherited to the CoP, and it is unclear how it can be that number resolution does not always give a plural CoP:

(111) a. [A good friend and an eager supporter] has died today

b. [A good friend and an eager supporter] have died today

If the features are semantic, it is unclear how agreement with other categories is not always limited to semantic considerations. These questions are valid within a language or even within a particular kind of structure. The problems will not be further discussed here; they have been discussed by many other linguists, such as Sag et al. (1985), Goodall (1987), Corbett (1979, 1983), Corbett and Hayward (1987), Pollard and Sag (1991b), Lasersohn (1995).

2.5.2. RECEIVING-TYPE EBC

There is a different kind of EBC which has received very little attention in the literature. That is the one where the unusual features seem to be assigned to the CoP from a head outside the CoP, i.e., where the features of a CoP must be different from those of a simplex phrase. Just as for UC, the archetypical example of the receiving-type EBC is case assignment, to be exemplified in this section.

English
The ten English sentences below all have at least a first conjunct with case different from the one expected in the position in which that CoP occurs. Six out of the ten sentences are clear examples of EBC, since the conjuncts are overtly case-marked by a case different from that assigned to that position: (112b,e,f,h,i) have accusative conjuncts in a CoP in subject position, while (112j) has nominative conjuncts in object position. I take the other sentences (112a,c,d,g), which all seem to have a deviant first conjunct only, to be instances of EBC as well. (The reason will be discussed below.)

(112) a. [Me and Scott] are going to go play video games
                                              (Stahlke 1984:360)

      b. [Them and us] are going to the game together
                                              (Stahlke 1984:360)

      c. By the time I was 19 I'd had enough so [me and my
          cousin] left for London
                              (*The Big Issue* 12:10, London 1992)

      d.[35] Shearer then revealed that Jack Walker, the club's Mr
          Moneybags, had given [he and his new team-mates] a pat
          on the back for their fairy-tale start.
          (*Daily Mirror*, 19 Aug. 1992, reported by D. Hudson, p.c.)

      e. 'When she kissed me, [myself and the rest of the class]
          were totally shocked,' he said.
                                        (*Today*, 6 June 1992, 17)

      f. [Him and me] ate it all
          (Jorge Hankamer, p.c., children, small rural town, Texas,
          1940s–50s)

      g. [Me and Robert] went to the fair yesterday
          (Leanne Hinton, p.c., children / teens, Texas and Califor-
          nia 1990s)

      h. Dinner-table conversation, U. of Texas, a married couple
          (A and B) and C:
          A: So. We decided to have a mutual adventure today. We
          hadn't seen each other for a week, and . . .
          C: Who?
          A: [Me and B].
          B: [Me and him].
                              (Leanne Hinton, p.c., recorded by L. H.)

      i. [Him and her] were always good friends
          (Malcolm Ross, p.c., children, suburban London,
          1940s–50s)

  j.   Joe wouldn't explain it to [she and I]

$\qquad$ (Susan Ervin-Tripp, p.c.)

The reason for considering all the sentences instances of EBC is that I have not encountered any example of unbalanced coordination in English in which both conjuncts were overtly case-marked pronouns, and where only the pronoun in the first conjunct had deviant case. (More will be said about the reason for this in Chapter 4.) The clear UC examples have a deviant second pronoun only. The examples above, which all have a deviant pronoun in the first conjunct, are therefore taken to be balanced coordination, where both conjuncts have deviant case. (112e) may seem slightly unusual in that the pronoun has the shape of an anaphor. However, it is common in English to use this form for the purpose of emphasis, rather than as a bound anaphor. It is included here, since, like the others, it has non-nominative case features and does never occur as a subject on its own. The examples (112f–j) are all reported on the basis of personal experience.

French

In French, only the emphatic forms of pronouns can be used in co-ordination. Thus, in the same position where a nominative, clitic form of a simplex pronoun is allowed, only emphatic pronouns can occur, if co-ordinated. In (113a), a simplex nominative clitic pronoun is in subject position; in (113b), two coordinated nominative clitic pronouns wrongly occur, while (113c) shows how only emphatic pronouns are allowed (although the sentence is slightly marked); (113d), with left dislocation, is the preferred structure.[36]

(113) a.   J'ai   soif
$\qquad$ 1SG.NOM have thirst
$\qquad$ 'I am thirsty.'

   b.   *Tu   et je,   nous   avons soif
$\qquad$ 2SG.NOM and 1SG.NOM 1PL.NOM have thirst
$\qquad$ 'You and I, we're thirsty.'

   c.   ?*Toi   et   moi   avons soif
$\qquad$ 2SG.ACC and 1SG.ACC have thirst
$\qquad$ 'You and I are thirsty.'

    d.   Toi   et moi,   nous   avons soif
        2SG.ACC and 1SG.ACC 1PL.ACC have   thirst
        'You and I, we're thirsty.'   (Paul Kershaw, p.c.)

Italian

Whenever a determiner is missing (or being empty) in a noun phrase in Italian, the interpretation should be indefinite. Furthermore, the only determiners can in general only be left out with plural or mass head nouns. However, as pointed out by Longobardi (1994:619), when nouns in an argument position are coordinated, they may occur without a determiner, and still give a definite reading:

   (114) a. Cane e   gatto si   erano giá   addormentati
           dog and cat   had already fallen asleep

       b. *(Un/Il) grande amico di Maria mi ha tilefonato
         a/the   great friend of Maria me has called
         'A/The great friend of Maria called me up.'
                             (Longobardi 1994:612–19)

Greek

In Greek, definite determiners are obligatory with proper nouns. Furthermore, definite determiners are also obligatory for a generic interpretation (Roussou and Tsimpli 1994:73). However, when coordinated, nominals may occur without the otherwise obligatory definite determiners, as has been shown by Eftichidhou, Manolessou, and Vassiliou (1995):

   (115) a. Dhiodhoros ke Kurtios anaferun oti . . .
           Diodorus   and Curtius mention that

       b. *(O) Dhiodhoros anaferi   oti . . .
         the Diodorus   mentions that
               (Eftichidhou, Manolessou, and Vassiliou 1995)

   (116) a. Jiatri   ke dhikighori plirononde adhra
           doctors and lawyers   are.paid   very.well
               (Eftichidhou, Manolessou and Vassiliou 1995)
       b. *(I) manavidhes kserun arithmitiki
         the greengrocers know   arithmetics
                     (Roussou and Tsimpli 1994:73)

Norwegian

The Bergen dialect, which may have unbalanced coordination of pronouns in subject position (as shown in Section 2.2.1.1), also has attested extraordinary balanced coordination, where both conjuncts have accusative rather than nominative case.

(117) a. Bare [meg og deg] ska' sitte på kjelken hans
        only me.ACC and you.ACC shall sit on his   sledge
        'Only you and me shall sit on his sledge.'

    b. [Meg og deg] hjalp no godt te', då
        me.ACC and you.ACC helped now well to then
        'But then me and you did help a lot, too.'
                                    (Larsen and Stoltz 1912:138)

This phenomenon is also attested in the Kristiansand dialect by the dialectician A. Johnsen, who writes (unfortunately without relevant examples):

Når den som taler, nevner seg selv og en annen, vil han gjerne bruke begge pronomener i avhengighetsform, uavhengig av ordenes syntaktiske stilling.
                                    (Johnsen 1942:160)
[When the one who speaks, mentions himself and somebody else, he will usually use both pronouns in the dependent form [accusative, translator's note], no matter the syntactic position of the words.]

Qafar

In Qafar, it is the rule rather than the exception that CoPs have different case from simplex elements. Conjuncts in a CoP in subject position get absolute case rather than the expected nominative case (118)–(121).

This has additional effects: the verb loses the possibility of agreeing with the subject; the two verb forms possible, when the subject is a CoP, are either the feminine singular, which can be considered a default form on the basis of other phenomena in the language (see Hayward and Corbett 1988:266–70), or a plural form determined by semantic number resolution. This plural form is one which, when the subject is a simplex phrase, is used for nouns only; the plural form used with pronouns is only possible when the subject is plural, but non-coordinated.

(118) [kàa-kee tèt] temeete / yemeeten
     he.ABS-and she.ABS came.F.SG / came.PL

(119) [kèn-kee   kèn]   temeete   / yemeeten
      they.ABS-and they.ABS came.F.SG / came.PL

(120) [yì qammii-kee   kày baxa]   temeete   / yemeeten
      my uncle.ABS-and his son.ABS came.F.SG / came.PL

(121) [woò baacoytaa-kee   kày toobokoyta] temeete   /
      that poor-man.ABS-and his brother.ABS came.F.SG /
      yemeeten
      came.PL   (Hayward and Corbett 1988:265–70)

Spanish

In Spanish, which, like English, has a contrast between nominative and accusative pronoun forms, the rule is that coordinated pronouns in object position must have nominative case. The contrast is seen below; in (122a), a CoP with nominative pronouns is the object of a preposition, which, when having a simplex object, assigns accusative case to it, as seen in (123).

(122) a. para [tú   y   yo]
          for   you.NOM and I.NOM
          'for you and me'

      b. *para [ti   y   mí]
          for   you.ACC and me.ACC
          'for you and me'

(123) a. para ti / *tú

      b. para mí / *yo   (Goodall 1987:47–8)

2.6. Summary

In this chapter, we have looked at two classes of coordination data; unbalanced and extraordinary balanced coordination (UC and EBC). UC can be schematically represented as *[X & Y]* vs. **[Y & X]*, i.e., where the order of the conjuncts is essential for the acceptability of the whole construction. EBC can be represented as $*X_{[\phi]}$ / Z; $*Y_{[\phi]}$ / Z; $[X_{[\phi]} \& Y_{[\phi]}]$ / Z; or as $[Y_{[\phi]} \& X_{[\phi]}]$ / Z, i.e., where a conjunction phrase with certain morphosyntactic features cannot sit in a syntactic position which is perfectly fine for a simplex phrase with the same features, or vice versa: where a conjunction phrase can sit in a position not allowed for an equivalent simplex phrase.

Neither phenomenon has been studied in any depth previously. It seems clear that UC and EBC are widespread and occur in many languages systematically. I have found 32 languages (from closely related to unrelated) in which UC occurs regularly. Furthermore, it seems that the direction of the unbalancedness correlates with the general direction of head-complement in each language: out of 12 OV-languages, 11 have the deviant UC conjunct in the first position; out of 14 VO-languages, all have the deviant UC conjunct in the second position. There are six languages whose word order is mixed or unclear, and which must hence refrain from the generalizations.

The strong correlation of UC with the general word order in these languages shows that UC should not be dismissed as a phenomenon caused by relative distance or processual factors. Corbett (1991:266) says that most cases which involve agreement with one conjunct involve the nearest conjunct. This does not seem to be generally true, although it does seem to hold for Czech, Old Norse, some Arabic and Hebrew varieties, and Serbo-Croat, all in which only predicates preceding the subject agree with a single conjunct (i.e., the first). EBC does not seem to be as common as UC; I have found data from six languages. However, in these languages, it does occur regularly, a fact that shows that it should be taken into an account of coordination.

Notes

1. Some examples are Corbett (1991:266–7), Goodall (1987:46–9), Hayward and Corbett (1988:271), Kiparsky (1968: appendices I and II), Lorimer (1935:381), Martin (1975:159), van Oirsouw (1987:231–5), Rouveret (1990:73 n.29). Höhle (1989) is an exception who discusses the topic with regard to one particular construction.

2. Such languages include, among others, Turkish, Eastern Mari, Welsh, and languages with so-called serial verbs; such as Fulfulde and Sidaamu Afo.

3. As we shall see in Section 2.4, Ross (1970) suggested that gapping was a phenomenon which was closely linked with the general word order of the language. Therefore, gapping rightly should be included as a special case of UC.

4. The term *conjunction phrase* (*CoP*) must be regarded as synonymous with *coordinated structure* throughout this chapter. In Chapter 4, we shall look at its

structure in detail; for the moment it is enough to understand it pretheoretically as the constituent consisting of the conjuncts and the conjunction(s).

5. I have chosen to keep Lorimer's case-classification, but from a more modern point of view, Burushaski seems to be an ergative language, where the category NOM.ACC. probably is the equivalent of ABSOLUTIVE, and TRANS.NOM. AG. of ERGATIVE.

6. I am grateful to Trond Trosterud for making me aware of these data.

7. Not all morphosyntactic properties are subject to unbalancedness; e.g., for most speakers, possessive is obligatorily expressed in each conjunct, as is seen in the contrast between (ia) and (ib), and between (iia) and (iib) (ILL = illative case).

(i) a. %Annan   [ydər   den ergəže]   školəško   kajat
    Anna.GEN [daughter and son.3SG.POSS. school.ILL go.3PL
    'Anna's daughter and son went to school.'

  b. Annan   [ydəržö   den ergəže]   školəško
    Anna.GEN [daughter.3SG.POSS and son.3SG.POSS. school.ILL
    kajat
    go.3PL
    'Anna's daughter and son went to school.'

(ii) a. *Məj Annan   [ydər   den ergəžəm]   palem
    I   Anna.GEN daughter and son.3SG.POSS.ACC know.1SG
    'I know Anna's daughter and son.'

  b. Məj Annan   [ydəržö   den ergəžəm]
    I   Anna.GEN daughter.3SG.POSS and son.3SG.POSS.ACC
    palem
    know.1SG
    'I know Anna's daughter and son.'

8. It is unacceptable for both conjuncts in an object CoP to have nominative case (i), (although one exception is included in the section on EBC), and it is unacceptable for the first conjunct only to have accusative case in a subject CoP (ii).

(i) a.   *Gramps will kiss [he and she]

  b.   *Gramps expected [he and she] to sing   (Schwartz 1985:167)

(ii) a.   *[Him and she] will drive to the movies

b. *It would be better if [her and he] drove to the movies

                                    (Schwartz 1985:165)

These intuitions are confirmed by the English speakers I have consulted.

9. I am grateful to Trond Trosterud for making me aware of the Estonian data.

10. Tom Cravens made me aware of the Italian data, for which I am grateful, and Hallvard Dørum kindly supplied me with references.

11. I am grateful to Kirsti Koch Christensen for this information.

12. Accusative case on both conjuncts can be found in the Bergen dialect, see Section 2.5.2.

13. I am grateful to Elie Wardini for helping me with the translation of the examples.

14. This information is due to Fredrik Otto Lindeman, who has kindly made me aware of the data presented here.

15. I am grateful to Elisabeth Silva for the information on Tamil.

16. Arnfinn Vonen informs me that he no longer believes that the plural form of *pele* 'dear' is actually *p[e]pele*; instead this lexeme has the same realization in singular and plural, like many other Tokelauan words. However, the example is the only one in their Tokelauen text corpus which has attested the unbalanced second conjunct. It must be noted that in spite of the lack of much evidence in their corpus, this type of unbalanced coordination is very common in Tokelauan as well as in the closely related language Samoan:

(i) a. [le   tama lelei ma le   mānaia]
        the.SG boy   kind and the.SG handsome.SG
        'the kind and handsome boy'
    b. [Ø   tama lelei ma le   / *Ø   mānanaia
        the.PL boy   kind and the.SG / the.PL handsome.PL
        'the kind and handsome boys'   (Arnfinn Vonen, p.c.)

17. However, Bernt Brendemoen (p.c.) has informed me that exclusive disjunction is formed in a different way: in the "exclusive" counterpart of (37), each conjunct has its own question-particle, and each conjunct is fully inflected. The verb has also moved in front of the last conjunct:

(i) [elmaları]   mi yediniz   [armutları]   mi
    the.apple.PL.ACC Q eat.PAST.2PL the.pear.PL.ACC Q
    'Did you eat the apples or the pears?'

Adversative DP coordination is formed without overt conjunction, but with a preference for marking both conjuncts:

(ii) [Ahmed'i   değil Mehmed'i]   gördüm
     Ahmed.ACC not   Mehmed.ACC see.PAST.1SG
     'I saw Ahmed but not Mehmed'

18. There are, however, also some examples where the order is reversed, i.e., nominative followed by vocative. Kiparsky (1968:54–5) claims that the latter type is the marked case; that in poetry, it is possible for the second conjunct (with its attached clitic conjunction) to be "shifted into the first position" (the two other theoretically possible types, *Voc+ca & Nom*, and *Nom & Voc+ca*, never occur):

(i) indraś ca vāyav
    NOM   VOC
    'Indra and Vāyu'   (Kiparsky 1968:54)

19. The initial sound in *chaws* has undergone spirant mutation (from *kaws*) triggered by the conjunction *a*, and is not further mutable.

20. Interestingly, only overtly marked agreeing elements are unacceptable. A few words are neutral with respect to marking of agreement features; one of them is the adjective *rosa* 'pink'. It does not cause a conflict:

(i) a.   huset   er rosa / blått
         the.house.N.SG is pink / blue.N.SG
         'The house is pink.'

    b.   hytta   er rosa / blå
         the.hut.F.SG is pink / blue.F.SG
         'The hut is pink.'

    c.   huset   og hytta   er rosa / *blått   / *blå
         the.house.N.SG and the.hut.F.SG is pink / blue.N.SG / blue.F.SG
         'The house and the hut are pink.'

21. Whether resolution rules are used or not depends on the syntactic construction. When the predicate follows the coordinated subject, resolution rules are used—but when it precedes the subject, the result is UC, where agreement is determined by the first conjunct. (This is shown in the subsection on Old Norse below.)

22. Trygve Skomedal informs me that the general rules by which conflict resolution is handled (in the cases where the verb follows the subject) invoke rather complex semantic and pragmatic considerations. As a rule, coordination of DPs with different gender triggers neuter agreement, while singular conjuncts will result in plural agreement. But in (i) below, the verb, participle, and adjective that agree with the respective CoPs, follow the rule with respect to gender

only. With respect to number, they surprisingly have singular agreement features. This can only be explained semantically by assuming that what is denoted by the conjuncts is understood as a singular group.

(i) a. [konur   ok bǫrn]   var   rekit   í   eitt hús
   woman.F.PL and child.N.PL was.3SG driven.N.SG into one house
   'Women and children were driven into a house.'

   b. hvárt   honum væri [kapp   sitt ok metnaðr]
   whether for.him was competition.N.SG his and prestige.huntM.SG
   einhlítt
   one-way.N.SG
   'whether he could trust his own competition and hunt for prestige.'

   c. [ǫnnur   kinn   hans ok svá nef]   var   hálft
   one.M.SG cheek.M.SG his   and also nose.N was-3SG half.N.SG
   snjóhvítt
   snow-white.N.SG
   'His other cheek and also half the nose was snow-white.'
   (Nygaard 1966:69–71)

23. What is the reason to assume that one suffix is a conjunction while the other is a serial suffix? Why are not both considered to be conjunctions? Generally, the answer will have to do with similarities and differences between the two within a language, and cross-linguistic evidence. E.g., cross-linguistically, it seems that most OV languages have a conjunction which is tied to the first conjunct, while in VO languages it is tied to the second conjunct (when the conjunction is situated between the conjuncts). If serial affixes were conjunctions, they would most likely be prefixes in VO languages. This does not seem to be the case, however. For Amharic, a language-internal reason to keep them separate is the fact that serial affixes have agreement features while conjunctions do not.

24. I am grateful to Nils Berg for assisting with the glosses.

25. Surface phonological form:

(i) Kakkaddenna 'angate seiseha 'ikkikkiro, k'olte ka''e galagalchite k'ishshe la''anno.

26. Cathrine Fabricius Hansen informs me that the same generalization holds for case-assigning prepositions:

(i) a. Die Kinder kommen [mit und ohne] Mäntel   /
   the children come   with and without rainclothes.ACC /
   *Mänteln
   rainclothes.DAT
   'The children come with and without rainclothes.'

    b.   Die Kinder kommen [ohne   und mit] Mänteln   /
        the children come   without and with rainclothes.DAT /
        *Mäntel
        rainclothes.ACC
        'The children come without and with rainclothes.'

27. I am grateful to David Adger for having brought the example to my attention.

28. If anything, the second conjunct might be seen as a deviant conjunct, since it is not incorporated. I have not been able to find out whether noun-incorporation is obligatory. If it is, then the second conjunct is, in fact, a deviant conjunct, and the construction is an example of UC (for a different reason than discussed, though).

29. Coordination can usually not happen at a level before syntax, i.e., at a word-internal level. However, sometimes coordination can take place within compounds, as in (i), where both first and second members of compounds are coordinated (in (ia,b) and (ic), respectively). Derivational and inflectional affixes cannot be coordinated (ii). The examples are from Norwegian. It can be noted that word-initial coordination is much more common, and that word-final coordination occurs in written language only.

(i) a.   av- og påkledning
         off and on.dressing
         'undressing and dressing'

      b.   jule-   og nyttårsmat
         Christmas and new.year.food
         'food at Christmas and new year'

      c.   barneblader   og -bøker
         child.magazines and books
         'children's magazines and books'

(ii) a. *fisker og -ing
         fish.er and ing
         'fisherman and fishing'

      b.   *flytter og -et
         move.s and ed
         'moves and moved'

30. I am very grateful to Trond Trosterud for having collected the information on Estonian from Mati Erelt for me.

31. It should be stressed that whether the stem is vowel-final or not is of no importance, as the following examples show:

(i) tubagi   toagi   *tubaga   toaga   *tubas
room.too room.GEN.too   room.COM.   room.GEN.COM.   room.INE.
toas
room.GEN.INE.

32. The phenomenon is assumed by Johnsen (1988) to be closely related to the empty object construction discussed in Åfarli and Creider (1987), exemplified below:

(i) Jens hugg   ved   og stablet Ø opp
Jens chopped firewood and piled   (it) up

(Åfarli and Creider 1987:339)

However, this construction, while being entirely normal in Old Norse and even Modern Norwegian a hundred years ago, seems unacceptable by most speakers today, and I will not discuss it here.

33. I am grateful to Ana von Klopp for having pointed out this fact for me.

34. Information on the word order of the majority of the languages in the table is obtained from Bright (1992); for a comparison of the kind presented in this table, I see it as a virtue that as much information as possible comes from the same source (although admittedly, the different languages are described by different contributors). The following is a complete list of the sources of word-order information on the languages in the table: Afrikaans(Bright 1992:i.379,381), Amharic (Bright 1992:i.55), Burushaski (Lorimer 1935:469), Czech (Bright 1992:iii.455), Dutch (Bright 1992:i.381), Eastern Mari (Bright 1992:iv.208), English (Bright 1992:iv.245), Estonian (Haman 1962:13), Fulfulde (Endresen 1992a:50), Gã (Williamson 1989:28–30), German (Bright 1992:ii.66), Homeric Greek (Bright 1992:ii.92), Hopi (Bright 1992:iv.213), Italian (Bright 1992:ii. 241), Japanese (Bright 1992:ii.250), Latin (Bright 1992:ii.317), Norwegian (Bright 1992:iii.378), Old Hebrew (Gil 1982:128), Old Irish (Fredrik Otto Lindeman, p.c.), Old Norse (Sigurðsson 1988), Palestinian Arabic (Bright 1992: iii.416), Qafar (Hayward and Corbett 1988:271), Samoan (Bright 1992:iii.248), Serbo-Croat (Bright 1992:iii.455), Sidaamu (Bright 1992:i.328), Slovene (Bright 1992:iii.455), Swahili (Bright 1992:iv.105), Tamil (Bright 1992:iv.135), Turkic (Bright 1992:iv.188,194), Vedic (Bright 1992:iii.371), Welsh (Bright 1992:i.234), West Greenlandic (Sadock 1985:394–5), Yagnobi (based on data in Bright 1992:ii.229–30).

35. This sentence seems to be exceptional, in that none of my English informants can accept it.

36. I am grateful to Paul Kershaw for having drawn my attention to these data, which he presented at a seminar at the University of Minnesota, 1992.

3

Conjunctions as Heads

3.1. Introduction

In this chapter, I will investigate the idea that conjunctions may be heads. The term *head* has been used a long time; Hudson (1987:109) dates it back to Henry Sweet (1891) (quoted in Matthews 1981:165), who used it to refer to any word to which other words are subordinate. In recent years, the term has had a renaissance, being used for the most prominent and super-ordinate word in endocentric constructions. The emergence of X-bar syntax (Chomsky 1970; Jackendoff 1977) has made its existence absolutely crucial, since the head is what projects into an X-bar phrase. Other modern, syntactic theories also rely on the notion *head*, e.g., Generalized Phrase Structure Grammar (Gazdar et al. 1985), Head-driven Phrase Structure Grammar (Pollard and Sag 1987), and dependency grammar (see references in Hudson 1987:109).

The chapter is divided into two parts. Section 3.2 considers conjunctions as heads in a pretheoretic sense, applying the criteria in Zwicky (1985), Hudson (1987), and Svenonius (1992), who are among the few in the literature to have examined such criteria at all. It will be concluded that conjunctions are heads. Section 3.3 discusses whether conjunctions can be counted as functional rather than lexical heads. The criteria to be considered are those of Abney (1987) and Åfarli (1991), as well as Fukui and Speas (1986). It will be concluded that from most perspectives, they are functional heads.

3.2. The head-status of conjunctions

In spite of the interest in lexical projection and heads in the linguistic literature in recent years, very little is written about how one might determine whether an element is a head or not. Zwicky (1985) and Hudson

(1987) are notable exceptions to this trend. Zwicky discusses several criteria for determining head-status, and concludes that the criteria do not consistently point to one and the same head in a syntactic construction. Hudson, however, re-examines the criteria and concludes, after having shown that Zwicky's analyzes are "irrelevant or open to improvement" (Hudson 1987:112), that they do in fact point to the same head category in the syntactic constructions Zwicky discusses. Svenonius (1992), in applying the criteria to the Norwegian noun phrase, and showing how they point to an analysis which is consistent with the determiner being interpreted as head, adds a few more criteria.

In the first seven sections below, the conjunction is examined as a head by the criteria of Hudson and Zwicky. It is discussed whether the conjunction is: (a) a semantic argument or functor; (b) a determinant of agreement; (c) a morphosyntactic locus; (d) a subcategorizer; (e) a distributional equivalent of the phrase in which it occurs; and (f) obligatory.[1] The three subsequent sections apply the additional three criteria suggested by Svenonius to see whether the conjunction is: (a) unique, (b) an X^0 element, and (c) a determinant of word order. Finally, we shall apply a criterion of projected properties to CoP.

3.2.1. SEMANTIC ARGUMENT OR FUNCTOR

Zwicky's description of semantic heads is given in (1) (a description which Hudson shows concerns semantic functors rather than semantic arguments, as Zwicky suggests).

(1) We could take the head/modifier distinction to be at root semantic: in a combination X + Y, X is the "semantic head" if, speaking very crudely, X + Y describe a kind of the thing described by X.
(Zwicky 1985:4)

In a PP, the DP is standardly taken to be the argument. The preposition is hence a head, and this is supported by the description above: the PP in (2) describes a kind of direction rather than a kind of penguins.

(2) toward those penguins

Being a semantic functor is taken by Hudson to be the most important property for a head, and we should therefore expect the conjunction *and* to be one. This is not so straightforward, however, when we consider some typical coordination examples.

(3) a. apples and oranges

    b. in and out

    c. singing and dancing

We can establish that at least the conjuncts are certainly not semantic functors: (3a) is not a description of a kind of apples or a kind of oranges. The same can be said about the directional adverbs in (3b): the whole coordination is not a kind of in-direction or a kind of out-direction. Neither is (3c) a kind of singing or of dancing. However, the problem is that neither do the conjunctions seem to be functors: the phrases in (3) are not a kind of *and*. The same kind of comments can be made for other conjunctions:

(4) a. an apple or an orange
    b. Mary does not like baking but fishing

In (4a), what is described is not a kind of apple or a kind of orange, nor a kind of *or*. Similarly, (4b) is not a description of what Mary does not like or of what she likes, or of *but*. However, conjunctions are typically grammatical function words from a closed lexical class rather than contents words from an open lexical class. It is therefore not surprising that they cannot be modified by (lexical) elements. At this point, the criterion cannot be applied. We shall, however, get back to it in Section 3.3.5.

3.2.2. DETERMINING AGREEMENT

Hudson dismisses that in an endocentric construction with internal agreement (in English) the head is what determines the appropriate agreement features. He explains his point by showing that the relevant agreement features can be lexically fixed on the noun, no matter whether the noun is a head or not (1987:116–17). Agreement is therefore not a head property, he concludes. Besides, in copular predicate constructions, with a DP in both subject and object positions, where the DPs should ideally agree with each other, it can be seen that semantic considerations are as important as syntactic ones:

(5) a. He is my friend
      SG SG SG

b. They are my friends
    PL   PL PL

c. They are a nuisance
    PL   PL SG

d. ?My main problem is these scissors
    SG   SG PL

Hudson is probably right that overt agreement is governed by semantic rather than syntactic resolution rules (see Chapter 2) in English. For co-ordinated structures, however, we do not need to take a stand in this discussion. Although we shall make use of spec-head agreement in this book (Chapter 4), there is no overt morphological agreement within a CoP (see the English and Norwegian examples in (6)). There are no agreement features on the conjunction itself, and the agreement features that may be present on one conjunct (such as person, number, or case, depending on the particular language and the particular categories of the conjuncts) occur independently of the features of the other conjunct:

(6) a. [one chair]_{SG} and [two houses]_{PL}

     b. [en grønn stol]_[M.SG] og [et grønt hus]_[N.SG]
         a green chair   and a green house

     c. [en grønn stol]_[IND.SG] og [de grønne husene]_[DEF.PL]
         a green chair   and the green houses

The fact that the features in (6) are indeed agreement features is, of course, indisputable: the features within a conjunct have to be compatible, as is seen in (7):

(7) a. [one chair which is/*are green] and [two houses which
         SG   SG/PL   PL
         are/*is white]
         PL/SG
     b. *[en   grønt   stol]   og [et   grønn
         a.M.SG. green.N.SG. chair.M.SG. and a.N.SG. green.M.SG.
         hus]
         house.N.SG.

Overt CoP internal agreement cannot be a relevant criterion, then, to determine the head-status of any element within the CoP.

3.2.3. MORPHOSYNTACTIC LOCUS

The head is the morphosyntactic locus of its phrase, i.e., the element in which the morphosyntactic features of a phrase are expressed. Hudson (1987:122–3) shows this point by referring to German, where determiners are the only elements in the DP to receive some of the morphosyntactic features. For English, he uses examples with determining pronouns, which carry the case features of their phrase:

(8) a.   You children must behave yourselves /*themselves

    b.   We / *us students work hard

    c.   The government is against us / *we students

The conjunction itself is not a morphosyntactic locus in this way. It never changes shape (other than for phonological reasons), and never carries features determined by a particular construction. On the other hand, the other possible morphosyntactic loci, i.e., the conjuncts, are even less plausible, since, although they may carry the features of the whole construction, they may also sometimes carry features that are positively conflicting with those of the whole CoP.[2] Consider, e.g., gender resolution in Old Norse, where a conjunct with feminine gender and one with masculine gender agree with a participle with neuter gender (repeated from Chapter 2):

(9) [Gunnhildr ok synir þeira]   váru farin   til Danmerkr
    G.F.SG   and their sons.M.PL were gone.N.PL to Denmark
    suðr
    South
    'G. and their sons had gone South to Denmark.'

                                                        (Nygaard 1966:71)

The well-known case of singular conjuncts agreeing with a plural verb (semantic number resolution) also, of course, illustrates this point:

(10) [An apple]$_{[SG]}$ and [an orange]$_{[SG]}$ are on [the table]$_{[PL]}$

The morphosyntactic locus is not the conjunction itself, but it cannot be the conjuncts either, as we have seen, since they have features which may be contradictory to the whole conjunction phrase.

For this particular criterion I conclude that neither of the elements in the conjunction phrase is particularly well suited for head-hood, but that the conjunction is the only possible candidate. This conclusion is not far-fetched when seen in light of the comments for the semantic criterion above; although the morphosyntactic features are not located on the conjunction, it is clearly the conjunction which determines the morphosyntactic features of the whole phrase, in virtue of its function as a collector of single elements that are grouped together.

3.2.4. SUBCATEGORIZER

The head is the element that subcategorizes for other elements. Therefore, determiners are readily seen as heads: some of them have obligatory complements, others do not, as in (11). Also, they combine with different kinds of nouns, e.g., count nouns and mass nouns (12):

(11) a. The winners were lined up and each was given a standing ovation

   b. *The winners were lined up and every was given a standing ovation

(12) a. each penguin / *penguins / sand

   b. much *penguin / *penguins / sand   (Hudson 1987:121)

Conjunctions are clearly heads from a subcategorizing perspective. E.g., the Norwegian conjunction *for* can only coordinate uncomplementized finite clauses: [3]

(13) a. Jeg gikk   til byen   for jeg hadde ikke penger (CP & CP)
         I   walked to the.town for I   had   not money
         'I walked to the town for I had no money.'

   b. *Jeg gikk   til byen   for handlet mat   (IP & IP)
         I   walked to the.town for bought food
         'I walked to the town for bought food.'

    c. *Jeg gikk   til byen   for alle gatene   (DP & DP)
       I   walked to the.town for all the.streets
       'I walked to the town for all the streets.'

The conjunction *så* 'so' has the same subcategorization restriction; it can only coordinate CPs.

(14) a. Jeg hadde ikke penger så jeg gikk   til byen   (CP & CP)
        I   had   not money so I   walked to the.town
        'I didn't have any money so I walked to the town.'

     b. *Jeg handlet mat så gikk   til byen   (IP & IP)
        I   bought food so walked to the.town
        'I bought food, so walked to the town.'

The conjunction *men* 'but' also seems to be restricted in its subcategorization. Although there are examples where the conjuncts look like DPs they are probably best analyzed as something else. Consider first an example:

(15) Jeg har sett [Per, men ikke Marte]
     I   have seen Per but not Marte
     'I have seen Per, but not Marte.'

(15) is a problem since the negator *ikke* does not normally precede directly the conjunct it modifies if the conjunct is first in the CoP; rather it is in the ordinary adjunct position of the clause, after the finite verb:

(16) Jeg har ikke sett [Per, men Marte]
     I   have not seen Per but Marte
     'I haven't seen Per but Marte.'

Since *men* is a conjunction which requires its conjuncts to have adversative meaning, and forces one onto the conjuncts if it is not explicitly stated, we realize that *men* in this sentence cannot coordinate the DPs only. There is no forced interpretation here; the adversity is obviously linked to the presence of a negator in the first conjunct, and the absence of one in the second conjunct.[4] (16), and possibly also (15), therefore are examples of clausal coordination with some deleted elements (see Chapters 5 and 6). Thus, at least three Norwegian conjunctions are heads with respect to the subcategorization requirement.

3.2.5. DISTRIBUTIONAL EQUIVALENT

The head of an endocentric construction is the element that can function as a distributional equivalent of that construction. Hudson (1987:118) shows how Aux is the head of Aux + VP because Aux can function alone where VP cannot:

(17) a. He is controlling those penguins (Aux + VP)

    b. He is (Aux)

    c. *He controlling those penguins (VP)

This point is not as straightforward for coordinated constructions. It is clear that in some cases, it is one of the conjuncts that can be the distributional equivalent of the whole phrase, while the conjunction can never be such an equivalent:

(18) a. Apples and oranges are good for you

    b. Apples are good for you (first conjunct)

    c. Oranges are good for you (second conjunct)

    d. *And are good for you (conjunction)

However, there are also many cases where the conjuncts cannot be equivalents:

(19) a. An apple and an orange are good for you

    b. *An apple are good for you (first conjunct)

    c. *An orange are good for you (second conjunct)

(20) a. Ruth and Ursula embraced

    b. *Ruth embraced

    c. *Ursula embraced

(21) a.   We talked with Sam and Becky, respectively

      b.   *We talked with Sam, respectively

      c.   *We talked with Becky, respectively

The two examples (18) and (20) are constructions where a plural subject
is needed as a subject by the particular verb, the first one because of
agreement-features, the second one (the "symmetrical predicate") probably because of its inherent plurality features.[5] In (21), it is the adverb
respectively that requires features that cannot be fulfilled by an individual
conjunct alone (see also Section 5.3.2.2 for a discussion of *respectively*).

The discussion above seems to suggest that if the conjunction were a
head, it ought to be a distributional equivalent, occurring on its own in a
position that can be filled by a major category projection. This is contrary
to what we saw in the first examples in this section. However, there is
reason to question the relevance of this criterion: the conjunction is a
grammatical closed class item. Like other grammatical words it cannot
normally occur on its own.[6] It is therefore not surprising that it cannot
alone represent a whole phrase. We shall postpone further discussion until
the section on functional categories (Section 3.3).

3.2.6. OBLIGATORINESS

Obligatory elements are heads. Hudson (1987:118–19) illustrates this
point with categories whose subcategorized arguments can be elided but
retrieved from the previous discourse. Thus Aux is again the head of Aux
+ VP, and the clause is the complement of the complementizer:

(22) a.   I can swallow goldfish but you can't (swallow goldfish)

      b.   I've not seen him since (he left)

3.2.6.1. *Overt conjunctions*

Coordinated structures cannot easily be described as having a distinction
between obligatory and facultative or elided elements, since usually, all
elements are obligatory. However, they are not alone in this class. E.g.,
it is not clear that PPs have facultative or elided elements either: prepositional objects are usually not deletable except in constructions of so-
called "phrasal verbs" (intransitive prepositions), where the preposition

is often regarded as a particle, and where the meaning of the whole expression is often not compositional. Consider the Norwegian (23):[7]

(23) a. Vil du   sitte *på*?
      will you.SG sit   on
      'Do you want a lift (in our car)?'

     b. Har du   gått *ned*?
       have you.SG gone down
       'Have you lost weight?'

     c. Ta *i* her!
       take in here
       'Give (me) a hand!'

This kind of special case can in fact be found with coordinated structures as well. Even if these are special cases, we expect the elided element not to be the head-candidate, but one of the conjuncts, since the head should be more stable in the constructions it heads. Our expectations are borne out:

(24) a. Har du   vært bortreist, *eller*?
      have you.SG been away-gone or
      'Say, have you been away?'

     b. Hun likte det ikke, *men*.
       she liked it not, but
       'Well, she didn't like it.'

     c. Han har vært i Afrika *og*.[8]
       he has been in Africa and
       'He has even been to Africa.'

     d. *Men* er du   her alt   'a?
       but are you.SG here already then
       'Oh, are you here already?'

     e. *Og* det ble   lys
       and it became light
       'And there was light.'

Just as with the preposition examples above, these constructions have a
specialized meaning: the conjunction has not, or only marginally so, retained its meaning as an element for creating a collection. It is therefore
not clear whether these examples are relevant to the question of obligatoriness. However, it does seem reasonable to assume that the prepositions and conjunctions in these constructions are the same as those in
ordinary PPs and CoPs, and one might then ask how this development
could possibly have happened had the missing elements been heads, given
that obligatoriness is a characteristic of heads.[9] We can conclude that if
something is more obligatory than something else, it is the conjunction.

3.2.6.2. *Empty conjunctions*

In spite of the difficulty of eliding anything but non-heads, assumed to be
the conjuncts rather than the conjunctions, there is ample evidence of
empty conjunctions (resulting in what is often called asyndetic coordination) in various languages. Here, I will provide evidence that they are not
elided. We shall see five arguments for counting unexpressed conjunctions as empty conjunctions rather than no conjunctions. Finally, we shall
see that not all conjunction-less constructions should be counted as constructions with empty conjunctions.

First, while most languages seem to have some kind of conjunction
phrase, the way in which conjunctions are realized varies a lot between
as well as within languages. Gazdar et al. (1985:179) put it this way:
"Realization of coordinating morphemes is a highly parochial matter."
In many languages, coordination can be expressed facultatively with or
without conjunctions (the latter is often called asyndetic coordination).
This is the case for DP coordination in Sarcee, an Athapaskan language
spoken in Alberta (25a,b), and for VP coordination in Sissala (a
Niger–Congo Voltaic language) (see (28) below).

(25) a. [dítòò   dóó-ʔĩ]   iná áání-là
         own.father own.mother-DET she told
         'She told her own father and mother.'

     b. [dítòò   dóó   ìhílà] áásnì-là-à
         own.father own.mother-DET CONJ. she.told
         'She told her own father and mother.'
                              (Cook 1984:87, cited in Mithun 1988:339)[10]

Furthermore, in many languages, empty conjunctions are used for the coordination of certain categories, but not for others. One such example is Cayuga, a Northern Iroquoian language of Ontario, in which noun phrases are systematically coordinated with a conjunction *hni'*, while verbs and clauses cannot be coordinated by means of an overt conjunction (see Mithun 1988:342). DP coordination is shown in (26a), and clausal coordination in (26b):

(26) a. Ne:' tshō: ne' [onēhē' sahe'tá' hni'] ōkwayēthwē hne:'
          it   only the corn   beans   also we.planted CONTR
          'No, we only planted corn and beans.'

      b. Tho tshō: nhe:yóht ake'tré' atká:ta'
          there only so.it.is   I.drove it.stopped
          'I was just driving along and it stopped.' (Mithun 1988:342)

This kind of variation seems no different from the one in languages where the variation is between overt conjunctions. One such example is Sissala, which distinguishes between CP-coordination, VP-coordination, and "non-verbal" coordination (outlined in Blass 1989). Sentences are co-ordinated by *ká* (27), VPs by means of *a* or nothing (28), and non-verbal constituents by *rí* (or *arí*) (29).

(27) Betúú coŋgoroŋ pérí méétré bɛllɛ ká ú zíŋ má
      Elephant height   reach meters two and his weight also
      peri   kííló buɪ-ammuɔ
      reach kilos thousand-five
      'The height of the elephant reaches two meters and his weight
      reaches five thousand kilos.'   (Blass 1989:15)

(28) [I   sɪsényé sɪé [tɔk niŋ (a) mú (a) coki yɪɓuú ná (a)
      You now   so take fire and go and cut mound DEF and
      nyɪkɛ (a) ɓa yɪla vɪva
      light and cut mound IMP.walk]
      'You clear the mound place there and burn (the place). You
      now form the mounds while walking.'   (Blass 1989:12)

(29) [Pilɛ́kɛ́   rí wɔ́wúlɛ́nɛ́rɛ́] nɛ́ muɛ́ hé baksɛ
      Chameleon and spider   SDM went put farms
      'The chameleon and the spider went and made their farms.'
                                                  (Blass 1989:1)

Another example of a language in which coordination of different syntactic categories is expressed by different conjunctions is Nguna, a Melanesian language of the Central New Hebrides. There, VP coordination is expressed by the conjunction *poo*, and clausal coordination by *go*:

(30) a. A [ga   vano poo tape na-peka seara]
         I NON-PAST go and get yam some
         'I go and get some yams.'
                    (Schütz 1969:3.8, cited in Mithun 1988:343)

     b. Eu munu na-maloku go eu   sale poogi
         they drink kava   and they dance night
         'They drank kava, and they danced all night.'
                    (Schütz 1969:240.39, cited in Mithun 1988:348)

Given that empty conjunctions seem to function on a par with overt conjunctions in such a variety of cases as those above, it seems to me that languages with no audible coordinating conjunctions should be regarded as having empty conjunctions rather than lack of a head-conjunction and a conjunction phrase. Two such cases are the Turkic language Old Uighur (31a), and Dyirbal (31b); serial verb constructions—here represented by Fulfulde (31c)—can also be taken to be conjunction-less. ((31a,c) are repeated from Chapter 2. (31a) may look like apposition or even compounding, but there is ample evidence in Chapter 2 that it is coordination.)

(31) a. [äwdä   barqta]
         house.LOC home.LOC
         'house and home'

     b. Bayi yaṛa baŋgul gubiŋgu mundan (bayi) (yaṛa) baŋgun
         NOM. man ERG. gubi   brought NOM. man   ERG.
         ḍugumbiṛu balgan
         woman   hit
         'The man was brought here by the gubi and (he) was hit by
         the woman.'   (Dixon 1972:154)

     c. Baaba nyaami, haari,   looti   juude
         father eat.SP become.full.SG.SP wash.SG.SP hands
         muudum, wi'i . . .
         his,   say.SP
         'The father ate, became full, washed his hands, and said . . .'

Second, languages that have empty conjunctions for the conjunctive meaning, often have overt conjunctions for other conjunctions such as disjunctive or contrastive ones. Since such languages do have conjunction phrases, it is plausible to assume that there is an opposition between empty and overt conjunctions, in the same way as in morphology: absence that contrasts with presence of a marker of a particular category within a paradigm is taken to be one way of realizing a value of that category.

Several examples from Old Turkic languages (Grønbeck 1979) show that the disjunctive conjunction 'or' is overtly expressed even if conjunctive conjunctions are not. Consider, e.g., al-Kashgari (32a), Ottoman (32b), and Uighur (32c):

(32) a. kälirmüsän *azu* baryrmüsän
        are.you.coming or are.you.going
        'Are you coming or are you going?'

    b. bän *joksa* biradärim
       I   or   my.brother
       'I or my brother'

    c. uluš saju, balyq sajukim bägläri   *azu* qary
       land all   city all   prince.PL.POSS or   old
       bašlary   ärsär
       head.PL.POSS be.CONDITIONAL
       'whatever princes or elders there may be in all realms and
       cities'   Grønbeck (1979:53–4)

Similarly, Modern Turkish has an overt conjunction expressing adversity, *fakat* 'but', although conjunctive coordination can be expressed without a conjunction:

(33) pastahaneye gid-er-di-k   fakat dondurma
     patisserie.DAT go.HAB.PAST.IPL   but   ice-cream.NOM
     ye-mez-r-di-k
     eat.NEG.HAB.PAST.IPL
     'We used to go to the patisserie but we did not use to have ice-
     cream.'   (Bernt Brendemoen, p.c.)

Japanese, too, was shown in Chapter 2 to have conjunction-less coordination of clauses. However, for clausal coordination with non-conjunctive meaning, overt conjunctions are used, as is seen below, with the adversative conjunctions *ga* 'but', the stronger *keredo* 'but', and the disjunctive *mo* 'or':

(34) a. kanojo wa   utsukushii *ga* taikutsu desu
         she   as.for beautiful but boring   is
         'She is beautiful, but boring.'

     b. kono apato   wa   benri   da *keredo* takasugiru
         this apartment as.for convenient is but   too.expensive
         'This apartment is convenient, but too expensive.'

     c. futte *mo*   tette   *mo*   dekakemasu
         falling whether shining whether leave
         'Whether it is raining or shining, I shall leave.'
                                              (Bleiler 1978:99–100)

Third, in the languages from which I have found evidence of UC, the direction of unbalancedness correlates with the direction of head complements more generally (see Chapter 2). E.g., both Japanese and Old Turkic are OV languages, and they typically have the would-be complement conjunct before the would-be empty conjunction, just as expected. Similarly, Fulfulde is a VO language, where the would-be empty conjunctions precede the would-be complements, as expected.

Fourth, historically, many languages have not had conjunctions, but have recently borrowed conjunctions from other languages, or developed them from other constructions within the language (see also Chapter 7). Mithun (1988:356) assumes that, in such languages, conjunctions have emerged as a result of bilingualism, especially as a result of contact with written languages (assuming that there are more occurrences of coordination in written than in spoken language). Grønbeck (1979:52), too, assumes that the emergence of conjunctions in Turkic languages is due to the influence of foreign languages. These new conjunctions have had no syntactic consequences. If there was not already a conjunction phrase with an empty head present in such languages, it is difficult to see how a conjunction could come into the language with no further consequences.

Fifth, child language, too, seems to consist of conjunction-less CoPs. E.g., while the child is at a stage where "sentences" have not exceeded the two-phrase stage, they employ coordination of the type in (35). If this is not interpreted as involving a CoP the child would have to be described as having poly-phrased sentences (with, e.g., four independent DPs preceding a verb, as below) where coordination is involved. This is highly unlikely. Furthermore, the later insertion of conjunctions does not, to my knowledge, involve any syntactic consequences. Again, then, the most plausible explanation is one in which a coordination-phrase has an empty head.

(35) [Mamma, pappa, Anna, Maria] spise

(Elisabet Engdahl, p.c.)

It is interesting to note here that Kayne (1994:11–12) argues against the possibility of sentences such as (36). His argument is that without a conjunction the conjunction phrase would not be "adequately asymmetric"—an important point in his antisymmetry theory. Thus, with different arguments, he arrives at the same conclusion as this author—that coordination requires a conjunction that is a head (although his English data bias him against the idea that there are empty conjunctions).

(36) a. *I saw the boy the girl

b. *The girl the boy were discussing linguistics

(Kayne 1994:11)

Finally, it must be pointed out that not all instances of juxtaposition of categories involves empty conjunctions. In many languages, coordination exists side by side with apposition, which seems to be a different phenomenon: the structure of an apposition would not necessarily be a legitimate conjunct structure, as seen in (37b,c). Apposition constructions should not be considered conjunction-less CoPs.

(37) a. Kari Pettersen, også kjent   som gulljenta,   er hjemme
        Kari Pettersen also known as   the-gold-girl is home
        igjen
        again
        'Kari Pettersen, also known as the golden girl, is home
        again.'

b. *[Kari Pettersen og også kjent   som gulljenta],   er
    Kari Pettersen and also   known as   the-gold-girl is
    hjemme igjen
    home   again
    'Kari Pettersen, and also known as the golden girl, is home
    again.'

c. *[Også kjent   som gulljenta   og Kari Pettersen] er
    also   known as   the-gold-girl and Kari Pettersen is
    hjemme igjen
    home   again
    'Also known as the golden girl and Kari Pettersen is home
    again.'

Furthermore, in many languages, such as English and Norwegian (38), all conjunctions but one can be phonologically null in multiple coordination. I do not see this as an allomorph of the overt conjunction which happens to have a very limited distribution. The main reason is that any conjunction can be null in this context. In contrast to the empty conjunctions above, the null allomorph would have occurred in conjunctive as well as disjunctive coordination (39). Instead, I see it as a special kind of deletion, unlike other deletions, in that one non-deleted element must be present within the same overall phrase.

(38) a.   Louise, Ø Michael, Ø Linda, and Gemma

      b.   Astri, Ø Syver, Ø Marit og Kristoffer

(39) a.   Louise, Ø Michael, Ø Linda, or Gemma

      b.   Astri, Ø Syver, Ø Marit eller Kristoffer

I conclude, therefore, that there is reason to claim that empty conjunctions can head conjunction phrases. This must not be confused with deletion of conjunctions, which is assumed not to take place, with the limited exception of deletion in multiple coordination. In sum, therefore, while deletion of conjuncts can happen marginally, this is not the case with conjunctions, and the point of obligatoriness holds.

3.2.7. UNIQUENESS

Svenonius (1992) takes uniqueness to be a characteristic of heads. He shows how the verb is unique while adverbs can be iterated, and takes this as support for the head status of the verb:

(40) slowly, mysteriously evaporated

(Svenonius 1992:96)

Applying this criterion to conjunction phrases, we see that the conjunction is the only possible candidate:

(41) a.   again and again

    b.   *a girl and a boy and

It is, of course, never wrong for there to be at least two conjuncts, even identical ones as in (41a), as opposed to (41b). There are, however, two possible types of counter-example to this: one is languages where there can be a conjunction attached to each conjunct, as in Latin and Modern Greek (42a,b), the other is multiple coordination.

To the first charge it can be said that it is possible that CoP initial "conjunctions" should be more accurately analyzed as CoP adverbs (Section 4.7). This is at least a plausible analysis for Modern Greek and Latin, where a facultative, initial conjunction-like element has the same effect as English *both* or Norwegian *både*, intensifying the conjuncts individually, and in particular the first one.

(42) a.   et   ego et   Cicero meus flagitabit
     and I   and Cicero my   will-demand.3SG.

    b.   ke egho ke o   petros to thelume
     and I   and the Petros it want.1PL
     'Both Peter and I want it.'

To the second charge it can be said that multiple coordination is analyzed in this book as repeated binary coordination, in which case there is, of course, only one conjunction in each conjunct (Section 4.6). In sum, it is never the case that conjuncts are more unique than conjunctions. The latter are more often than not unique. From this perspective too, the conjunction can be seen as a head.

3.2.8. X^0-ELEMENT

Svenonius (1992:104) shows how a DP analysis is consistent with a single-word analysis of determiners such as *this* or *my* and Norwegian *denne* or *min*. In a conjunction phrase, there is only one element which can never be anything but X^0, and that is the conjunction. The conjuncts can be single words, but they can also be maximal projections:

(43) a. min og din hemmelighet (X^0 & X^0)
         my and your secret

    b. min hemmelighet og din historie (XP & XP)
        my secret   and your story

For this point, too, the conclusion is that the conjunction is the only head-candidate.

3.2.9. DETERMINING WORD ORDER

A head should be expected to behave like a head also when it comes to word-order facts (Svenonius 1992:96). In a language that is predominantly head-initial (VO), such as English and Norwegian, any head should occur before its complement, and in a head-final language (OV), the complement should precede its head.

In Chapter 4, a structure of CoP is going to be suggested in which the conjuncts occupy specifier and conjunct positions in an X-bar type CoP. We would then expect UC constructions to provide evidence: if one conjunct is normal and one is not, it is expected that the specifier one, which is in every sense closer to the rest of the sentence outside CoP, is the normal one, while the complement conjunct can be deviant, given its closeness to the conjunction rather than to the outside. The prediction that the deviant conjunct is therefore the complement conjunct, following the head in head-initial languages and preceding it in head-final languages is explicit and easy to test. And the prediction is borne out. Two examples from Chapter 2 illustrate this, (44) from Eastern Mari, an OV language, and (45) from Bergen Norwegian, a VO language:

(44) Məj Annan   [ydəržö   den ergəžəm]
    I   Anna.GEN daughter.3SG.POSS and son.3SG.POSS.ACC
    palem
    know.1SG
    'I know Anna's daughter and son.'

(45) Det sku'   bare mangle at [eg   og deg]   ikkje sku'
    it   should only lack   that I.NOM and you.ACC not   should
    gjere det
    do   it
    'Of course you and I would do it.'

3.2.10. PROJECTER OF FEATURES TO CoP

One very important criterion for head-hood is whether a category projects
to a maximal category, and can thus be considered its head.[11] This can be
tested if that maximal projection is subcategorized for in virtue of those
features. For example, one argument in favor of DPs might be that the
choice of determiner can be important for the syntactic context. This can
be illustrated by Norwegian, in which the general rule of presentation
constructions is that the presented category is indefinite: [12]

(46) a. Det satt en dame   på trappa
        it   sat a woman on the.stairs
        'There sat a woman on the stairs.'

    b. *Det satt denne dama   på trappa
        it   sat this   the.woman on the.stairs
        'There sat the woman on the stairs.'

Turning to the relationship between CoP and its immediate syntactic context, it is obvious that the conjuncts have an important role to play in determining the distribution of CoP. This need not be discussed; it is beyond
question that, e.g., a CoP[DP] has a distribution like DPs rather than
something else, given that the conjunction is a grammatical function category with very limited distribution. This is going to be recognized in
Chapter 4, where it will be argued that all the features of the specifier
conjunct are inherited by the CoP. However, we also know—from earlier
in this Chapter—that CoP must have additional features, since there is no
conjunct alone that can be equivalent to the whole CoP.

In this section, we shall see some examples where the CoP has a behavior which indicates that the conjunction indeed has to be maximally projected—since CoP behaves differently from what a phrase containing only one of the conjuncts would do. Let us first look at an example in which the presence of CoP rather than a simplex phrase results in a different acceptable word order. In Norwegian, there is such a distinction in the distribution of (unstressed) pronouns:

(47) a. Silja så   han / henne / dere   ikke
         Silja saw him   her   you.PL not
         'Silja didn't see him / her / you.'

     b. *Silja så   [han og meg] ikke
         Silja saw him and me   not
         'Silja didn't see him and me.'

In (47a), an unstressed pronoun can occupy the position before the negator, no matter whether it is ordinary singular (*han*), is bisyllabic (*henne*), or is bisyllabic as well as plural (*dere*). However, in (47b), the unstressed simplex pronoun is substituted with an unstressed conjunction phrase. From (47a) it is clear that an unstressed element of two syllables is allowed in the pre-negator position. Reducing the three-syllable CoP in (47b) to two syllables by phonologically reducing and cliticizing one or both of the conjuncts is not possible, however, even though this process is usual for pronouns in general (see, e.g., Johannessen 1989), as shown in (48a) vs. (48b):

(48) a. Silja så   'n / 'en' / d'r'   ikke
         Silja saw him   her   you.PL not
         'Silja didn't see him / her / you.'

     b. *Silja så   ['n   og meg] / ['n og mæ] / [han og mæ] ikke
         Silja saw him and me   not
         'Silja didn't see him and me.'

A Norwegian CoP with pronoun conjuncts cannot be unstressed in the way that simplex pronouns can. There is, therefore, a distributional difference between the two kinds of category, a fact which supports the claim that CoP is a category in its own right, different from other categories.

A second type of example that supports the claim that the conjunction does lend some features to CoP comes from EBC constructions. In Chapter 4, it will be argued that extraordinary balanced coordination can be accounted for if we accept that a category X[pl] is treated differently by the grammar from a category CoP[X], also plural. In some languages, or for some speakers, case, for example, might be a feature which can only be assigned to pure [+N] categories, not to a CoP category, not even one with [+N] as one of its features.

The Qafar example, repeated from Chapter 2, shows how case is not assigned to the subject CoP (absolutive case being the default case; the subject normally being nominative). The incompatibility of an agreement phrase (feminine verb-form is the default found in other non-agreeing contexts as well) and a CoP, which is normally accompanying the subject, is further syntactic evidence for the claim that the conjunction does indeed lend features to CoP[X], making its syntactic distribution different from that of X.

(49) [woò baacoytaa-kee   kày toobokoyta] temeete
     that poor.man.ABS-and his brother.ABS came.F.SG

The other examples of extraordinary balanced coordination in Chapter 2 equally suggest that the conjunction has features that makes the whole phrase different from just a combination of two component phrases. Longobardi (1994:619), in order to explain a sentence such as (50) (repeated from Chapter 2), actually suggests that when definiteness can be achieved without definite determiners in coordinations of nouns, the reason might be that conjunctions have in common with determiners the property that they can be understood as quasi-operators giving rise to quantifactional structures.

(50) [Cane e   gatto] si erano giá addormentati
     dog   and cat   had already fallen asleep
     'The dog and the cat had fallen asleep.'
                                        (Longobardi 1994:619)

In addition, there are semantic differences between CoP[X] and X. One is that, for some speakers, the adverb *respectively* can only occur with a CoP:

(51) a. *The boys loved the pupil and the teacher, respectively

    b. [Anthony and Peter] loved the pupil and the teacher, respectively

These points show that the conjunction does influence its phrase in a way which makes it distinct from an ordinary (plural) phrase of any other category. Since the conjuncts do not have this ability, the conjunction must definitely be seen as head.

3.2.11. SUMMARY

The results of applying the various head-criteria to the participants of CoP are summarized in the table (52) below. It is easy to see that no matter which criterion is used, conjunctions are better candidates for heads than conjuncts are.

(52)

Criterion	Conjuncts	Conjunctions
Semantic functor	NO	MAYBE
Determining agreement	Irrelevant	Irrelevant
Morphosyntactic locus	On the contrary	MAYBE
Subcategorizer	NO	YES
Distributional equivalent	NO	MAYBE
Obligatoriness	MOSTLY	MOSTLY
Uniqueness	NO	YES
X^0-element	NO	YES
Determining word order	NO	YES
Projecter of features to CoP	NO	YES

3.3. Is the conjunction a functional or a lexical head?

What kind of category does a conjunction project? In recent years, it has become usual to divide syntactic categories into lexical and functional ones, and we should like to establish to which category conjunctions belong.

Lexical categories can possibly be classified as those that are analyzable by the features ±N and ±V, following Chomsky (1970), i.e., N,

A, and V, with the addition of P. The notion of functional categories is more recent, but it has triggered very much work, and many suggestions as to which and how many functional categories there are (or should be). A different distinction (suggested to me by Teun Hoekstra) can be made in which lexical categories are descriptive, denoting properties, and assign theta-roles (DPs are assumed to assign theta-roles in small clauses).

Some functional categories suggested in the literature include not only CP and IP (Chomsky 1986a), but also AgrP (subject and object), MoodP, TopicP, NegP, FocusP. Some work can be seen in Abney (1987), Chomsky (1988), (1995), Fukui and Speas (1986), Ouhalla (1991), Platzack and Holmberg (1989), Pollock (1989), Tsimpli (1990), Åfarli (1991).

There are many unclear points pertaining to the two category types lexical and functional. One question is whether there is any distinctive difference between them. Another is whether the distinction has any consequences. One distinction might have to do with word-order facts: the presence or absence of a functional category means possible places for elements to move to. Two languages that differ with respect to functional categories, e.g., agreement, possibly have different word order.[13] (This is how Platzack and Holmberg (1989), and later work, explain one difference between some Germanic languages.) One consequence may be the order of acquisition. Radford (1990), e.g., argues that functional categories are acquired after lexical categories, and that this can be seen in the difference in children's syntax before and after acquisition of functional categories.

However, compared to the amounts of literature on functional categories, surprisingly little has been written about criteria one might apply in order to determine whether a certain category is functional or not. (I disregard the requirement that they must not be major lexical categories, and the theta-requirement.) Abney (1987) is an exception, and below, we shall apply his criteria. Åfarli (1991) has tried to constrain the possible categories. Fukui and Speas (1986), Speas (1990), and Contreras (1991) have suggested that the two types of categories project differently. We shall look at these proposals in turn.

3.3.1. CLOSED LEXICAL CLASS

Abney (1987:64 f.) suggests that functional elements constitute closed lexical classes. This criterion applies unproblematically to conjunctions:

in English, e.g., there are only five coordinating conjunctions; *and, or, but, for*, and *so*, in Norwegian the same: *og, eller, men, for*, and *så*.

3.3.2. PHONOLOGICAL AND MORPHOLOGICAL DEPENDENCE

Abney (1987:64 f.) says that functional elements are "generally stress-less, often clitics or affixes, and sometimes even phonologically null." This fits well with conjunctions in general; they are usually short and stressless, and generally cliticize onto some other element before or after. In Latin, e.g., the conjunction may be realized as a clitic which attaches either to the first word of each conjunct or only to the second conjunct (53).

(53) a. Marcusque Juliusque
          Mark.and   Julius.and
          'Marcus and Julius'

     b. senatus populusque romanus
          senate people.and Roman
          'the senate and the Roman people'

                                                  (McCawley 1988:525)

We have also seen (Section 3.2.7.2) that deletion of conjunctions and empty conjunctions is not unusual; e.g., in English, conjunctions may be phonologically null in multiple coordination in Japanese, certain syntactic categories are coordinated by a null conjunction, and in Dyirbal, conjunctions are always null.

3.3.3. ONLY ONE COMPLEMENT

"Functional elements permit only one complement, which is in general not an argument." Abney distinguishes between functional elements and thematic elements, which are predicates of the type $\langle e,t \rangle$ (functions from entities to truth-values) (Abney 1987:66–8). This point must be taken to mean that the complement of a functional element does not receive a theta-role, and is hence not an argument. (The possible arguments of functional categories are CP, PP, and DP, and seem to be a closed class in his view.)

Applied to conjunctions, the criterion of not selecting for a theta-assigned argument is unproblematic. However, Abney claims that functional elements select IP, VP, and DP. This is, obviously, far too restrictive as far as conjunctions are concerned, but clearly also for other functional categories suggested more recently, such as Agr, Neg, Mood, etc. Abney's claim can only be explained by taking into acount the fact that his thesis was written before most of the work on functional categories had seen the light of day.

The part of the criterion which requires there to be only one complement might be more problematic from the point of view of conjunctions. Although there is only one subcategorized category in the complement *position* of the CoP, clearly, the element in [Spec, CoP] is also subcategorized by the conjunction, and is also in some sense a complement. However, since the word *complement* can mean both "subcategorized element" and "element in complement position," we can maintain Abney's criterion by choosing one of the meanings; there is only one element in complement position.

If the strict sense of the word "complement" was taken to be the relevant generalization, clearly, conjunctions would not qualify as far as this criterion was concerned. However, Abney does not believe any of the properties he examines to be critical for classification as a functional element (in the sense that every criterion must be met, Abney 1987:64); it is therefore not crucial what the result of our discussion at this point is.

3.3.4. INSEPARABLE FROM THEIR COMPLEMENT

Abney (1987:64 f.) claims that functional elements are usually inseparable from their complements. This follows, of course, to a large extent from their morphological and phonological dependence. Conjunctions fit well into this criterion: many suggestions have been proposed in the literature to group the conjunction with the second conjunct for phonological reasons.

Ross (1986:99) suggests that the conjunction "forms a constituent with the following sentence," mainly for phonological reasons. Since we have established that the complement is the second conjunct in VO languages, and Ross's examples were mostly from such languages, this generalization seems to hold. In Qafar, which is an OV language, the conjunction cliticizes onto the first conjunct (Hayward and Corbett 1988), which must be considered its complement.

Most of the data in this book have written sources. It is therefore not easy to verify this point completely. However, to my knowledge, the data do not contradict this point.

3.3.5. LACK OF "DESCRIPTIVE CONTENTS"

The fact that functional elements lack "descriptive contents" is the one which Abney characterizes as the most crucial. Their semantic contribution is "regulating or contributing to the interpretation of their complement. They mark grammatical or relational features, rather than picking out a class of objects." For our purpose, this is the point which explains why conjunctions did not fit completely into the head requirements of the previous section: they are functional rather than lexical or referential elements. Let us consider the requirements again:

Semantic functor. A problem with characterizing the conjunction as a semantic functor (which a head ought to be) is the definition given by Zwicky, where the whole phrase describes a kind of the thing described by the head. Obviously, this definition works much better on referential categories than on functional ones. We said that neither of the elements in *apples and oranges* are descriptions of *and*.

However, if we regard *and* as a functional category, whose role is "contributing to the interpretation" of its complements, we are closer to seeing conjunctions as semantic functors, as we would like. E.g., if *collection* is the interpretation that the conjunction *and* contributes to the meaning of its complements, (3a) can be said to be a kind of *collection*, viz. of apples and oranges together. It seems reasonable, then, to say that the modifying elements (the conjuncts) make explicit the kind of collection in the phrase (e.g., of fruit).

Similarly, in *an apple or an orange*, what is described is a kind of *disjunction*; of a collection in which the members, in this case fruits, are picked out separately. In *Mary does not like baking but fishing*, there is a description of a kind of *adversative collection*, where two things, e.g., two activities, are contrasted.

Morphosyntactic locus. We saw previously that the conjunction itself is never the morphosyntactic locus of the phrase. However, the conjunction is crucial with respect to the morphosyntactic features of CoP, as we shall see in Chapter 4.

Distributional equivalent. In the previous section, a criterion for a head was that it ought to function as the distributional equivalent of its phrase. This is not possible when we look at conjunctions: *And are good for you* cannot replace *Apples and oranges are good for you*. However, if we take the functional content of *and* into account for this criterion, we find that the criterion is now applicable: many functional elements standardly taken to be heads, such as tense-affixes, prepositions (used as ordinary prepositions rather than in more or less idiosyncratic, idiomatic ways as particles), and determiners, cannot be viewed as distributional equivalents in a strict sense:

(54) a. Jack liked it there

　　b. *Jack -ed

(55) a. Rory sat on the box

　　b. *Rory sat on[14]

(56) a. Thomas saw a boy

　　b. *Thomas saw a

Instead of requiring that the head is itself a distributional equivalent of the whole phrase, we should ask whether a word that expresses the content of the head could act as an equivalent. This line of thought is also common in morphology: a morpheme (or a morphosyntactic category) can be realized by different allomorphs (or morphological operations). The head, from this perspective, will be the element that carries the grammatical content associated with that particular phrase.

With this modified requirement we get the right and expected results. Various phonologically independent while semantically rather empty elements (57) are distributional equivalents of the relevant phrases in (54)–(56).

(57) a. Jack did

　　b. Rory sat there

　　c. Thomas saw somebody

The only content in these elements is the grammatical one in the heads of those phrases, i.e., tense, location, and indefiniteness. That the analysis with functional heads is the right one can be seen if we try to substitute some equivalent more or less semantically empty element, or a lexical synonym, for what the analysis claims are the *non*-heads in the (a) versions of (54)–(56). As is seen in (58), these cannot be distributional equivalents.

(58) a. *Jack do / love

b. *Rory sat it / the stairs

c. *Thomas saw male / young

Turning to the conjunction *and*, we know from the discussion above that its main grammatical function is to assemble or gather entities or events into a collection. If a conjunct already carries the relevant grammatical contents, i.e., plural, we predict it to be fine as a distributional equivalent. The result is as we would now expect:

(59) a.   An apple and an orange are good for you

b. *It / a fruit / an apple are good for you

c. *It / a fruit / an orange are good for you

d.   They / fruits are good for you

The conclusion is, then, that what is expressed by *and* is what is necessary in that position. On this background, *and* is the (functional) head of its phrase. This is consistent with the discussion above on *and* as a semantic functor.

3.3.6. THE HEAD AS A D-STRUCTURE PROJECTION

Other researchers have included other features they take as necessary for an element to be head. Åfarli (1991:216) requires that for something to be a functional projection, it must be a projection of a functional element at D-structure. E.g., while a TenseP can be defended in, e.g., Norwegian on the grounds that it occurs in every sentence, a CP is not defendable in main clauses, where there is nothing for it to project.

For the present discussion, it means that there is no CoP unless there is a projected conjunction. Åfarli's requirement is fulfilled for coordination in languages such as English and Norwegian, where a conjunction is obligatory in coordinated structures (with the exception in enumeration mentioned above); the conjunction is clearly projected from the lexicon, a fact which is easily seen by the different subcategorization and different functions conjunctions have. In languages like Dyirbal and Old Turkic languages, in which coordination is never expressed by an overt conjunction 'and', I argued above that there is a phonologically null conjunction which projects its own phrase. An important reason for this point was the fact that although one of the conjunctions is never overt, other conjunctions with which it contrasts are overt. Empty conjunctions are just the unmarked category out of several conjunctions within the same paradigm. On this background, it is possible to retain Åfarli's requirement.

3.3.7. THE DIFFERENCE BETWEEN FUNCTIONAL AND LEXICAL PROJECTIONS

Few linguists have explored the structural differences between functional and lexical categories, but there are some exceptions: Fukui and Speas (1986:130), Abney (1987:76), and later Contreras (1991:64), among others, assume that only functional categories project up to X″-level, and have a specifier or subject position.

Fukui and Speas (1986:130–1) explain their position by the fact that "specifiers" in lexical categories may iterate, while "specifiers" in functional projections close off their projection:

(60) a. the very very old man

　　 b. Susan never could have been eating cabbage

(61) a. *the the old man

　　 b. *What who did buy?

To illustrate, their proposals for IP, DP, and CP are:

(62)

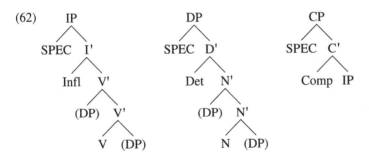

They suggest that the highest projection of lexical categories is adjoined to, thereby allowing the iteration effects. They argue for this analysis on the basis of data from Japanese and English. Their claim is that a language that lacks functional heads also lacks specifier positions. Therefore, since Japanese does not have determiners, it does not have a determiner phrase, and hence no specifier to close off a noun projection. This prediction is borne out:

(63) kireina   John-no ko-no hon
     beautiful John's   this   book   (Fukui and Speas 1986:134)

Proforms can also be modified by any type of category:

(64) (Did you meet with Taro yesterday?)
     Un, dem kinoo-no   kare-wa sukosi   yoosu-ga
     yes but yesterday-GEN. he-TOP. somewhat state-NOM.
     hendat-ta
     be strange-PAST
     'Yes, but yesterday's he was somewhat strange.'

This criterion applied to CoP suggests that CoPs are functional rather lexical projections. The evidence comes from multiple coordination, which is most likely analyzed as having a unique specifier (Chapter 4). The examples below from English (65) and Tamil (66) illustrate the point; only one conjunct (the specifier one) behaves normally with respect to case assignment. The others are exempt, which is explained by the fact that they are not in a spec-head relation with the conjunction, and do therefore not get the features assigned to the phrase.

(65)   We talked about [the dog, (and) that it was hungry, and that we gave it a bone]

(66)   [viiṭu   tooṭṭaŋ   kutiraikaḻaiyum]
       house.IND.NOM garden.IND.NOM horses.IND.CO.ABS
       koṭuttaaN
       he gave
       'He gave a house, a garden and some horses.'

3.3.8. SUMMARY

The application of criteria given in the literature shows overwhelming evidence for the assumption that conjunctions are not only heads, but functional heads. This is shown in the table (67).

(67)

Criterion	Conjunction
Belongs to closed lexical class	YES
Is phonologically and morphologically dependent	YES
Has only one complement	MAYBE
Is inseparable from complement	YES
Lacks "descriptive contents"	YES
Its head is a D-structure projection	YES
Has a specifier position	YES

3.4. Summary and concluding remarks

In this chapter, we have examined conjunctions with respect to criteria for head-hood in general given in the linguistic literature. The topic of heads has not been discussed to a very great extent, the work by Zwicky (1985), Hudson (1987), and Svenonius (1992) being exceptions. However, the criteria point in the same direction; conjunctions are heads. We have also looked at conjunctions with respect to functional categories. The applicable criteria, most of which are taken from Abney (1987), strongly suggest that conjunctions are functional heads.[15] The idea that conjunctions are heads is interestingly suggested in the literature as early as in 1980: "Parataktiske konjunksjoner som 'og,' 'eller' og 'men' utgjør kjerneledd i paratagmene." [Paratactic conjunctions like 'and,' 'or' and 'but' constitute the core elements in the paratagms.] (Dyvik 1980:263)

Notes

1. They also discuss head-hood in terms of "ruler," a theory-internal concept in dependency theory which I shall not pursue here.

2. In many cases of unbalanced coordination, the whole CoP does take the features of one of the conjuncts. I do not take this to indicate that in such constructions, a particular conjunct is head, since the reason for the asymmetry between conjuncts can be explained in general terms having to do with the structure of CoP and the lexical entry of the conjunction, as explained in Chapter 4.

3. Care must be taken to distinguish the coordinating conjunction *for* from the preposition *for* and the subordinating complementizer *for*. (They are probably all related etymologically—this has been difficult to get attested—having the same common core meaning of cause, reason, or intention.) It is only the coordinating

conjunction that does not have the possibility of preposing *for* + its complement:

    (i)   For penger gikk   jeg til byen
          for money walked I   to the.town
          'For money, I walked to the town.'

    (ii)   For å tjene penger, gikk   jeg til byen
          for to earn money walked I   to the.town
          'In order to earn money, I walked to the town.'

    (iii) *For jeg hadde ikke penger, gikk   jeg til byen
          for I   had   not   money walked I   to the.town

Notice also that, while coordinated IPs can have different tense, they cannot differ w.r.t. finiteness. As seen in (ii), this is no problem for the subordinating *for*; its complement may be the only non-finite clause in the sentence.

    4. An example of forced interpretation is the one below:

    (i)   He was a good father, but an excellent cook

There is nothing inherently adversative in the two conjuncts here, but the conjunction forces the interpretation that being a good father is normally incompatible with being good at cooking.

    5. It cannot be only the semantics of the verb that requires it to have a plural subject, since many other verbs that are inherently symmetrical, such as *marry*, can have a singular subject:

    (i) Sue married

    6. I am ignoring certain exceptions, like the Norwegian *men* 'but' being used as a pause-filler in a reduplicated form:

    (i)   Jeg liker det ikke. Men-men. Livet   må   gå videre.
          I   like it   not   but-but   life.the must go further
          'I don't like it, but, well, life must go on.'

    7. In these constructions, the verb and its particle often have a different intonational pattern from what they would have normally: in the (b,c) examples the toneme 2 would be used, while they would have had toneme 1 if followed by a DP, in which case they would also have the ordinary compositional meaning.

    8. In this example, intonation and stress are important. The intended intonational pattern is (i) rather than (ii), the latter being more readily interpreted as the modifier *too*, in which case *og* and *også* may be interpreted as synonymous.

(i) Han har vært i 'Afrika og
(ii) Han har vært i 'Afrika 'og

9. The fact that all conjunctions but one can be elided in multiple coordination is not taken to be an example of ellipsis in the same way as those discussed in this section, since unlike the latter cases, deletion of conjunctions requires the presence of the same element within the same overall CoP.

10. Mithun gives no explanation for the difference in the way "she told" is expressed.

11. I am grateful to Alan Munn (p.c.) for requiring an answer to this question.

12. There is one exception to this rule: the determiner may be definite in a subclass of cases where it is headed by a demonstrative, in which case the meaning conveyed by the DP is a modification of its original lexical meaning towards something unusual and spectacular.

(i) Det satt den dama   på trappa
    it   sat that the.woman on the.stairs
    'There sat an unusually attractive/ugly woman on the stairs.'

13. In a theory that assumes that languages have AgrP projections independent of their morphological features, such generalizations must obviously be reformulated.

14. Of course, prepositions can occur on their own without their object in other contexts, but that is not relevant here. The point is that a functional element is not automatically a distributional equivalent of its phrase.

15. It is fair to mention at this point that not everybody agrees with this conclusion. Borsley (1994) strongly disagrees that conjunctions are heads. This view will be discussed in the next chapter, after the theory of the present book has been presented in more detail.

4

The Conjunction Phrase

4.1. Introduction

In this chapter, we shall see how the UC and EBC data presented in Chapter 2 can be accounted for if we assume a theory of coordination which provides an internal structure for the conjunction phrase, following directly from X-bar theory. We shall see an outline of the CoP phrase and the important role of spec-head agreement. An account will be given of the correlation between CoP word order and word order in a language generally (Section 4.2). Unbalanced coordination is discussed with respect to coordination of different categories (Section 4.3), and ordinary and extraordinary balanced coordination are discussed—with the suggestion that ordinary balanced coordination is in fact the most complex type (Section 4.4). The analyzes in this chapter are then seen in light of language acquisition and universal parameters (Section 4.5). An analysis of multiple coordination being analyzed as repeated binary coordination is given (Section 4.6), while "initial conjunctions" are being analyzed as CoP adverbs (Section 4.7). Other approaches to conjunctions phrases are presented in Section 4.8, before a short summary (Section 4.9).

4.2. The structure of the conjunction phrase

The present book suggests that the conjunction phrase is as in (1). It is headed by a conjunction generated from the lexicon. The conjunction needs two arguments in order to have a saturated phrase, these are the conjuncts. The conjunction phrase follows the familiar format from general X-bar theory. Similar suggestions have been proposed in recent literature, by, in particular, Munn (1987a, 1987b, 1992) and Grootveld (1992), and Johannessen (1990, 1993c). The former two will be presented and discussed at the end of this chapter. Below is a CoP for head-initial languages (1a), and a CoP for head-final languages (1b).[1] (We shall postpone a discussion of multiple coordination until Section 4.6.)

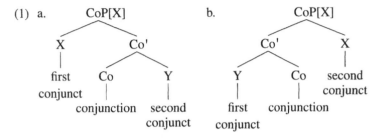

(1) a. CoP[X]   b. CoP[X]

The conjuncts are attached to [Spec, CoP] and [Complement, CoP], respectively. A few words are needed to clarify why the specifier in head-final languages is right-branching; after all, it does not follow from the position of other specifiers. I take as a starting-point the assumption that the position of specifiers does not correlate strongly with that of complements and heads.[2] When CoP specifiers are invariably the second conjunct in head-final languages, this might be explained by the nature of coordination: in most languages, the conjunction has a tendency to sit between the conjuncts. Since the complement position is occupied, the other position has to be the one on the other side of the conjunction. In head-initial languages, this position is to the left of the conjunction; in head-final languages the position is to the right. A more principled account is suggested by Richard Kayne. Given his Linear Correspondence Axiom (LCA) (Kayne 1994:6) and a general antisymmetry requirement, it follows that the specifier (an adjunct in his system) and the complement will always be on opposite sides of the head (Kayne 1994:35). Since CoP specifiers have no reason to move (unlike, e.g., subjects, which have to have their agreement features checked), they stay *in situ*, which results in a position on the opposite side of that of the complement.

It should be noted that the approach presented here is not totally akin to the antisymmetry thesis of Kayne (1994): Although the two possible CoPs in (24) are in accordance with the LCA, which can accept just those two constituent orders (specifier-head-complement and complement-head-specifier), Kayne puts forward the hypothesis that only the former is possible in UG (Kayne 1994:36). But how would one, following his hypothesis that there is only one basic word order, account for the parallel directionality between heads, such as verbs, adpositions, complementizers and conjunctions, and their complements? Accepting a directionality parameter in UG accounts for these parallels in a simple way.

The way the conjuncts are attached to the CoP, and the location from which the conjuncts are taken, will be discussed in Chapter 5; here it suffices to accept that the conjuncts are in the relevant positions in the CoP. Any category and any bar-level can in principle be coordinated. (This too will be discussed in Chapter 5.)

The X and Y in (1), therefore, are true variables that can stand for anything, e.g., N, I', VP, P, etc. From this, it follows that not only like syntactic categories can be coordinated, but categories of any kind. The fact that any categories can be coordinated means that CoPs diverge from X-bar theory in one respect: while specifiers and complements are generally considered to be maximal projections, in a CoP they can be categories of any bar-level: X^0, X', or X^{max}. It could be seen as a problem for the present approach that it accepts heads in specifier and complement positions. However, this depends on the way such notions are defined. In Chomsky (1994), a category that does not project further is a maximal projection XP, while one that is not a projection is a minimal projection X^0. Thus, a category is defined in terms of projection only. Looking at CoP in this light, we find that Co, the head, is not a projection, i.e., it is minimal. The specifier and complement are maximal projections by definition, since they do not project further. They might be minimal or not. There are no categories such as XP, X', etc. in the actual phrase-marker, these are simply notations (Chomsky 1994:9). The question of which categories can constitute conjuncts is discussed in more detail in Chapter 5.

What are the features of CoP? I shall propose, in a minimalist spirit (Chomsky 1995), that it inherits the syntactic category features from its specifier conjunct by spec-head agreement. Since a conjunction, the head of the CoP, must be considered a functional category (Chapter 3), we shall regard spec-head agreement as involving the unification of features, so that the head projects the features of its specifier. Thus, the features of the specifier will also be present at the maximal level, since this is a projection of the head, thereby bestowing ordinary lexical features on the CoP. The conjunct in the complement position takes no part in agreement, and offers no syntactic features to the CoP itself.

We can take unification (e.g., Shieber 1986) to be the situation in which two units which are combined with each other do not have conflicting features. Spec-head agreement with checking of features, as in Chomsky (1993), is an instance of unification; categories with the same features unify, those with conflicting features do not. However, the feature-checking approach implies that an item has certain features of its own which are then checked against those of another item. Unification can be seen as a wider concept, in which an item can also be under-specified with respect to certain features, and inherits those of the item with which it is unifies.

Since spec-head agreement is not normally assumed to let the category features of a specifier be projected to the maximal projection of a head, there must be something special about conjunctions (in contrast to, for example, I-heads, which do not project the DP features of their specifier). Conjunctions can be assumed to be lacking proper categorial fea-tures—they have a slot that must be obligatorily filled by such features, maybe in order to be interpreted at LF. This approach is in some ways akin to Rothstein (1992b:108), who suggests that, although conjunctions are heads, they do not project category features.

This has the advantage that CoP will be fully specified for syntactic categorial features, in contrast to some suggestions in the literature, such as the unificational theory of Gazdar et al. (1985) (discussed in Chapter 5), where the conjunction phrase has only the features that are common to all the conjuncts. In Johannessen (1990), I showed how, depending on the features chosen, there might be very few, if any, features left for CoP. Consider the example of unlike category coordination in (2).[3]

(2) Zoe is [a woman, rich and in the lucky position of owing a castle] (NP & AP & PP)

(Johannessen 1990:22)

If we adopted the feature system in Jackendoff (1977:56), the category features of the three conjuncts would be as in (3). Only one feature is common for all of them, [+Comp], which is the feature saying that the head has the ability to take a complement. This feature would also be shared by VP, however.

(3)
NP	AP	PP
+ Subj	− Subj	− Subj
− Obj	− Obj	+ Obj
+ Comp	+ Comp	+ Comp

If we took the features in Chomsky (1970), (4), the conjuncts would have no features in common.

(4)   NP   AP   PP
       $\begin{bmatrix} + \text{N} \\ - \text{V} \end{bmatrix}$ $\begin{bmatrix} + \text{N} \\ + \text{V} \end{bmatrix}$ $\begin{bmatrix} - \text{N} \\ - \text{V} \end{bmatrix}$

Thus, adopting a view in which CoP's major category features were the unification of all the conjuncts might lead to the undesirable situation in which CoP would have very few, if any, such features. Theories that see unlike category coordination as a unification of compatible features (see Chapter 5) have added an extra type of category such as PredP to the categories that are coordinatable, and to the new CoP-category, one reason for which has been to compensate for the lack of syntactic likeness between the conjuncts. The status of this kind of category is very unclear, however.

The idea of CoP getting its major category features from one conjunct only is akin to the suggestion in Chomsky (1994), in which the labeling of categories is discussed. In particular, the question of whether a super category should be labeled by the intersection of two categories a and b; the union of a and b; or one or the other of a and b is addressed. Chomsky's answer is the same as the one presented here: that one or the other must project—but not both. Here, the conjunction is the category that projects to a CoP. In effect this means that the features of the specifier will also project, given spec-head agreement and the under-defined nature of conjunctions. Thus, the projection of a conjunction is a Conjunction Phrase with properties inherited from the conjunction as well as from the specifier. The fact that the maximal CoP projection does not have exactly the same features as the conjunction (it has more) is also possible in the Bare Phrase Structure approach: "[. . .] the head determines the label, though not always through strict identity" (Chomsky 1994:10).

If the conjuncts are head-type categories, e.g., N, so that the CoP[N] will in fact be the head of an NP, we might ask if this does not mean that the conjuncts (at least the specifier one) do project, and are thus not maximal projections. To this I would answer no. The conjuncts of CoP do not themselves project anywhere. The higher NP is a projection of CoP[N], whose head has a dual nature. The conjunction part of it is maximal and does not project further, while the nominal part of it is not a projection, and is thus minimal.

The fact that one conjunct is in a specifier position whereas the other is in a complement position is a very important part of the account of unbalanced and extraordinary balanced coordination, as well as of the possible violations of the Coordinate Structure Constraint (Ross 1986), and the correlation beween general word order and the direction of unbalanced coordination. However, the structure of the CoP needs to interact with the rest of the grammar in important ways to enable the theory to handle such less straightforward kinds of coordination. The significance of these aspects of the theory will become clear in the discussion of other theories involving conjunction phrases, at the end of the present Chapter.

4.3. The role of CoP in unbalanced coordination

4.3.1. NOMINAL UC

As can be recalled from Chapter 2, UC is a type of coordination where the order of the conjuncts is crucial, since in one order, the coordination is acceptable, and in the other, it is not, i.e., [X & Y] vs. *[Y & X]. Let us take as an example the English (5) (repeated from Chapter 2).

(5) Can someone help [my wife and I] find housing in Texas . . .?

In order to account for the fact that only one of the conjuncts (the first one) has the expected case, it is necessary to assume a certain internal structure in the CoP.[4] The structure has to provide a principled explanation for the restriction of case assignment to the first conjunct only. The second conjunct is obviously in a local domain different from that of the first. The CoP structure shows that the first conjunct is in the specifier position, while the second conjunct is in the complement position.

(6)

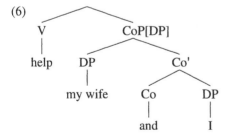

I shall give three different ways of showing how the difference in local domains is handled, in order to show that the same CoP structure is necessary independently of the particular formulation of the theory. The first way is to follow the barrier approach of Chomsky (1986a), the second way is the relativized minimality approach of Rizzi (1990), and the third way is the minimalist program of Chomsky (1995).

Following Stowell (1981) in assuming that case is assigned under government, the question of deciding why the second conjunct does not have case assigned in the ordinary way may be reduced to deciding whether it is in fact governed by the case assigner. We can start by applying the theory in Chomsky (1986a). We need the definitions in (7) for government, and the one in (8) for a minimality barrier:

(7) *Government*:
    a. α governs β iff α m-commands β and there is no γ, γ a
        barrier for β, such that γ excludes α
    b. α m-commands β iff α does not dominate β and every γ
        (γ a maximal projection) that dominates α dominates β.
    c. α excludes β iff no segment of α dominates β.
                                        (Chomsky 1986a:8–9)

(8) *The minimality condition*:
    α does not govern β in the configuration . . . α . . . $[_{\gamma}$ . . . δ . . .
    β . . .] if γ is a projection of δ excluding α. (δ is a zero-level
    category distinct from β, and γ is the immediate projection of δ,
    and γ immediately dominating β.)   (Chomsky 1986a:42)

The verb *help* m-commands the second conjunct, and it excludes it. However, in order for government to obtain, the governed element must not be separated from the governor by a barrier. The definitions in (7)–(8) show us that there is such a barrier present, viz., Co', which is a projection of the conjunction:

(9)

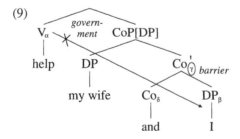

The fact that the second conjunct has not got the expected case can be derived, then, from the fact that it is barred from being governed, and thereby from being assigned case. The reason why the second conjunct has got case, albeit an unexpected one, has to do with head-properties of the conjunction, and will be discussed in Section 4.3.1.1. (See Section 4.4 for an account of balanced coordination, i.e., the instances in which both conjuncts have case.)

Let us then take a look at Rizzi (1990). The kind of government which accounts for (5) is head government. The relevant definitions are:

(10) *Head government*: X head-governs Y iff
    (i) X ∈ {A, N, P, V, Agr, T}
    (ii) X m-commands Y
    (iii) no barrier intervenes, i.e., no XP not directly selected by a [+V] element intervenes
    (iv) Relativized minimality is respected   (Rizzi 1990:6)

(11) *Relativized minimality*: X head-governs Y only if there is no Z such that
    (i) Z is a typical potential head-governor for Y, i.e., Z is a head m-commanding Y
    (ii) Z c-commands Y and does not c-command X
                                      (Rizzi 1990:7)

Let us make the minimal change of adding Conj to the list of possible head-governors (a step which is well motivated by the head-like properties of the conjunction). Let us then apply the definition to the example: the verb *help* is a head which governs the CoP, i.e., potentially anything being dominated by it, including the specifier and the complement of the conjunction. It also m-commands both conjuncts, and no barrier intervenes. However, while relativized minimality is respected for the first conjunct, since no head intervenes between it and the verb, relativized minimality is not respected for the second conjunct, since the conjunction is a typical potential head-governor for it.

(12)

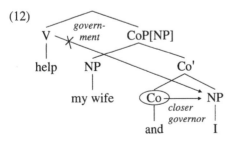

We have now accounted for the fact that only the specifier is in a domain governed from outside the CoP. It explains why case is only assigned to the first conjunct. The two ways which we have seen can solve the problem have had the same kind of explanation; an intervening head makes government by a head further away impossible. This supports the theory of coordination suggested here, in which the conjunction is head of its phrase.

However, although the two solutions above account for unbalancedness involving case assignment (typically the receiving kind of nominal UC in Chapter 2), there are several other kinds of UC which cannot be thus explained, viz., the receiving type of verbal UC, as well as the various assigning types, such as those where only one nominal conjunct determines verb agreement.

The third way of accounting for UC to be demonstrated here is within the framework of Chomsky (1988, 1995), the minimalist program. In that approach, case is not assigned by some head; instead, case is a spec-head relation between (elements in) two positions; e.g., (a verb in) a relevant Agr-position, and (a DP in) a [Spec, Agr] position. More generally, it is assumed that any lexical element has its inflectional features as an intrinsic property. Its features are then checked against the inflectional element in the relevant position. If the features match, the lexical element will be free to be realized at PF; if not, the inflectional features of that position will remain unmatched at PF, and the derivation will crash (Chomsky 1992:39). Here, the notion of government is irrelevant so that an analysis along the lines of Chomsky (1986a) or Rizzi (1990) is inapplicable. The explanation now depends on projections only.

Many morphological features have their own projections, and a category gets its features from the relevant position by sitting in it or by agreeing with a category with which it enters spec-head agreement. In our example, the syntactic category CoP[DP], situated in [Spec, Agr-O″], gets case from the verb, situated in Agr-O, via spec-head agreement. The features will be inherited by the head of CoP, i.e., the conjunction. The specifier of the CoP will get the same features via spec-head agreement. The complement of the CoP will not get these features, for the simple reason that it does not take part in spec-head agreement. There is, therefore, no need to postulate a barrier or blocking mechanism; the complement conjunct does not get the relevant features since it sits in the wrong position. This is illustrated below:[5]

(13)

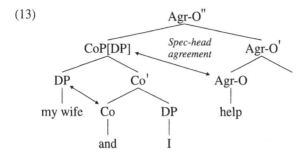

The rest of the nominal UC examples can be analyzed in the same way. For instance, the Burushaski example (14) from Chapter 2 is analyzed in the same way as the English (5).

(14) jε   kε u:ŋ   kε miyu   o:ltʌlik
     I.NOM/ACC and thou.NOM/ACC and us.GEN.sons two
     [i:mo   wʌzi:rtiŋ kε ʌka:bi:rtiŋεr]   sεnimi
     he.GEN wazir.PL and grandee.PL.DAT he said
     'I and thou and our two sons, he said to his wazirs and grandees.'

Burushaski is a head-final language, where only the last conjunct has the expected dative case-marking. In accordance with the correlation between UC and general word order, this is expected; the specifier position is the one where the normal features can be found. The conjunction bars the possibility of the complement receiving case. The complement in a head-final language obviously is the conjunct before the conjunction. It therefore does not get case.[6]

(15)

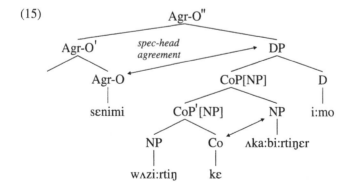

Most of the other nominal receiving-type UC languages from Chapter 2, e.g., Dutch, Eastern Mari, Estonian, Homeric Greek, Japanese, Old Hebrew, Old Irish, Tamil, Turkic, and Vedic, are unbalanced with respect to case. They can all be analyzed in the same way. We have seen two features apart from case that show up in UC: number (as in the Turkic languages) and phonological mutation (as in Welsh). These, too, can be explained in the same way as the others. Consider Welsh again (repeated from Chapter 2):

(16) Bwytais I [fara, menyn a   chaws]
     ate   I bread butter and cheese
     'I ate bread, butter and cheese.'

Since Welsh is a head-initial language, the first conjunct has to be the specifier conjunct, which in turn is the one that can cooperate with the clause outside CoP. In this case, the specifier cooperates with the preposed subject DP, which triggers the soft mutation of the specifier. The other conjuncts cannot take part in spec-head agreement with the conjunction, and thereby not with the rest of the clause.

This minimalist approach is advantageous compared with the other two approaches, since it can account for other kinds of unbalanced co-ordination in the same way, regardless of whether it is the receiving or the assigning type; government or avoidance of government is no longer a crucial factor. Every instance of UC can be explained by spec-head agreement. Above, we have seen the receiving type exemplified. Let us see how the assigning type of nominal UC can be accounted for. The example is from Czech (repeated from Chapter 2); only the first conjunct determines the agreement features of the verb.

(17) Půjdu   tam [já a   ty]
     will.go-1SG there I and you
     'You and I will go there.'

There is spec-head agreement between the first conjunct and the con-junction. This determines the features of the CoP; it gets the syntactic category features [+N,-V] (=DP), in addition to the morphosyntactic fea-tures of the first conjunct, among which are [1st person] and [singular]. There is also spec-head agreement between CoP[DP] and Agr-S, which determines the relevant agreement features of the verb.[7]

(18)

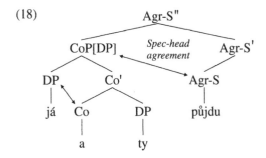

The other assigning-type languages can be analyzed in the same way, no matter whether the feature to be assigned is number (as in Hopi), gender (as in Latin and Swahili), or both number and gender (as in Old Norse, Palestinian Arabic, Qafar, Serbo-Croat, and Slovene).

Summarizing, we have seen three ways of accounting for the receiving type of nominal UC, viz., by an analysis based on the kind outlined in Chomsky (1986a), Rizzi (1990), and (Chomsky 1988, 1995). Only the third analysis can also account for the assigning kind of nominal UC in the same way, i.e., by means of spec-head agreement. The first two analyses were based on government for the receiving kind, and would have to resort to spec-head agreement for the assigning type.[8]

Two important questions at this point are: 1. If UC follows automatically from the spec-head agreement mechanism, how is it possible for languages to have balanced coordination, ordinary as well as extraordinary? 2. How have the deviant conjuncts got case? The first question will be discussed in Section 4.4, on extraordinary balanced coordination. The second question, however, will be answered below.

4.3.1.1. *Case: assignment, licencing, default, overcorrection*
In this section, we shall investigate the possible roles of the conjunction and the conjunction phrase with respect to case. The hypothesis of the conjunction being a case assigner will be rejected in favor of a view in which the conjunction is licencing a position for default case (or for the possibility of being case-less). Some special cases in English, sociolinguistically associated with overcorrection, will nonetheless be argued to be due to case assignment.

4.3.1.1.1. *The conjunction—a case assigner?*
Crucial in the present account of coordination is the fact that the conjunction is a head. As such it may have the potential of licencing and assigning features and categories. One possibility, in order to account for UC

with different case-features, is, then, that the conjunction can assign case, which may be different from the case assigned to the CoP itself. This stand would immediately explain how the complement conjunct of a subject CoP in Qafar may have absolutive case, and in Italian accusative case, when the specifier conjunct has nominative case, or how the complement conjunct of an object CoP in e.g. Dutch, English, Old Irish, and Vedic may have nominative case even when the specifier has the expected accusative case.[9]

If we assumed the case assignment hypothesis we would probably have to further assume that whenever at least one of the conjuncts was a DP, the conjunction assigned a particular case to its complement. However, it would be difficult to explain how the English *that*-complementized clause can occur in a case assigned position: if the complement of a conjunction either has the case associated with the position of CoP (which has to be a possibility for many languages and dialects), or it has the case assigned by the conjunction (e.g., nominative), how can we explain that the clause can receive such case, while not being able to receive case when being the single object of a preposition? Furthermore, what can be said about languages such as Burushaski, Eastern Mari, Tamil, and Turkish (see Chapter 2), in which the specifier conjunct has ordinary case while the complement seems to lack case, at least morphological case (according to the analyses given in the literature from which the examples are taken)?

4.3.1.1.2. *The conjunction—a licencer of default case*

An alternative to the case assignment hypothesis is a theory in which the conjunction *licences*, rather than *assigns*, case. Case licencing gives different predictions than those connected to case assignment. While case assignment is strong and gives case to any category that happens to be in the relevant position, case licencing is weaker, and does not allow case other than to categories that have to have it according to Chomsky's case-filter (Chomsky 1981). From this it follows that DPs will have case, while CPs will not. Second, while case assignment is linked to a specific case in a specific environment, case licencing is not linked to a particular case. Case licencing gives rise to the idea of *default case*, to be applied to an element in a situation where there is no case licencer.[10] The lexical entry for a conjunction like *and* would therefore be something like (19a) (to be further simplified below) rather than (19b).

(19) a. *and*, conjunction, arg1[α case],
                          arg2[β case].

   b. *and*, conjunction, arg1[α case],
                    arg2[nominative case].

The first conjunct of (19a,b) gets case from outside CoP; the second conjunct of (19a) gets default case (licenced by the Greek variable, which is
different from the one of the first conjunct), while the one in (19b) gets
assigned the particular case directly.

The default-case hypothesis is supported by evidence that the default
case of a (strongly inflected) language is often the one which is morphologically unmarked. (I exclude from this generalization languages that do
not have a clearly morphologically unmarked case—like Icelandic, Vedic, or Greek.) Good candidates are therefore nominative and absolutive;
these cases being the unmarked ones of "nominative-accusative" languages and "ergative" languages (Anderson 1985:181, Chomsky 1995:
176), respectively. The "case-less" complement conjuncts in the languages mentioned above indeed have the same lack of morphological
marking as the unmarked cases nominative and absolutive. Likewise, in
most of the languages where the complement conjunct seems to have
deviant case, i.e., different from the one of the specifier (and the one
assigned to the position of CoP), this deviant case is the same as the morphologically unmarked one. A distinction between languages where the
complement conjunct has deviant case, and those where it is case-less, is
therefore a false division based on the different analyzes of the linguists
involved in the description of these languages. The generalization that the
deviant conjunct in UC constructions has the morphologically unmarked
case is easily captured under the default-case hypothesis, but would remain a mystery under the hypothesis that conjunctions assign case.

If nominative and absolutive are universal candidates for default case,
what is the reason that in English, Italian and Norwegian, accusative
seems to be the default case? I suggest the answer has to do with the
extremely poor case inflection in these languages. Only pronouns are
distinguished with respect to case. The morphological build-up of pronouns is often obscure. It is, for example, quite unclear whether the pronoun pairs in English—*I–me, she–her, he–him, they–them, we–us*—are
possible to analyze as instances of stem plus inflection, and whether one
case is more basic than the other. Both members of each pair are therefore equally likely candidates for the default role.

What evidence is there that there is such a thing as default case? The
places to look are positions in which, for some reason or other, ordinary
case assignment is blocked. One candidate is the case in simple answers,

as in the English (20). The pronominal answer is the only word in the utterance, and cannot possibly be assigned anything by anything. (I disregard a deletion account of such utterances, since that would make the deviant case of the pronoun inexplicable.)

(20) A: Who talked about apples?
      B: Me / *I / *me did / I did

Another candidate is the case of nouns in exclamations. In the English (21a), there is more than one word in the utterance, but there is no finite verb which could be a possible case assigner. Also, the case of left dislocated (focused) pronouns is accusative (21b), as is the one in baby talk or idioms (21c). In both these cases, too, there is no obvious case assigner. The comment above on deletion is valid here, as well.

(21) a. What, me, worry?

      b. Me, I'm not interested.

      c. Me Tarzan, you Jane.
          (Paul Kershaw, p.c., presented at the University of
          Minnesota, Apr. 1992)

A third example of what may be considered an argument for default case is the use of nominative case in positions where there is no clear case-marking (left dislocation and topicalization[11]), as in Icelandic and Modern Greek:

(22) a. þessi hringur Ólafur   lofaði   Maríu   honum
          this ring.NOM Olaf.NOM promised Mary.DAT it.DAT
          'This ring, Olaf promised Mary it.'
                                              (Andrews 1982:433)

      b. o   paraksenos anthropos, dhen ton
          the.NOM strange.NOM person.NOM not   him.ACC
          idhame
          we.saw
          'The strange person, we didn't see him.'

A final point must be added to this discussion. The concept of default case presupposes an acceptance of Chomsky's (1981) case theory, in which every DP must have case. This is the background for the licencing account above. However, although there are doubtlessly many arguments for the theory, an alternative account might be that instead of default case there is lack of case. This was suggested by Jakobson (1936), who analyzed the Indo-European nominative as absence of case.

What evidence is there for this view? First, there is a morphologically unmarked case in many languages. Second, the unmarked case is the candidate for default case (to be used in contexts which lack ordinary case licencing). Third, the different case conditions predicted by the default case account of DPs and clauses in English CoP complements (that DPs get default case while clauses get nothing) would be eliminated—neither would have case. Fourth, there are other morphosyntactic categories that, in some positions, seem to lack a feature rather than have some default value of it. For example, complement conjuncts often have deviant number (Turkish and Eastern Mari being two examples, see Chapter 2). It would be difficult to claim that the unmarked number is really a default number, since the DPs unmarked for number can be interpreted as singular as well as plural.

There are, then, arguments for both the view that there is default case, and the view that there is lack of case. There seems to be no empirical way of choosing between them, and I shall not do so. The lexical entry suggested in (19a) will therefore be replaced with (23), which is compatible with both views:

(23) *and*, conjunction, arg1
              arg2.

In the view where a DP may lack case, the lexical entry (23) will simply lead to lack of case on the complement conjunct. In the view where a DP may have default case, again this case will only be licit on the complement conjunct, which is in no direct contact with a position that checks case. The specifier conjunct receives case by spec-head agreement in the usual way.

4.3.1.1.3. *Overcorrection in English*

The English examples in (20)–(21) above show that the accusative and nominative cases do not have the same status. Accusative is the only default case. The occurrence of nominative case in some UC constructions, such as (24), repeated from Chapter 2, must therefore have a different source.

(24) All debts are cleared between [you and I]

Emonds (1986) shows that there is no natural dialect of English in which nominative is the default case. The nominative case which occurs in some coordinated constructions, he claims, is due to overcorrection (also called hypercorrection) of rules for certain normative, but "grammatically deviant prestige constructions." Such rules have to be learned almost one by one, often with the help of grammatical handbooks, and identify a certain social and educational background. Since the conditions for identifying the proper contexts for these rules are not met in modern English (e.g., because morphological case is not productive), many speakers who want to be associated with a certain sociological class overgeneralize the rules:[12]

(25) A pronominal NP following *and, or, but, than, as* is subjective.
(Emonds 1986:116)

The case in such constructions is not due to the internalized grammar of any speaker, given the fact that it only occurs in the speech of people past their childhood and with obvious sociolinguistic connotations. I shall therefore assume, with Emonds, that the nominative case in such constructions is a lexical exception which has overridden the more general rule; the entry (26a) has been replaced by (26b), to generate constructions like those in (24). As argued above, case assignment by the conjunction cannot be the general way in which DPs get whatever case they need. However, given that the conjunction is a head, it is not implausible that it can assign case, e.g., in the special instance that overcorrection must be considered to be. Since we assume that the overcorrected case is not internalized, we hypothesize that it is assigned by the speaker's choice rather than by the grammar proper. The entry for the conjunction is therefore still the same; (26a), which happens to have been instantiated as (26b).

(26) a. *and*, conjunction, arg1,
          arg2.

    b. *and*, conjunction, arg1,
          arg2[nominative].

If the overcorrection hypothesis is right, which it seems to be, it is still important to emphasize that not just any construction in a language can be the target of it. There must be some general conditions present for overcorrection to be allowed to apply at all. These conditions are, I assume, met when there is no assignment of features by the general mechanisms of the grammar. We have already argued that default case (or no case) occurs only in positions which are not assigned case in the ordinary way by spec-head agreement. Such positions should therefore be predicted to be possible positions for overcorrection. Emonds mentions the following examples of overcorrection.

(27) a. They prefer not to think about James and I more than necessary

    b. She and Bill we ought not to mention

    c. John told no one other than I

    d. Who, if not he, could he have hired?

    e. It was she that John discussed in detail

    f. Mary expected the messenger to be she who had called earlier

    g. We democrats the voters expect to be more enlightened

    h. For they to be understood correctly, ... (produced by a College English professor)   (Emonds 1986:115)

The examples involve coordinated objects (27a,b); the object of a comparative complementizer or the subject of an understood predicate (27c); an appositive to an object (27d); predicate nominals (27e,f); a pronominal determiner of an object or a pronominal object with a nominal complement (27g); and a demonstrative pronoun in a for-to construction (27h).

It is not quite clear how the sentences have all got nominative case. However, from the point of view of this book, the important fact is that the overcorrection in coordination can be accounted for within the present theory. We can assume that it is unlikely that an ordinary case assigned position should have a different case assigned to it by sociolinguistic factors. From what we know about CoP (that the complement conjunct is in a position which is not directly checked for case features), we can see the complement position as a likely candidate for being targeted by a rule of extra-linguistic origin. It is, as it were, ready to be picked, since there is nothing in the grammar as such that provides it with case.

How can we account for (27b), which is really a case of EBC rather than UC? First, we can assume that the topic position in English is caseless, at least for non-typical case-receivers, on the basis of the fact that clauses subcategorized by prepositions can stay in that position, contrary to the *in situ* position:

(28) a.   That we wanted to go to the beach, we talked about a lot

b.   *We talked about a lot that we wanted to go to the beach

Second, as we shall see in Section 4.4, when a category such as CoP is not assigned case, the conjuncts get default case (or stay case-less), or, they get, of course, whatever is assigned. In the case of (27b), which is an example of EBC, we can assume that the speaker's entry for conjunctions before and after assignment is (29):

(29) a.   *and*, conjunction, arg1[α features],
                       arg2[α features].

b.   *and*, conjunction, arg1[α features],
                       arg2[nominative].

The general entry that ensures the same features on both conjuncts is the one in (29a). The particular instantiation might be (29b), by the speaker's intentional choice caused by sociolinguistic factors, which immediately causes both conjuncts to get nominative case.

We see, then, that a linguistic phenomenon which is learnt in more or less adult age for most speakers, and which is therefore not part of their internalized grammar, can still be explained in a principled way. It shows that it is possible to explain sociolinguistic influence on language as a constrained possibility: only where the grammar seems to lack the possibility of direct checking (as when there is no case or default case) is it possible for sociolinguistic factors to operate. It is, then, not accidental that sociolinguistic overcorrection can work on CoPs rather than on simplex verbal or prepositional objects.

4.3.2. VERBAL UC

While nominal UC can be explained by the fact that one conjunct is closer (in terms of spec-head agreement) than another conjunct to some category outside CoP this is not the way that all non-nominal UC constructions can be accounted for; in nominal coordination, unbalancedness affects a whole conjunct. In non-nominal coordination, on the other hand, the "unbalanced elements" may only be part of the conjuncts; if the conjunct is a VP (or AgrP or some other higher category) it may well be that only the verb of the conjunct has deviant features. If so, it is evident that it is not the entire conjunct which does or does not sit in a position which makes it different from the other conjunct; rather, it is only the verbs themselves which sit in different positions. This means that a verb has moved out of CoP to a position which makes it different from the other verb. (This is, strictly speaking, a violation of CSC–ATB, but even so, acceptable. See Chapter 6.)

Let us first, however, look at an example of a UC construction which can be explained in much the same way as nominal UC. (30) is from Yagnobi, repeated from Chapter 2.

(30) Man [a-šáw-im   a-tiraš]
     I   PAST-go-ISG PAST-fall
     'I went and fell.'

Here, we shall analyze the coordinated structure as being one consisting of V^0-conjuncts.[13] Since both verbs are inflected for tense, while only the first verb has person-number agreement features, we can assume that Agr-S″ dominates TP in this language, and the analysis will be the one in (31).

(31)

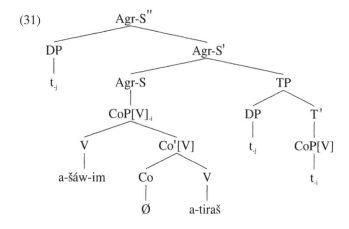

Both verbs are assumed to have independently moved to a TP each, before becoming coordinated (the details of the pre-coordinated stage can be found in Chapter 5). Then, after the two verbs in T^0 have been coordinated, the conjuncts move together as a CoP to Agr-S. It is at this point that the analysis is similar to the ones for nominal UC: only the first conjunct receives agreement features in the ordinary way by spec-head agreement; the second conjunct is left without such features. The technical details of tense features are easily accounted for. If we assume feature checking in the sense of Chomsky (1992:39), we can simply understand the morphological form of the particular verbs to have inflectional features lexically. These features are checked against the features in T (before coordination) and then disappear as the features match each other. The fact that we can assume an intermediate stage, prior to the movement of CoP[V] to Agr-S, in which the CoP[V] was sitting in T, and where consequently, the complement conjunct was not in a spec-head agreement position with that T is irrelevant, since the verb in the complement conjunct has already had its features checked prior to coordination.

This kind of analysis, however, is not possible for verbal UC in which the verb is only part of a conjunct. Let us take as an example the unbalanced Fulfulde example (repeated from Chapter 2).[14] It is a serial verb construction; while the first verb has full aspectual inflection (distinguishing between the two imperfective forms habitual and progressive) the subsequent verbs instead have a serial suffix, which is less informative, not distinguishing between several imperfectives, and also being used for other purposes.[15]

(32) Janngo   mi yahay,   mi foonda   ki, mi ndaara. . .
     Tomorrow I go.SG.HAB I investigate.SG.SI it I   see.SI
     'Tomorrow I shall go and investigate it and see . . .'

The difference between the Fulfulde example and the Yagnobi one above
is that here, only part of a conjunct is deviant: each conjunct consists of
a subject, a verb, and one also has an object. The verbs alone make up
the unbalancedness. Since the conjuncts obviously consist of more than
just the unbalanced verbs, they cannot be accounted for in a simple spec-
head agreement configuration.

The analysis I shall suggest includes two projected aspectual phrases,
Asp1″ and Asp2″. Asp1″ dominates the agreement phrase (following
Ouhalla 1991:117), which I have left out in figure (34). This order can
be argued for by the fact that both verbs are marked for number agreement with their respective subjects, while it is in aspectual features that
they differ, and that at this point in the derivation they have received
agreement features already. The subjects are treated as clitics, which is
why they are situated in a verbal complex with the verbs.

Asp1″ is where verb stems pick up features which determine whether
the aspect is perfective or imperfective. Asp2″ is the one which further
refines the kind of aspect given by Asp1″. In the present case, Asp2″ is
where the verb gets marked for either habitual or progressive features.
The analysis of two aspectual projections can be argued for morphologically as well as semantically. Morphologically, Asp1 is -*a*; Asp2 is either
a prefixed *d-on-* (for progressive aspect), or a suffixed -*n* (for habitual
aspect), see (33). It is important to notice that in both Asp2 cases, the
Asp1 suffix -*a* is retained. The step-by-step analysis can, therefore, be
defended on morphological grounds.

(33) *nyaam* 'eat':
     nyaam-a   (Aspect-1, Imperfective)
     d-on-nyaam-a   (Aspect-2, Progressive)
     nyaam-a-n   (Aspect-2, Habitual)

Semantically, Asp2″ is a refinement of Asp1″; the Asp2″ features are
hyponyms of the supercategory Asp1″, which subsumes them. Here, too,
a step-by-step analysis seems plausible.

There is no overt conjunction in the serial verb constructions. Nonetheless, a CoP is postulated, with an empty head (see also the discussion in
Chapter 3). This is done on basis of the fact that conjunctions do exist for

other syntactic categories in the language, and that cross-linguistically, empty conjunctions can be defended. Notice that the serial suffix cannot itself be regarded as a conjunction, since it carries verbal properties, viz. aspectual marking (here: imperfective). In (34), we see the tree representation of (32).[16]

(34)

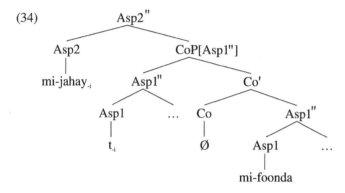

The important question with respect to UC is this. How can it be that only the first verb is fully inflected? The answer is illustrated in figure (34); while both verbs move to an Asp1 position, only the first verb moves further to an Asp2 position. (This movement is a violation of the CSC–ATB principles of Ross 1986; it will be discussed in Chapter 6.) The Asp2″ is obligatory in simplex contexts, with some exceptions (such as negation, subjunctive, and focus).

One question should be answered with regard to the analysis above. Coordination of Asp2″ conjuncts is unacceptable. Why? I cannot see a general answer which would follow automatically from the present theory. It seems to me to have to do with lexical properties. The Asp2″ category is limited in distribution. As mentioned above, it cannot occur together with negation, subjunctive, or focus. The fact that it cannot occur in a CoP, then, does not seem to be related only to CoP, but rather to something which can be generalized to hold for the other phenomena, too, whatever that "something" is.

Let us finally look at an assigning-type verbal UC. The example (35) (repeated from Chapter 2) has a CoP with simplex verbs as conjuncts, and where only the last conjunct determines case.

(35) Maria [begrüsste und half]   dem   / *den   Mann
     Maria greeted   and helped] the.DAT / the.ACC man
     'Maria greeted and helped the man.'

German is a language with mixed surface word order (verb first, second or final), and the direction of UC is also mixed, a fact which is unusual (as discussed in Chapter 2). It is therefore not straightforward to determine the structure of CoP; whether it should be head-initial or head-final. I assume in this kind of example that it is head-final, i.e., that the complement of CoP is initial.

(36)

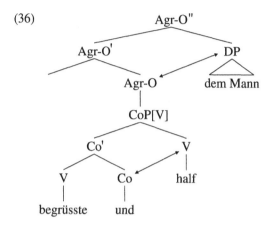

The structure of CoP now accounts for the unbalanced distribution of case. The checking verb is in the specifier position of CoP, which enables it to take part in spec-head agreement with the conjunction, and hence determine the features of CoP, in particular those that have to do with case. The object DP agrees with CoP, also via spec-head agreement, which results in the CoP features determining its case features, i.e., dative.

4.3.3. CLAUSAL UC

The cases of clausal UC also have an explanation along these lines. Let us take the German example (37) from Chapter 2 as a case in point. The first conjunct has subordinate word order with a final verb, as expected, while the other conjunct has main clause V2 word order, in spite of it too being a subordinate clause.

(37) wenn jemand   nach Hause kommt und da   steht$_i$ der
     when somebody to   house comes and there stands the
     Gerichtsvollzieher vor   der Tür t$_i$
     bailiff   in front of the door
     '. . . when somebody comes home and there stands the bailiff in
     front of the door.'

The analysis in (38) is different from the one in Höhle (1989:5), which
assumes that the conjuncts belong to different syntactic categories (V^m
and I^2, respectively). It is usual to assume that the Germanic V2 phenomenon can be explained in terms of a filled or a vacant C position
(e.g., Holmberg 1986; Platzack and Holmberg 1989). If there is a complementizer in C, the finite verb stays in some lower position; if the C
position is empty, the verb moves there. With an analysis of this kind the
conjuncts are obviously both CPs; the first conjunct has a complementizer in C; the second conjunct has main clause word order, and the
finite verb in C.

(38)

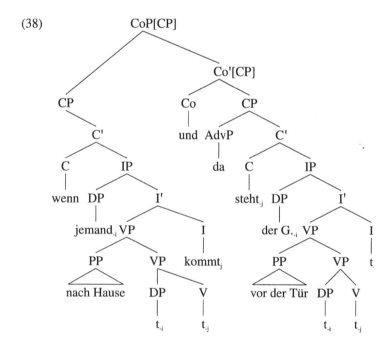

The analysis in (38) is straightforward, with few points to explain. The fact that two CPs are coordinated is, of course, quite unremarkable. Only one of the CPs contains the complementizer, in contrast to Höhle's analysis, in which the complementizer is shared by both conjuncts. Empirically, there is nothing to require the complementizer to be shared by both conjuncts. First, it is often the case that subordinate clauses are introduced without complementizers, as when an initial conditional clause has the order of a yes/no question (e.g. *kommst du nach Hause [. . .]*, taken from Höhle 1989:8), or when closely related languages like English and Norwegian can have complement clauses without complementizers (as in *I heard she was there* and *Jeg hørte hun var der*). (The fact that the complementizer only belongs to the first conjunct does not mean, then, that the second conjunct is not subordinated.) Second, with the analysis of V2 mentioned above, empirically, the second conjunct cannot in fact share the complementizer, since that would leave it a mystery how the main clause word order can occur.

However, we must explain why the reverse order of conjuncts is not possible. Why cannot the conjunct with main clause word order precede the conjunct with a complementizer? The answer has to do, as before, with the structure of CoP. First, we must assume that, in general, the reason a simplex subordinate clause needs a (certain) complementizer, is because it is required by the rest of the sentence, whether the clause (with its complementizer) is subcategorized or not subcategorized (with a complementizer required as a marker of subordination). In either case, the features of the complementizer are inherited by the maximal CP from the C-head (via spec-head agreement).

Coordinated CP conjuncts are not in the same position in CoP; one is in the specifier and one in the complement position. The one in the specifier of CoP is the one which gives its features to the head of CoP (by spec-head agreement). The complement conjunct has no role to play in the feature exchange. Whether there is a complementizer or a verb in its C-position, the former triggering subordinate word order and the latter main clause word order, is therefore of no relevance.

Why is it the first conjunct that is specifier, given that German can be seen as a mixed word-order language? As discussed in Chapter 2, the order of verb and sentential complement is always VO. Also, the order of CP is head-complement (complementizer before rest of clause)—and there are more prepositions than postpositions in German. In fact, most categories in German, except verbs and adjectives, are head-inital. The order of conjunction and head seems to be mixed, however, (36) vs. (38). It is possible that headedness is something that the conjunction inherits from its specifier, but this remains speculation.

We have to require an answer to what mechanism constrains the same kind of UC in languages like Norwegian, in which, too, there are different word order types, but in which both conjuncts must be of the same type. The answer seems to me to have to do with the existence of empty operators in Norwegian. Consider example (39) from Chapter 2. The CoP, itself a subordinate clause, has a main clause type first conjunct (an interrogative clause, which is a possible realization of subordinate clauses) and a subordinate clause type second conjunct.

(39) [Har jeg penger, og ikke gidder å gå]   tar jeg toget
      have I   money and not   bother to walk take I   the.train
      'If I have money, and can't be bothered to walk, I take the train.'

The difference between the German examples above and the Norwegian example here is that the second conjunct in Norwegian has subordinate clause word order in spite of there being no complementizer to bar the verb from moving to C. In fact, it is also acceptable for the verb to move, but this would yield a question type rather than a declarative main clause type, which would have had material in the [Spec,CP] as well. The structure is unbalanced, in that such a non-complementized subordinate clause is not possible in the first conjunct. In this respect the sentence has something in common with the German sentence above.

In (40), I have suggested a simplified structure for the sentence. (The empty subject of the second conjunct should be ignored at the moment; deletion and sharing are introduced in Chapter 5.)

(40)

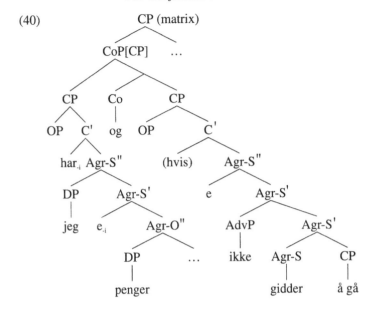

What all subordinate clauses have in common in general is lack of overt material in [Spec,CP] (with the exception of wh-phrases, which are the only phrases to be allowed to occupy that position).[17] I therefore assume that this position is filled by an operator (either empty or a wh-phrase), which must in turn agree with a head in C; a verb or a complementizer. When the second conjunct lacks a complementizer, this must be a PF phenomenon; complementizers in certain positions can, to a limited extent, be deleted. (We know (that) this is possible from the possible deletion of *at* 'that'.) When only a complementizer in the second conjunct can be deleted the reason for this is possibly that a deleted complementizer can only be deleted if it is c-commanded by a category with similar features. In the present sentence, the empty operator is assumed to have features of conditionals. These features are present at the first conjunct CP by spec-head agreement between the operator and C. The CP c-commands the whole of the second conjunct, including the complementizer. It is less clear to me why the complementizer of the second conjunct must be obligatorily deleted.

I would claim that the reason that German, but not Norwegian, allow declarative main clause word order in the second conjunct has to do with the existence of empty operators in Norwegian, but not in German. They occupy the [Spec,CP] position in Norwegian, and make it impossible for anything to land there. The highest place to which anything can move in a subordinate clause, is then, C. Empirically, this is correct, since verb-first question-type clauses as well as complementized clauses (C occupied by a verb or a complementizer, respectively) are possible realizations of subordinate clauses. The lack of empty operators in German makes it possible for any kind of clause-type to occupy the second conjunct in a subordinate CoP.

4.4. The role of CoP in balanced coordination

4.4.1. EXTRAORDINARY BALANCED COORDINATION

The first thing to be noted about extraordinary balanced coordination is that it seems to be the unmarked or default case that shows up in these constructions. Thus, in English and French (both of which have poor case morphology), it is accusative; in Qafar, it is absolutive; and in Spanish, it is nominative. The discussion at the end of Section 4.3.1 on nominal UC therefore carries over to this section. If the conjuncts in EBC are unmarked, this again is evidence that the conjunction is not a case assigner (which has been suggested by Kershaw 1992); either the conjuncts have default case, or they are caseless (cf. the discussion in Section 4.3.1.1.2).

Descriptively, what happens in EBC is that the case of a particular position, such as nominative in the Agr-S″ of the Bergen variant of Norwegian (41), repeated from Chapter 2, is not assigned to the element in that position when the element is a CoP.

(41) [Meg   og deg]   hjalp   no   godt te', då
     me.ACC and you.ACC helped now well to then
    'But then me and you did help a lot, too.'

This could be explained by assuming that different case is assigned to different categories; e.g., nominative to a DP, and accusative to a CoP. Another explanation could be that the conjunction assigns case to both its conjuncts. However, both these explanations are unable to capture the generalization that it is the unmarked morphological case which takes part in EBC. Why should the conjunction assign case, and thus override the case of the position in which it is situated, if the case is the most unremarkable one?

A different explanation, and the one to be adopted here, is one which is an extension of the explanation for unbalanced coordination. First, we assume that the unmarked case (or the caselessness) only shows up in positions which are not a direct case position. This is where the similarity to UC shows up. Second, we assume that some languages or language varieties only assign case to categories of a special kind, such as "pure" DPs. A CoP[DP] would not be a possible receiver of case, and the conjuncts would be left without case or receive the default case (as before, the choice between the latter two options is irrelevant). This explanation is more general than the one above, since nothing needs to be said about CoP or the conjuncts. The only thing which does need to be said is whether the language is "CoP sensitive" or not (with respect to some feature), i.e., whether case and other features can be given to "unpure" categories such as CoP[DP] in addition to such "pure" categories as DP.

The account relies on the assumption that there is a difference between the categories DP, even DP[pl], and CoP[DP]. There is some evidence for this distinction in Chapter 3, where we have seen that in Norwegian, a phrase of coordinated pronouns may have a different syntactic position from simplex pronouns, even when the latter are polysyllabic.

Furthermore, the idea that what shows up in EBC constructions is default case (or lack of case) rather than case assigned from outside CoP is supported by facts such as the following (from Kershaw 1992; the judgements are his): [18]

(42) a. %[Me and him] went out

      b.   [He and I] went out

      c.   %They know [he and I]

      d.   *[Me and him] know [she and I]

The sentence (42a) is fine; it is an example of ordinary EBC ("ordinary" since it sounds normal or natural for most speakers). Sentence (42b) is fine; it is either an example of EBC, with overcorrected nominative case assignment on the complement conjunct, or ordinary balanced coordination, where the ordinary case-features have been distributed to both conjuncts. (The details of the mechanism of EBC will become clear later in this section.) The three sentences cannot be uttered by the same speaker within the same dialect/sociolect/idiolect, since they presuppose different kinds of lexical entries for the conjunction and different case assignment (default vs. overcorrected).[19] Importantly, therefore, (42d) is predicted to be out: the subject CoP has accusative conjuncts, which shows that the speaker has the EBC-parameter (i.e., is CoP sensitive), with accusative as default case. The object CoP could have nothing but accusative conjuncts here; either because the speaker also has the EBC-parameter for objects, and the default case is expected to be the same, or because the object gets ordinary case assignment, i.e. accusative. The converse argument can be made for nominative case. There is no way that the conjuncts could just swap ordinary case, as is done in (42d). This example supports the theory presented in this chapter. It also supports a default theory rather than a theory with the conjunction being a case as-signer, since the latter option could in principle make possible an arbitrary choice of case for each position, there would thus be nothing in principle stopping (42d).

The analysis of EBC involving category-specific case assignment may seem to undermine some well-accepted analyzes, such as when subjects are assumed to have to sit in the position they do, or even exist at all (in the case of weather verbs and passive), it is because INFL has to assign nominative case to something. The present analysis with category-specific case does not have to contradict these analyses. First, notice that while a CoP[DP] may not be pure enough to get case in EBC constructions, it does have DP features even so. These features must be visible to EBC-speakers, since sentences such as (43), with no such features, are never heard:

(43) a. *[$_{\text{CoP[PP]}}$ On the table and in front of the garden] are outside

      b. *[$_{\text{CoP[VP]}}$ Paint the wall and wash the clothes] are waiting

Second, there are already well-known examples of subjects that we would not normally claim have case:

(44) a. [$_{\text{CP}}$ To be nice] is the most important thing in her life

      b. [$_{\text{CP}}$ That she was nice] perplexed her neighbours

We must therefore conclude that subjects not receiving case is quite straightforward when the category is of a certain kind. With respect to the minimalist program, we must assume that while what discharges inflectional features from (wrongly) appearing at PF is usually a checking of features on the lexical item, there is an additional way of discharging such features: when the syntactic category is of a kind appropriate for the position but not for some of the accompanying features of that position, such as case. This explanation accounts for the facts in (43), (44), and the EBC, and presupposes that there are other features than case which determine which category is possible in a certain position. At the same time, it retains the insight that case is a trigger for the filling of lexical material in certain position.

We now have a parallel between UC and EBC: in both cases, a position is left without case. In UC, it is only one conjunct, the complement conjunct, which is left caseless, while in EBC, it is both conjuncts: the complement conjunct in the same way as the UC one, and the specifier conjunct for the reason that the whole CoP is unassigned case, thereby having no case by spec-head agreement, in contrast to UC and ordinary balanced coordination.

4.4.2. ORDINARY BALANCED COORDINATION

The previous sections have accounted for coordination which is in some sense unusual, in that either one conjunct or both conjuncts are different from what would normally be expected in a given position. But of course, it is often the case that conjuncts have the same features, as in ordinary balanced coordination (OBC). This is typically the situation in Oslo Norwegian with respect to case:

(45) a. Jeg   gikk   til skolen
        I.NOM walked to the.school
        'I walked to school.'

   b. [Hun   og jeg]   gikk   til skolen
        she.NOM and I.NOM walked to the.school
        'She and I walked to school.'

(46) a. Jeg så   deg
        I   saw you.ACC
        'I saw you.'

   b. Jeg så [deg   og dem]
        I   saw you.ACC and them.ACC
        'I saw you and them.'

This situation is accounted for by features of the conjunction. The types of coordination we have seen so far have had nothing in the lexical entries of the head-conjunction to indicate anything about features in their respective arguments. However, ordinary balanced coordination can be accounted for by the kind of lexical entry below: [20]

(47) *og*, conjunction, arg1[α feature],
                      arg2[α feature].

The entry in (47) must be interpreted thus: whatever feature is received by one conjunct must also be present in the other conjunct. E.g., if the specifier conjunct receives case from the position in which the CoP is situated, the other conjunct also gets that case. Notice that the bracketed features in the lexical entry of a conjunction only make sense for receiving-type features. Features that are inherent in a conjunct, such as a particular number or gender on DPs or a particular tense on verbs, do not have to be the same in OBC constructions. More work has to be carried out with respect to determining the exact nature of the class of a features, the extent to which they vary across languages, etc.

In the next section, we shall see some justification for why this entry, in spite of it belonging to the "ordinary" kind of coordination, is more elaborate than those for UC and EBC.

4.5. UC, EBC, and OBC, and (parametric) variation

We have seen that there are two possible lexical entries which seem to be universal for conjunctions. The simplest one (48a) is the one that is used in UC and EBC contexts, English, while the slightly more elaborate (48b) is the one used in OBC, Norwegian.

(48) a. *and*, conjunction, arg1,
                          arg2.

       b. *og*, conjunction, arg1[α feature],
                               arg2[α feature].

Languages vary with respect to which of the two entries is utilized for conjunctions. In addition, while languages differ with respect to whether they have UC, EBC, or OBC, there may also be language-internal variation. English is one example. While there is an abundance of cases of unbalanced coordination in nominal conjuncts, there are none in other categories:

(49) a. *Mary [slept and dream]

    b. *Martha is [sleeping and dream]

    c. *Down the hill [walked a man and a woman ran]

It therefore is necessary to extend the lexical entries of conjunctions to include categorial restrictions:

(50) a. *and*, conjunction, $arg1_{[+N]}$,
                $arg2_{[+N]}$.

    b. *and*, conjunction, $arg1_{[-N]}[\alpha \text{ feature}]$,
                $arg2_{[-N]}[\alpha \text{ feature}]$.

It might seem almost counter-intuitive that ordinary balanced coordination is the only kind of coordination which is actually specifically marked in the lexicon. However, the situation is partly blurred by the names given to the different coordination types. The choice of the names 'ordinary" and 'extraordinary" has been based on the conception in previous literature that coordination involves conjuncts that are alike in category and features (e.g., The Law of Coordination of Likes, Williams 1981a). It is nevertheless possible to imagine an alternative analysis of OBC within an X-bar type analysis of coordination, in which head-head agreement plays a crucial role. This analysis will be discussed and rejected in the section on multiple coordination.

The unbalanced coordination data, and more evidence from language acquisition and cross-linguistic sources, as well as from multiple coordination (all to be discussed in the subsequent sections), together show that likeness in categorial features does not have to be the norm. Indeed, all these phenomena are evidence for an X-bar theoretic conjunction phrase, in which one conjunct is specifier and one is complement, i.e., an unbalanced situation. Under this consideration, it is hardly surprising that what is called "ordinary balanced coordination" is in fact less common than might have been expected.

4.5.1. COORDINATION IN LANGUAGE ACQUISITION

The idea that UC and EBC are more basic than OBC seems to be further justified from the standpoint of language acquisition: if the lexical entries in the previous sections reflect ones that speakers have in their heads, the simplest one (used in UC and EBC) should be preferred to the more elaborate one of OBC. This seems indeed to be the case for English and Norwegian (the only two languages of which I have had information about children's usage). Of the English examples of EBC in Chapter 2, many are from children who have grown up in very different parts of the English-speaking world (Texas, California, London, and other parts of England).

Many linguists have informed me explicitly that children use EBC: Leanne Hinton (p.c.) writes: "Among children and teens in the United States, it is now extremely common to hear [EBC]." Susan Ervin-Tripp (p.c.) writes: "In child speech we commonly hear 'him and me + V' long after 'me' has vanished as a unique subject." Malcolm Ross (p.c.) writes: "From my peers and other children I acquired structures like your [EBC]." Jorge Hankamer (p.c.) writes: "I am pretty sure the general rule for coordination of pronouns was an example of your [EBC]. We would say 'Him and me ate it all.' and would have to be taught to say 'He and I ate it all.' (which still sounds wrong and artificial to me)."

Helge Lødrup has informed me that his Norwegian children (in Oslo) used and use constructions like those in (51) (the adult pronoun is the one in brackets).

(51) a. [Meg   og Julie] skal gjøre det   [jeg]
         me.ACC and Julie shall do   it
         'Julie and I shall do it.'

     b. dukkene til [Julie og jeg]   [meg]
        the.dolls to Julie and I.NOM
        'The dolls (belonging) to Julie and me.'

                                              (Helge Lødrup, p.c.)

The examples show that EBC is the most common type in child language. What is then the status of UC in this context? If it is correct that the difference between OBC and EBC is that the former has a more complex lexical entry for conjunctions, we have an account of why EBC occurs in child language. But why does not UC seem to be as common as EBC? An answer can only be speculative. The difference between UC and EBC cannot lie in the lexical entry of the conjunction, which is the same for both, being completely unmarked for features. Rather, the difference can be assumed to lie in the different treatment of categories that can have case. Only DPs are typical case-receiving categories, therefore, only DPs receive case from the relevant positions. CoPs, even of the CoP[DP] type, are possibly not conceived of as typical DPs by the child. CoPs are thus "unpure" and cannot be checked for case. The only case the DPs in a CoP can get, then, is the default case (or no case).

To summarize so far; there are three main types of coordination: UC, EBC, and OBC. The first two, UC and EBC, are the expected ones. Speakers who have this kind of coordination utilize conjunctions which are lexically unmarked for morphosyntactic features. The complement conjunct in these constructions is always marked by default case (or have no case); the specifier either gets its features via spec-head agreement or by default (or has none). In OBC, on the other hand, the conjunction is specifically marked; both arguments get the same features, whatever they are.

There are thus two parameters that must be set: one concerns the syntactic features of possible case-receiving categories, in particular, whether $CoP_{[DP]}$ is a possible receiver of case. This distinguishes EBC from UC and OBC. The other concerns the make-up of the conjunction phrase, i.e., whether the arguments of the conjunction phrase have restrictions with regard to their features or whether they are unmarked. This distinguishes OBC from UC and EBC. Default case (or lack of case, which is the alternative explanation) can occur only in contexts where there is nothing else to provide case. Default case is the morphologically unmarked case in most languages, but in morphologically poor languages the default case is less predictable.

4.6. Multiple coordination

The examples of coordination we have considered so far have involved two conjuncts, which have fitted nicely with the theory of a conjunction phrase with two positions; one for specifiers and one for complementizers. An immediate problem arises as to the structure of coordinated constructions with more than two conjuncts (multiple coordination): if every conjunction phrase has the structure of a simple X-bar phrase, with a head, one specifier and one complement position, how is it that we often find coordination with several conjuncts?

(52) a. [Lesley and Jackie and Dawn] went to Keable's

b. [Lesley, Jackie and Dawn] went to Keable's

There are two possible analyses within the theory of binary coordination. Both are probably employed by in language, and both involve a situation in which one or more conjuncts is itself a coordinated structure. (52a) could be represented this way:

(53) a. $[_{CoP}$ $[_{CoP}$ Lesley and Jackie] and Dawn] went to Keable's

b. $[_{CoP}$ Lesley and $[_{CoP}$ Jackie and Dawn]] went to Keable's

A paired reading is less likely for (52b), where the conjuncts seem to have equal status within the top CoP. However, if we accept binary branching as in Kayne (1984), the default direction of branching is to the right in head-initial languages. In the present theory of coordination, this would mean that a semantically unmarked structure as regards pairing of conjuncts would be like (54). It would then represent both a situation in which all conjuncts have equal status, and one in which they were paired as in (53b).

(54) $[_{CoP}$ X conj $[_{CoP}$ Y conj $[_{CoP}$ Z . . .]]]

There is a question of whether a binary solution to multiple coordination is desirable. Would it not be better to assume a multi-headed structure? It might not be appropriate with respect to X-bar theory, but at least it would make transparent an analysis in which all the conjuncts are interpreted at the same level. The answer to the question is that a binary structure is still desirable. The reason is that there is usually only one conjunct with normal features in each multiple CoP (see below). In a multi-headed CoP for multiple coordination, we would have had to postulate an additional linearity principle to account for this: only the left-most specifier counts as a specifier for the overall, top CoP. With multiple coordination as binary structures, however, it is predicted that only one conjunct is normal.

In a structure such as (54) (an unmarked structure for head-initial languages like English), X (the first specifier) would be the normal conjunct; it would agree by spec-head agreement with the conjunction, and thus get the features from the top CoP. No other conjunct would be in such a privileged position. In the marked case, (55), in which the specifier is itself a CoP (etc.), it is still predicted that only one conjunct is normal:

(55) $[_{CoP1} [_{CoP2} X \text{ conj } Y] \text{ conj } Z]$

CoP2 receives all features from CoP1 by spec-head agreement, and X receives all the features from CoP2 by spec-head agreement. Y and Z are not in specifier positions, and will not receive features. Below, we can see that empirically, this is what happens (the examples are from Chapter 2 unless otherwise stated).

Different word order in Dutch
Multiple coordination of subordinate clauses in Dutch tends to favor the situation in (56a), where only the first conjunct has ordinary subordinate clause word order, while the rest of the conjuncts have deviant (i.e., main clause) order. The situation in (56b), in which the first two conjuncts have subordinate clause word order is much less likely. (These are the intuitions in van Zonneveld 1992, and are supported by Alma Næss, p.c., although countered by Marjan Grootveld, p.c.) There is thus only one proper specifier in the multiple CoP.

(56) a. [Als je   gepakt wordt, je   bent al   eens veroordeeld
       if   you caught get   you are already once convicted
       geweest en je   hebt geen goed verhaal,]   dan hang je
       been   and you have no   good explanation then hang you
       'If you get caught and you have been convicted before and
       you have no good explanation, then you're a dead man.'

     b. ?[Als je   gepakt wordt, je   al   eens veroordeeld bent
        if   you caught get   you already once convicted   are
        geweest en je   hebt geen goed verhaal,]   dan hang
        been   and you have no   good explanation then hang
        je
        you
        'If you get caught and you have been convicted before
        and you have no good explanation, then you're a dead
        man.'
                 (van Zonneveld 1992, quoted by Marjan Grootveld, p.c.)

Agreement in English

In English presentation constructions, the verb agrees with the post-verbal argument. When that argument is a CoP, the verb agrees only with the first conjunct—i.e., the specifier of CoP.

(57) There is/*are [a man, a woman, and a cat] waiting outside
                                            (Terry Langendoen, p.c.)

Case-marking in Estonian

In Estonian, only the final conjunct—the specifier—is case-marked if the case in question is among the CATE suffixes (see Chapter 2).

(58) [mehe, laste ja   koeraga]
     man   child and dog.COMITATIVE.SG.
     'With a man, a child and a dog'

Serial verbs in Fulfulde

In a serial verb construction, only one verb is allowed to have ordinary aspect features: the first one, which is the specifier. The rest of the verbs have serial suffixes with impoverished aspect-marking.

(59) Janngo   [mi yahay,   mi foonda   ki, mi ndaara...]
     Tomorrow I go.SG.HAB I   investigate.SG.SI it I   see.SI
     'Tomorrow I shall go and investigate it and see . . .'

Different case in Old Irish

In Old Irish poetry, all the conjuncts but the first, the specifier, have a deviant (default) case.

(60) rí   do.rigni (-gne MS) [aéar n-úar   ocus tene réil
     king has.made   air. cold.ACC and fire clear
     rorúad   ocus talam bladmar brass]
     very.red.NOM and earth glorious great.NOM
     'The King made the cold air, and the clear red fire, and the
     glorious great earth.'

Finite and non-finite verbs in Sidaamu Afo

In multiple serial verb constructions, only the last verb is finite and has a tense suffix. Since Sidaamu Afo is a head-final language, it again shows only one specifier conjunct.

(61) [kakkad-te-nna 'anga-te sei-se
tread-3SG.F.having.done-and hand-for it.was.ready-for.her
-ha 'ikki-kki-ro k'ol-te
-NOMINALISER-OBJ it.was-not-if turn-3SG.F.having.done
ka'-te galagalch-te
(empty.verb)-3SG.F.having.done do.again-3SG.F.having.done
k'ish-te la'-tanno.]
squeeze-3SG.F.having.done look-she.NON.PAST.
'If it is not ready for her hands (= feels good to knead) after she
has trodden on it, she turns it and squeezes it again, and then
looks at it (= investigates it again).'

Different case in Tamil
In UC constructions in Tamil, only the last conjunct, the specifier, has the
normal case-marking.

(62) [viiṭu tooṭṭaŋkutiraikaḷaiyum] koṭuttaaN
house garden.horses.CO.ACC he.gave
'He gave a house, a garden and some horses.'

Soft mutation in Welsh
Soft mutation in Welsh, which is triggered by the morphosyntactic, not
the phonological, features of the preceding phrase, occurs only on the
first conjunct, the specifier: the subsequent conjuncts are all treated like
complement conjuncts.

(63) Bwytais i [fara, menyn a chaws]
ate I bread butter and cheese
'I ate bread, butter and cheese'

Finite and non-finite conjuncts in Welsh
In a sequence of coordinate clauses, only the verbal head contained in the
first conjunct, the specifier, is morphologically specified for tense, person, and number, the following ones containing a verbal noun instead of
an inflected form, thus behaving like complements.

(64) [Aethant i 'r ty ac eistedd a bwyta]
go.PAST.3PL to the house and sit and eat
'They went to the house, sat and ate.'

The structure of multiple coordination with overt conjunctions is then as in (65) (for reasons of simplicity, only the VO-type is given, but there is of course an equivalent OV-type), where either X or Y or both may be a CoP, but where the unmarked case is that it is the complement Y which branches into a new CoP. This is consistent with the usual ideas behind binary branching.

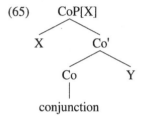

(65)   CoP[X]

At this point it is interesting to note that there are other ways of analyzing multiple coordination with the same theoretical assumptions. Zwart (1995) suggests that one should take the fact that many languages (such as Dutch, French, Greek, and Latin) seem to be allowed to have one conjunction per conjunct, as a sign that each conjunct has its own conjunction (in the next section, it will be argued against the view that the CoP initial words in these languages are conjunctions, even if they are homonymous with proper conjunctions). This would not only give a simple account of OBC (achieved by head-head agreement within CoP). It would also have as a consequence that group readings (i.e., where two conjuncts together are interpreted as a group as opposed to some other conjunct in the CoP) in multiple coordination would have a structural representation in which an additional conjunction had the group part of the CoP as its complement. Below, conjunctions appear in bold print, while conjuncts are represented as A, B, C:

(66) a. [&P1 [&P **&1** [&P2 A [&P **&2** [&P3 B [&P **&3** C]]]]]]

b. [&P1 [&P **&1** [&P2 A [&P **&2** [&P1' [&P **&1'** [&P2'
    B [&P **&2'** C]]]]]]]]

(Adapted from Zwart 1995:12)

The CoP in (66a) contains a multiple CoP in which all conjuncts are distributed evenly. The (66b) one, however, contains an additional conjunction (&1'), which ensures that the CoP following it is treated as a group. The difference in interpretation is illustrated below:

(67) a. A and B and C

    b. A and [B and C]

The conjunction &1' would either be comparable to English *both*, which would give a distributive reading of the group (68a), or to an empty conjunction (in English and Dutch) in a non-distributive reading of the group (68b).

(68) a. A and both [[B] and [C]]

    b. A and [[B and C]]

Although this analysis would give an attractive account of OBC, it involves some problems. First, an additional empty conjunction would have to be added to every non-distributive CoP (i.e., to every conjunct not preceded by a word like *both*). In all languages (as far as I am aware), this conjunction is always empty, an idea which is rather unattractive. Second, and most importantly, the analysis assumes that the element *both* is an ordinary conjunction. This point, however, is empirically questionable. In English, *both* cannot take a CoP consisting of CPs. In contrast, its suggested non-distributive counterpart, the empty Ø, can take this kind of CoP (since Ø is always present in non-distributive CoPs). This is an unexpected gap. Furthermore, in Dutch, the distributive "conjunctions" *en* ('both') and *of* ('either') are impossible (or only acceptable with several question marks) in a triplet when heading the complement of a phonologically similar (though not identical—the distributive one is stressed) "conjunction", even when the distributive meaning is intended:

(69) a. *A en en B en C kochten een auto

    b. *A of of B of C kochten een auto

    c. A en of B of C kochten een auto   (Alma Næss, p.c.)

According to the group analysis (68b), there is a conjunction position which is filled in either case (as long as a group reading is intended), by an overt distributive conjunction or an empty non-distributive one. If there were such a position available, it is difficult to understand why the overt conjunction should be unavailable, especially since the effect of the prohibition is to add ambiguity to the construction.

The equivalent words that trigger a distributive reading in Norwegian and German will be discussed extensively in the next section. There is strong evidence against a conjunction analysis of these words—indeed, they have more in common with adverbs. This fact is a final argument against an analysis of multiple coordination as one in which each conjunct has its own conjunction.

In a series of conjuncts without conjunctions, the only interpretation is one where the conjuncts have equal status, and certainly not one where, e.g., the two left-most of three conjuncts are interpreted as a group. The interpretation is reflected in the structure—(70) rather than (71). All the conjuncts that are sisters to a null head are complements, and must be in the right-hand branch in a head-initial language.

(70) a.

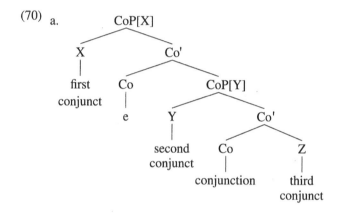

b.*

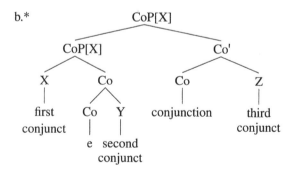

However, a group reading is sometimes intended. Although there is no overt or covert conjunction present, the group reading can be expressed phonologically by a little break or additional stress on some suitable conjunction. In this, it looks very much like Focus Phrases, which are usually taken to be projections of a Focus head (see e.g. Brody (1990) for Hungarian). I suggest that group readings, when "focused," i.e., when contrasting with one or more conjuncts not in the group, have moved to the specifier position of a Group Phrase which has an empty head. The analysis of (67b) above would be:

(71) $[_{CoP} \text{ A } [_{GroupP} [_{CoP} \text{ B and C}]_i \text{ Ø }] \text{ t}_i]$

It is important to note that the Group Phrase does not occur in every group reading, such as when there are only two conjuncts. It is only used as a special disambiguating device, when there are at least three conjuncts altogether. In this respect it parallels the concept of focus. There is a focus in every clause, which usually coincides with an unmarked constituent. A Focus Phrase is only present whenever focus falls on an unpredictable item. In the same way, whenever there are two conjuncts, a group reading is predictable. The Group Phrase will only be necessary to disambiguate an otherwise ambiguous, multiple CoP.

To sum up, there are three possible kinds of phrases within multiple coordination: (i) the unmarked CoP, which is unspecified with respect to grouping between the conjuncts, (ii) the Group Phrase, which gives a group reading to the conjuncts in the phrase (these conjuncts should be interpreted as closer to each other than to other conjuncts in the overall CoP—usually accompanied by a break or additional stress), and (iii) the distributive reading, introduced by CoP adverbs such as *both, either*, and *neither*.

It has been considered a problem in the literature that multiple coordination rarely occurs with CoP adverbs, and never if the CoP is headed by an empty conjunction:

(72) *both Kim, Lee and Sandy

(73) *Kim, both Lee and Sandy   (Borsley 1994:238)

How would we account for this here? Let us make certain assumptions explicit. First, the CoP of which the empty conjunction is a head, is marked with a feature [+ empty]. Second, CoP adverbs like *both* have very specific requirements with respect to what kind of CoP they can adjoin to (*both* can only adjoin to CoPs headed by *and, neither* to *nor*, etc.; these must be [– empty]). Third, since they always co-occur with at least two (in English, exactly two) conjuncts, we can take it that they form a group out of the CoP they adjoin to.

(72) can be accounted for by the assumptions just given: *both* needs a CoP that has the features [and] and [– empty]. The second of these requirements is not met. (73) is interesting because it is not the fact that the word *both* follows an empty conjunction which makes the phrase unacceptable, since (74) is fine. (To my knowledge, this has not been discussed previously in the literature. It would not be accounted for by, e.g., the elaborate rule schema for empty conjunctions and CoP adverbs in Gazdar et al. (1985:171), which is one of the most detailed accounts of the interplay between conjunctions and conjuncts in the literature.)

(74) Kim, both Lee and Sandy, and Mary.

(73) is impossible because the necessary interpretation cannot be given: empty conjunctions need an enumerative interpretation which can be found only if there are at least three conjuncts (of which the complement of the empty conjunction is not the last one) in the CoP. CoP adverbs like *both* create a group interpretation out of the following CoP. The two last conjuncts in (73) therefore must be a group. Enumeration would then only count two conjuncts altogether. In (74), there are three conjuncts, (of which the second one is itself a (Group) CoP)—it is therefore acceptable. (75) illustrates the unacceptable (73), which, from an interpretation point of view, consists of only two conjuncts, *Kim* and *both Lee and Sandy*.

(75) *

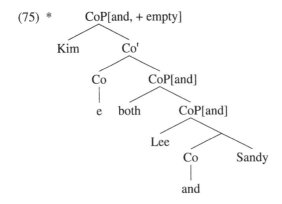

(76) illustrates (74), in which there are three main conjuncts: *Kim, both Lee and Sandy*, and *Mary*. It is therefore acceptable.

(76) ok

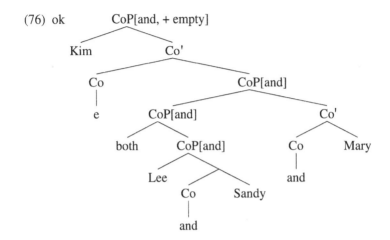

So far, we have established that in multiple coordination, there is one conjunct which is typically normal (a specifier), while all the subsequent conjuncts are complements. While it is evident how the specifier gets case (and generally interacts with the rest of the clause), since it is in the same way as for specifiers of binary coordination, it might not be quite as clear how the rest of the conjuncts get their features. The answer is simple. The same lexical entry accounts for multiple as for binary coordination:

(77) *and*, conjunction, arg1,
                          arg2.

As mentioned in Section 4.3.1.1.2, the conjunction licences case rather than assigns it. The specifier usually gets case from outside the CoP. In multiple coordination only one conjunct spec-head agrees with the conjunction. The rest of the specifiers (and the final complement) have nowhere to pick up case from, and therefore receive the default case. This is why only one specifier looks normal, and all the rest are deviant.

It is interesting to notice that a group reading within the CoP and the role and position of the specifier in CoP are unrelated phenomena. Thus, there are two different group readings of a three-member CoP, but, in

English, there is only one specifier that determines agreement, as noticed by Terry Langendoen (p.c.):

(78) a. There is/*are [[a man and a woman] and a cat] waiting outside.

    b. There is/*are [a man, and [a woman and a cat]] waiting outside.

We have to remark that even if the unmarked case is for a single conjunct to be the specifier, we must account for how there seems to be two or more specifiers, since there is evidence (as mentioned above for Dutch) that this may happen, however marginally. The explanation offered here is that the conjunctions involved in the multiple CoP are of a different kind; the specifier of the topmost CoP is itself a CoP, whose conjunction is of the type used in OBC, i.e., one which explicitly requires its two conjuncts to have the same features. The conjunction of the top CoP, on the other hand, is of the ordinary unmarked kind. Since this seems like a rather unusual situation, we can assume that it is not common. In fact, this seems also to be the case empirically. E.g., the English (79a) sounds much worse than (79b):

(79) a.*[He and she and that their father went to France] worry me

    b. [He and her and that their father went to France] worry me

We can conclude, then, that binary structures along with the general mechanisms already established (like spec-head agreement and licencing of case) can account for the empirical fact that only one conjunct is normal in multiple coordination. A multi-headed analysis would have had to postulate an additional linearity rule.

4.7. CoP adverbs

In the literature (Grootveld 1992; Kayne 1994; Zwart 1995), there have been suggestions that "initial conjunctions" (such as *either, neither, both*) are actually conjunctions.[21] I will argue instead that they are adverbs. There are several arguments in favor of this analysis. Let us first, however, take a look at some of them, exemplified by English and

Norwegian (80)–(81) (the negative adverb *ikke* is superfluous for the meaning of (75a)).

(80) a. I didn't see *neither* [Peter nor Paul]

   b. She likes *both* [walking and cycling]

(81) a. Jeg så   (ikke) *hverken* [Per eller Pål]
       I   saw (not)   neither   Per or   Paul
       'I didn't see neither Peter nor Paul.'

   b. Hun liker *både* [å gå   og å sykle]
       she likes both   to walk and to cycle
       'She likes both walking and cycling'

There is no position within CoP in which these particles naturally belong, since each CoP can only have one head, and we do not want an analysis in which they also head CoPs (as was briefly discussed in the previous section). But in order to discuss their position, it is important to determine what kind of category they are.

It soon becomes clear that they are not conjunctions in an ordinary sense of the word, since they do not conjoin anything. On the contrary, they have to be initial to an extreme extent; they must be at the top of a CoP which is itself not preceded by a conjunction, as shown by (82b) and (83b).

(82) a. neither [$_{CoP}$heat, nor [$_{CoP}$ frost, nor thunder]

   b. *neither heat, neither frost, nor thunder

(83) a. hverken [$_{CoP}$ varme eller [$_{CoP}$frost eller torden]

   b. *hverken varme hverken frost eller torden

Furthermore, both in Norwegian and German, these particles behave like adverbs rather than conjunctions with respect to word order when they occur with CP conjuncts: they trigger subject-verb inversion. Let us consider Norwegian main clauses first.

(84) a. Per gikk   til jobben, og Marit tok trikken til
        Peter walked to.work, and Mary took the.tram to
        skolen
        the.school
        'Peter walked to work, and Mary went by tram to school.'

     b. Både gikk   Per til jobben, og Marit tok trikken til
        both walked Peter to.work, and Mary took the.tram to
        skolen
        the.school
        'It is both the case that Peter walked to work, and that Mary
        went by tram to school.'

     c. *Både Per gikk til jobben, og Marit tok trikken til skolen

     d. *Både gikk Per til jobben og tok Marit trikken til skolen

In (84a), there is an ordinary coordinated CP with normal V2 word order
(here: subject-verb) in both clauses. In (84b), *både* triggers subject-verb
inversion in the first conjunct, just as if some constituent (e.g., an adverb)
had been fronted, giving the order *både* -verb-subject. The second conjunct is not affected by this, and retains its original order. (84c,d) shows
that neither the original word order nor the *både* -triggered one can occur
in both conjuncts. The other two initial particles *enten* ('either') and
hverken ('neither') behave in the same way:

(85) a. Enten har Per   gått   til jobben eller Marit har tatt
        either has Peter walked to.work or   Mary has taken
        trikken.
        the.tram
        'Either Peter has walked to work, or Mary has gone by tram.'

     b. Hverken har Per   gått   til jobben eller Marit har tatt
        neither has Peter walked to.work nor   Mary has taken
        trikken
        the.tram
        'Neither has Peter walked to work, nor has Mary gone by
        tram.'

The similarity between these particles and constituents in general with respect to V2 can be seen by comparing the word order in the first conjuncts of (84) above with the one in the sentences below—both types require a restructuring of the clause in order for the verb to occupy the second position of the clause.

(86) a. Per gikk til jobben
Peter walked to the.work
'Peter walked to work.'

b. I går gikk Per til jobben
yesterday walked Peter to the.work
'Yesterday, Peter walked to work.'

c. Jobben gikk Per til
the.work, walked Peter to
'To work, Peter walked.'

There is, in contrast, never an inversion effect following subordinating or coordinating conjunctions in general. The latter can be seen in the second conjunct in (84a,b) and (85) above, and the former, below:

(87) a. Hvis Per ikke går til jobben, blir han syk
if Peter not walks to the.job, becomes he ill
'If Peter doesn't walk to work, he gets ill.'

b. *Hvis går ikke Per til jobben, blir han syk
if walks not Peter to the.job, becomes he ill

It is clear, then, that these CoP initial particles are syntactically more like adverbs, since they trigger inversion in exactly the same way as proper constituents.[22] Interestingly, a certain urge for parallelism in the structures actually gives (88) as a common alternative to (85a): a semantically rather empty adverb *så* ('then') has been inserted in front of the second conjunct, probably in order to gain the order verb–subject there as well.

(88) Enten har Per gått til jobben eller så har Marit tatt
either has Peter walked to the.work or then has Mary taken
trikken.
the.tram
'Either Peter has walked to work, or then Mary has gone by tram.'

In German, too, CoP initial particles affect word order, although the situation, described in Wesche (1995), seems more complex than in Norwegian. Some of the initial particles trigger V2 in the first conjunct (like Norwegian) (89), others trigger inversion in both conjuncts (90):

(89) a.   Entweder kocht Hans heute oder Maria ruft   den
           either   cooks Hans today or   Maria calls the
           Pizzaservice.
           pizza-service
           'Either Hans cooks today or Maria calls the pizza-service.'

     b.   Nicht nur   kocht Hans heute sondern Maria ruft
          not   only cooks Hans today but   Maria calls
          (auch noch) den Pizzaservice.
          also   the pizza-service
          'Not only cooks Hans today, but Maria also calls the
          pizza-service.'

(90) Weder kocht Hans heute noch ruft Maria den Pizzaservice.
     neither cooks Hans today nor   calls Maria the pizza-service.
     'Neither does Hans do the cooking today nor does Maria call
     the pizza-service.'

                                                    (Wesche 1995:68)

The V2 order is usually assumed to result from the finite verb sitting in C while any constituent can occur in the only position to the left of C: [Spec,CP]. If we now assume that the initial words are adverbs, the behavior of the first CP conjunct is accounted for; the initial CoP adverb sits in the [Spec,CP] of the first conjunct, and since the verb must sit in C, it follows that the subject must find its place further down in the tree. (This would not readily explain the fact that the German (90) has inversion in both conjuncts. However, notice that its English translation also has inversion. The explanation is possibly linked to so-called negative inversion.)

(91) [CoP [CP Adv [C Verb [IP Subject . . .]]] [Co' and [CP Subject [C Verb . . .]]]]

Having decided that the CoP initial particles are actually CoP adverbs, we can also explain their position in subordinate clauses. A subordinating conjunction blocks C, and the verb is left in a lower I position. As adverbs, there is only one possibility for the CoP adverbs, and that is to adjoin—the adjunction site being partly determined by what kind of adverbs they are. Sentential adverbs can adjoin to IP and to I', exemplified by the Norwegian *ikke* 'not':

(92) a. Hun spurte [CP om   [IP ikke [IP Per har gått   til
         she asked   whether   not   Per has walked to
         jobben]]]
         the.work
         'She asked whether Per hasn't walked to work.'

     b. Hun spurte [CP om Per [I' ikke [I' har gått til jobben]]]

(93) a. . . . [CP om [IP enten [IP Per har gått   til jobben]] eller
                      whether either   Per has walked to the.work or
         M.   has taken the.tram
         Marit har tatt   trikken]
         '. . . whether either Per has walked to work or Marit has taken
         the tram.'

     b. . . . [CP om Per [I' enten [I' har gått til jobben]] eller Marit
         har tatt trikken]

Like other adverbs, CoP adverbs do not trigger inversion in subordinate clauses; they adjoin to some inflectional projection. In German, too, adjunction is the only possibility in subordinate clauses:

(94) . . . [CP dass [IP entweder [IP Hans heute kocht]]
              that   either   Hans today cooks
                                   oder Maria den Pizzaservice ruft]
         or   Maria the pizza-service calls
         '. . . that either Hans cooks today or Maria calls the pizza-
         service.'
                                                      (Wesche 1995:67)

The idea that these particles are adverbs makes sense from a semantic perspective. While the main role of conjunctions is to link one constituent to another, CoP adverbs have no such function. Rather, they modify the contents of the CoP they adjoin to: *både* 'both' makes the conjunctive function of *og* 'and' very explicit; *enten* 'either' makes the disjunctive function of *eller* 'or' explicit—and they both add a distributive reading to the modified CoP. The adverb *hverken* 'neither' adds a negative aspect to the disjunctive CoP.

Adverbs in general usually have a limited number of categories they can adjoin to, such as either a clause (CP), a predicate (IP or I'), or an adjectival or adverbial phrase (AdjP/AdvP). We do not have evidence for the position of CoP adverbs in relation to the different kinds of CoP categories. Although we have seen that with CP and IP coordination, CoP adverbs sit in the same positions as other adverbs, we know little about their placement in other phrases:

(95) a. Jeg ønsker *enten* melk eller brus
I   want either milk or   fizzy.water

    b. Jeg sa   at   jeg *enten* ønsker melk eller brus
I   said that I   either want   milk or   fizzy.water

In (95a), the adverb is clearly next to the nominal CoP, but we do not know whether it is adjoined to the CoP itself or to the first conjunct within the CoP. In (95b), the adverb looks as if it is detached from the nominal CoP, but an alternative account is one in which the CoP is verbal (*[CoP ønsker melk eller brus]*), with a deleted verb in the second conjunct. In the latter case, we still do not know whether the adverb is adjoined outside or inside CoP. However, since we do know from clausal coordination that CoP adverbs adjoin to a category inside the CoP (i.e., in the specifier conjunct), we might assume that this is also the case for other kinds of coordination.

The adverb account is compatible with the fact that there is a close relationship between the CoP adverb and the conjunction within CoP. It is not uncommon for adverbs or adverbial phrases to have their adjunction site determined by functional or lexical features. For example, an adverbial denoting 'a certain length of time' cannot be adjoined to a verb of an aspectual type like achievement: **He reached the top for five days.* The CoP adverb is sensitive to the type of CoP it attaches to (determined by the head of CoP), so that, e.g., *both* can only attach to a CoP headed by *and*; *either* can only attach to one headed by *or*, etc.:

(96) a.   He wants both [milk and coffee]

     b.   *He wants both [milk or coffee]

(97) a.   She either [walks or talks]

     b.   *She either [walks nor talks]

Furthermore, the fact that some of these modifiers can only occur with CoPs consisting of two conjuncts, as in some variants of English, see (98), can be accounted for: it can be assumed that the modifiers are sensitive to whether the conjunction in the modified CoP is empty or not. Only in the latter case would the modifier be licit.[23]

(98) a.   *He saw both [a car, a bicycle and a wheelchair]

     b.   *He goes either [by car, by bicycle or by wheelchair]

Although there is thus no evidence for the view that the initial CoP particles are conjunctions in Norwegian, English, and German, one might legitimately ask whether the same conclusion carries over to languages in which the initial particles have the same form as proper conjunctions (such as Dutch, French, Greek, Japanese, and Latin). As mentioned already, some researchers believe initial particles to be conjunctions (Grootveld 1992; Kayne 1994; Zwart 1995), contrary to the view presented in this book. Let us look at Modern Greek (99), and French (100), which both can have a CoP initial particle that looks exactly the same as the proper conjunction:

(99) a.   [o   Janis tha erthi sto   parti] i [tha mini spiti]
         DEF John FUT come to.DEF party or FUT stay home
         'John will come to the party or (he will) stay at home.'

     b.   i [tha erthi o   Janis sto   parti] i [tha mini spiti]
         or FUT come DEF John to.DEF party or FUT stay home
         'Either John will come to the party or (he) will stay at
         home.'   (Joseph and Philippaki-Warburton 1987:58)

(100) a.   Jean connaît [Paul] et   [Michel]
         Jean knows   Paul and Michel
         'Jean knows Paul and Michel.'

b. Jean connaît et   [Paul] et   [Michel]
    Jean knows and Paul and Michel
    'Jean knows both Paul and Michel.'

(Kayne 1994:58 and Antin Rydning, p.c.)

There are two or three things that count against a conjunction analysis of the initial particles even in these languages. First, the initial particles contribute strongly to change the meaning of the CoP. The translations given are the English CoP adverbs *either* and *both*—and like the English counterparts, the meaning is to give a distributional interpretation of the conjuncts in the CoP. The point is explicitly given in Joseph and Philippaki-Warburton (1987:58): "The coordinators *ke* ['and'] and *i* ['or'] can occur at the beginning of both conjuncts to give a more emphatic sense, i.e. *ke . . . ke* 'both . . . and' (literally "and . . . and"), [. . .], and *i . . . i* 'either . . . or' (literally "or . . . or")." If the initial particles were the same as the ordinary conjunctions, these differences in meaning would be rather surprising.

Second, the initial particle is different phonologically, in that it is emphasized or stressed (for Greek, see Mackridge 1987:240). For a functional category (which conjunctions have been argued to be) regularly to carry stress is no less surprising. Third, the initial particle can affect word order, as in (99a) vs. (99b). As discussed extensively above for the Germanic languages Norwegian, English and German, this fact is something one does not expect from conjunctions.

I conclude on the basis of the above discussion that no initial particle is a conjunction. Their actual categorial status may differ in each language, but in no language are they ordinary conjunctions.

4.8. Alternative approaches to conjunction phrases suggested in the literature

The idea that conjunctions are heads follows from the emergence of functional categories (Chapter 3). Various other versions of a CoP have therefore been suggested; Johannessen (1990), Larson (1990), Hartmann (1991), Tait (1991), Grootveld (1992), and Munn (1987a, 1987b, 1992) are some examples. However, few of these works have taken seriously the role of the conjunction as a head in its phrase, with the corollary of one conjunct being more complement-like syntactically than the other (I disregard the only partly developed solution in Johannessen 1990). For example, the complement-like conjunct in Munn (1987b, 1992) is in fact the only argument of the conjunction, while every conjunct, on the other hand, is a complement in Grootveld (1992); Larson (1990) and Tait (1991) only mention the CoP in passing. The suggestions in Munn (1987a, 1987b, 1992) and Grootveld (1992) will be discussed in this section. We shall also look at a position that takes the opposite view of these—that of Borsley (1994)—which is opposed to the idea that conjunctions are heads and to CoP as it is presented here.

Below are illustrated the suggested CoPs in Munn (1987b, 1992), (101a), and Grootveld (1992), (101b), as well as the one suggested in this book, (101c). As can be seen, both (101a) and (101b) assume that there is only one conjunct within the projection of the conjunction.

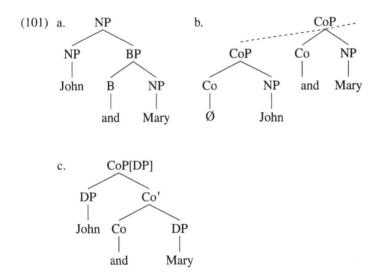

(101)

4.8.1. MUNN'S THEORY

Munn's analysis (Munn 1987b, 1992) stresses the fact that the conjunction and the second conjunct form a strong unit together. The conjunction, B (for Boolean), takes the second conjunct as a complement, and projects to a BP, which is in turn either a complement of the first conjunct (Munn 1987b:16) or adjoined to it (Munn 1992:18).

The UC data have shown us that there is a special relationship between the conjunction and its complement. Munn (1987a, 1987b, 1992) has no

UC data, but refers to Ross (1967/86) for such evidence.[24] Structurally, Munn's analysis is reminiscent of the one advocated in this book, it therefore has the potential of accounting for many of the phenomena discussed here in the same way. However, the lack of a coordinate-alpha transformation and the categories of CoP ("CoP" is to be interpreted here as a projection of the conjunction including the specifier and complement, not in the sense of BP) in his theory leads to several problems.

4.8.1.1. *Some advantages of Munn's theory*

The similarity between Munn's analysis of coordinated structures and the one advocated in this book shows up in the fact that UC (but not EBC) constructions can actually be accounted for in Munn's theory (though not mentioned by him), due to the hierarchical structure of the CoP. Take agreement as an example. In the Czech (17) (above), only the first conjunct determines the agreement features of the verb. This can be straightforwardly accounted for by Munn's analysis; the category of the first conjunct (the specifier), including all its morphosyntactic features, is inherited by the top node, which in turn determines verb agreement. The same reasoning goes for case; whenever the whole CoP is in a case position, only the top category receives case. This category is (presumably) the same one as the specifier conjunct, which, therefore, receives the same features. The complement of the conjunction has no direct connection with the specifier or the top node, and therefore does not get any of those features. With a theory of default case (or lack of case), the case on the complement can be accounted for.

4.8.1.2. *Some problems in Munn's theory*

A very important difference between Munn's theory (Munn 1987b, 1992) and the one advocated in this book are the categories of CoP. In Munn's theory, the conjunction and its complement together form a BP (which is either adjoined to the first conjunct or is a complement of it, see above). The first conjunct is not part of the whole conjunction phrase (it belongs to the CoP by way of being one of two arguments which are, he says, theta-marked by the conjunction, see Munn 1987b:136).[25] Also, importantly, the top node of the CoP is identical to the first conjunct. While this point has the same advantages as those mentioned for the theory of the present book, by accounting for UC, the fact that the top node is not marked as a CoP leads to difficulties, some of which we shall see below.

Munn (1992:18) defends the choice of having no conjunction features on the top level by the claim that there is no category that selects for a CoP. Nevertheless, there are, as I have shown, at least four reasons to assume the necessity of a top CoP. One reason has to do with semantics; coordinated singular DPs usually have a plural interpretation (see (102)).

(102) [A man$_{[sg]}$ and a woman$_{[sg]}]_{[pl]}$ were$_{[pl]}$ / *was$_{[sg]}$ arrested

This requires a CoP to receive the plural features (forced by the lexical entry of the conjunction). It is inconceivable to assume that the top category inherited from the first conjunct should select and perhaps change features depending on some category that is either adjoined or the complement of a conjunct, as would be necessary for Munn's analysis.

Second, there are cases where a CoP has a different syntactic position from both singular and plural simplex DPs. (103) (repeated from Chapter 3) shows an example from Norwegian. Such examples would remain unexplained without a CoP category.

(103) a. Silja så   han / henne / dere   ikke
          Silja saw him   her   you.PL not
          'Silja didn't see him / her / you.'

      b. *Silja så   [han og meg] ikke
          Silja saw   him and me   not
          'Silja didn't see him and me.'

Third, I have shown how EBC constructions are best explained in the same way as UC constructions, but that the difference is that in the former case the syntactic context in which the CoP occurs treats CoPs differently from simplex categories. The Norwegian (41) shows an example where both subject DPs have got accusative case. The fact that it is the default case in a language which occurs in an EBC construction, can be easily accounted for by assuming that the CoP is deprived of normal case assignment. It is not easy to see how a theory without CoPs could account for it.

Fourth, in the case of CoP adverbs ("initial conjunctions"), we have seen that they adjoin to a CoP marked for the relevant conjunction features. Thus, *both* adjoins to *CoP[and]*, *neither* to *CoP[nor]*, etc. There is probably no way of accounting for the distribution of such adverbs, unless one has access to a maximal category marked by conjunction features, i.e., a CoP.

There are other problem cases, too: how would Munn's theory account for the fact that the conjuncts have to be similar, if not identical, category-wise, i.e., [DP and DP] or ordinary OBC? It seems implausible for a grammar to state such a principle explicitly, and implausible to have to state it for two categories that belong to different categories, and have little more in common than that one is part of the complement or adjunct of the other.

Furthermore, the status of conjunctions is not clear. They are supposedly non-lexical and not able to be proper governors (Munn 1992:22–3), but they are still able to theta-mark, as mentioned above. Since we know that, apart from theta-marking, Munn's conjunctions only relate to their complement conjunct, it seems difficult for the conjunctions to be able to require things like kind of category in the other conjuncts.

The lack of an equivalent of a coordinate-alpha transformation (to be presented in Chapter 5) in Munn's theory also makes some phenomena unaccounted for; it is not clear where the conjuncts come from. Traditional problems such as non-constituent coordination, gapping, unlike categories, etc., therefore have no immediate explanation.

4.8.2. GROOTVELD'S THEORY

Grootveld (1992) proposes three-dimensional structures to account for coordination (figure (63b) above). Each conjunct is a complement in a phrase in which a conjunction (empty or not) is head. A CoPhrase (I shall not use the term CoP for the phrases in her theory; "CoP" is restricted to mean a phrase with two conjuncts and a conjunction, as before) therefore consists of only one conjunct; a coordinated structure with two conjuncts would be represented by two CoPhrases, where the second CoPhrase is represented behind the first one. In Grootveld's theory, the concept of *behindance* is as important as precedence or dominance.

4.8.2.1. *Some advantages of Grootveld's theory*

Grootveld's theory has some of the same advantages as other CoP theories; it can account for the fact that different choice of conjunction causes different syntactic behavior, and it can account for different interpretation caused by different linear order of the conjuncts (the CoPhrases behind will be realized after the front ones at PF). EBC constructions can possibly be accounted for in the same way as in the coordinate-alpha theory; the presence of a CoPhrase whose coordination features are visible for the rest of the clause may be considered deviant from a "pure" simplex category with otherwise the same syntactic category features.

4.8.2.2. *Some problems in Grootveld's theory*

One of Grootveld's reasons for having a conjunction position for each conjunct is the possibility of it being the host of pre-coordination elements (in the present book called CoP adverbs) like *both* (1992:68). However, I have shown that these elements must rather be considered adverbs. In addition, they are not always directly followed by the nearest conjunct (something which is a problem in a non-transformational approach like Grootveld's):

(104) Hun har *både* likt [å gå   og å sykle]
       she   has both liked to walk and to cycle
       'She has enjoyed both walking and cycling.'

It is not clear whether the CoPhrase is the top node, in some sense. However, it seems reasonable to assume that the front phrase has priority over the phrases behind. In that case, it is possible, in principle, that the first conjunct is in a privileged position, e.g., to receive or assign case in a UC construction. However, since the behindance relation is clearly something other than a hierarchical relation, it is not clear what constrains the other conjuncts from either getting the same features as the first conjunct, or completely different ones in an unconstrained way.

4.8.3. BORSLEY'S VIEW

Borsley (1994) argues against conjunctions being heads, and against conjunction phrases in general—amongst them an earlier version of the one presented in this book. I will present and answer some of his criticisms against my approach. Let it first be said that Borsley does not present an alternative theory, but expresses support instead to the view suggested in Pollard and Sag (1994) (Borsley 1994:243). However, there is very little about coordination in Pollard and Sag's book—they simply make it clear that there are no heads in conjunction phrases; the mother category subsumes (i.e., is less specific than) the daughter categories (Pollard and Sag

1994:203). This is a very simple theory, whose main goal is to be able to account for conjuncts that have different categories. However, as we saw at the beginning of this chapter, this may lead to severe difficulties in finding a category for the mother at all—if the conjuncts are very different from each other. Also, it lacks a way of determining for the grammar what categories are constrained from being coordinated, and which are not. Of course, the types of coordination presented in this book—UC and EBC—are also unaccountable for.

Borsley accepts that Pollard and Sag's theory is not enough, but what he argues for, is not quite clear. On the one hand, he maintains that "a single conjunct is sometimes the head of a coordinate structure in some languages" (Borsley 1994:243), to account for the unbalanced coordination data in Johannessen (1993c). On the other, he thinks it is plausible that "conjunctions are heads of conjuncts" (1994:244). The reason for the latter is to accommodate the facts from languages which have conjunctions that are homonymous with (what is called here) CoP adverbs. The order between conjunction and complement correlates with that of other heads and complements in these languages, therefore Borsley calls conjunctions heads. But he makes a point of the lack of effect this has: "the categorial makeup of the mother" is determined by the complement, not the head (ibid.). One might ask what it means for something to be a head in Borsley's sense. There is no hint to this in his paper.

Another problem for Borsley (1994:227) is my approach to spec-head agreement—in which major category features (not just ϕ-features) are projected from the specifier to the projection of the head conjunction. This is discussed in Section 4.2—it is claimed that conjunctions lack proper category features.

Borsley (1994:228) believes it is a problem for my analysis that it is the second conjunct in English which is marked with the possessive 's. This, in my opinion, depends on the status of the possessive. Borsley refers to Zwicky (1987), who argues that it is an inflectional affix. However, this stand is at best controversial. Zwicky's reason for assigning it inflectional status is that certain morphophonological facts are easier formulated in GPSG rules that way. The fact that the possessive is always attached to the right-hand periphery of the whole nominal phrase, irrespective of the part of speech of the last word (e.g., *People who hurry's ideas*), still is a weighty argument for its status as a clitic. As such, my analysis with respect to the possessive is unproblematic.

Borsley (1994:224) finds it a problem that in my analysis, CoP specifiers are head-final in head-final languages, while other specifiers in the same languages are often head-initial, when Kayne (1994) claims that specifiers are universally head-initial. This point, which is not a problem, is discussed in Section 4.2, where I claim that Kayne's idea is a hypothesis rather than a conclusion.

Borsley (1994:231) says that the fact that conjuncts sometimes have different categorial status is a problem for an analysis like mine. However, the opposite is true. Both my (previous) merging analysis and my (present) deletion analysis account for unlike category coordination in a principled way. This is in fact a rather important aspect of the theory (see Section 4.2 and Section 5.4), and one of the main reasons for (i) the idea that CoP inherits the whole category from its specifier conjunct (no underspecified category), and (ii) the idea that the input structures to coordination are always full CPs.

Borsley (1994:233) also questions the idea that complements (and specifiers) of conjunctions can be non-maximal. I have commented on this in Section 4.2. He also discusses multiple coordination and what I call CoP adverbs in this book. These are accounted for in 4.6 and 4.7. I conclude that none of the problems that Borsley points out are left unaccounted for.

4.9. Summary

In this chapter, we have seen a theory in which coordinated structures are represented in simple X-bar conjunction phrases. The conjuncts are placed in different positions; one is specifier and one is complement of CoP, while the conjunction is head. The theory can account for the existence of UC and EBC constructions: the former is a result of the different ways in which the conjuncts relate to the clause outside CoP; the specifier is in a spec-head agreement with the conjunction (the head), and gets direct access to the top node, whether it assigns or receives features. The complement conjunct, on the other hand, has no direct contact with the rest of the clause. The features it receives—if any at all—are either default features (licenced by the conjunction), or features inherited from the specifier because of a special conjunction entry thus specified. In rare cases, the conjunction can itself assign case, which is how overcorrection in English is explained.

EBC constructions are explained partly in the same way as UC constructions; the entry of the conjunction is the same. EBC and UC constructions differ from each other not because of internal CoP structure, but because the language (or variety) in which EBC occurs is particularly sensitive and does not accept grammatical features to or from "unpure" categories. An example of an unpure category is CoP[DP] (compared to, e.g., an ordinary plural DP). If the CoP does not receive case, the specifier does not get any. It will therefore get default case (or none at all), just like the complement conjunct. OBC constructions are assumed to be due to a particular feature of the entry of the conjunction, where it is specified that both conjuncts should have the same features. If the specifier gets features from outside CoP, the complement gets the same features. (EBC constructions can also appear this way.) This way, OBC turns out to be the most complicated and marked type, which seems to be correct, according to child language data.

The present theory can furthermore explain the regularities to be found; that UC constructions pattern as head-complement structures with other word-order phenomena, and that in multiple UC, only one conjunct is normal, while irregular features are present at the complement conjunct(s) rather than the specifier one. "Initial conjunctions" are regarded as CoP-modifying adverbs.

We have seen examples of two other theories that also support a CoP analysis (albeit different from the one suggested in this book). Some of their features make them able to account for either UC or EBC, but probably not both. Both theories will have problems accommodating the facts concerning CoP adverbs discussed in this chapter.

Notes

1. Since this book is written within the minimalist program, the structures in (1) should ideally have been presented as in the figure below, in which there is an agreement projection where agreement between specifier and head can take place, and one where the particular case-licencing of the complement, to which we will return later, happens. However, since nothing ever intervenes between the specifier and the complement (apart from the conjunction), such structures will be avoided in this thesis. The types in (i) may however be regarded as abbreviated versions of this structure:

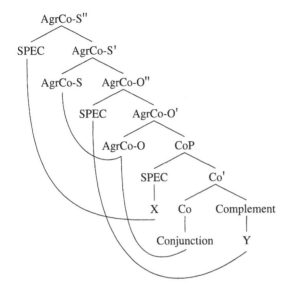

2. There seems to be a general consent in the literature for the assumption that the position of specifiers, as opposed to that of complements, is less closely linked to that of other elements. E.g., in Greenberg (1963), subjects play little role among the categories that behave in a universal manner. Furthermore, it is controversial or at least disputable in which position the subjects are generated. It is not clear whether they are specifiers of VP or of IP (see references in, e.g., Haegeman 1991), and it is not even clear that they are specifiers at all. Contreras (1991: 64), e.g., suggests that subjects are adjoined at D-structure to the predicate in which they occur. There may even be more than one subject position in the same language; e.g., in Spanish, there are two positions (Contreras 1991:64–5):

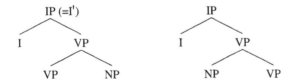

Georgopoulos (1991), on the other hand, sticks to the traditional specifier analysis of subjects. She even assumes the existence of a "specifier parameter," which is independent of the head-complement parameter, but which is consistent within each language, and determines the position of all specifiers in terms of direction in relation to the X'-sister. The specifier of CoP does not seem to follow any such generalization; in an SOV language like Japanese, the [Spec, IP] (the clausal subject) is presumably to the left of I′, but the [Spec,CoP] is to the right of Co′.

3. In the present theory, multiple conjunction is seen as repeated binary co-ordination (see Section 4.6), so there would never be a tripartite CoP to share features, but the fact remains that the number of features of CoP would vary depending on the similarity of the conjuncts; and a CoP might still end up with no syntactic features as when a CoP would consist of AP and PP conjuncts.

4. As mentioned in Chapter 2, Section 2.2.1, there is good reason to assume that the first conjunct has accusative case, since substituting the DP with a nominative case-marked pronoun yields a completely unacceptable result.

5. The verb is only temporarily sitting in Agr-O; it will move further up to T and Agr-S, (maybe) among others.

6. The tree is simplified. The fact that the CoP is a DP, while the category that is in a case position is a DP may look like a problem. It is not, though, since in any DP-analysis, there must be a way that the categories within DP (such as DPs and AdjPs) get to agree with each other. Usually, one assumes that there are many more positions in the whole DP, in which its components have moved and been in a spec-head relation with each other. The tree here can be thought of as the top of the DP tree in which D and CoP[DP] have spec-head agreed at an earlier stage in the derivation.

7. The verb is only temporarily situated in the Agr-S position.

8. It must be emphasized here that the discussion concerns agreement which is determined by syntactic position alone. Agreement which involves computation of both conjuncts, such as when two singular conjuncts give plural agreement, is determined by language-specific resolution rules, and are briefly discussed in Chapter 2.

9. Paul Kershaw has informed me that he suggested this solution for English unbalanced coordination in his talk "Conjunction and Case-Assignment: A Parameter," at the Second Language Research Forum, University of Minnesota, Apr. 1992.

10. This idea has been suggested by Peter Svenonius (p.c.), but it has also been discussed by others, such as Paul Kershaw (p.c.), who eventually rejected it, and Schwartz (1985: 164).

11. Greek usually has a clitic object in addition to the lexical object, which makes it difficult to draw the distinction between left dislocation and topicalization.

12. Incidentally, *than* is regarded as a conjunction in Napoli (1983).

13. The sentence could also be analyzed as the Fulfulde sentence further below, but that is not relevant here.

14. I am grateful to Rolf Theil Endresen for having provided me with data on Fulfulde.

15. Neither the imperfective nor the perfective serial suffixes have a two-way distinction, in contrast to their non-serialized counterparts. The serial imper-

fective suffix is also used in subjunctive moods, while the serial perfective suffix is the one used in non-coordinated relative constructions (such as focus constructions).

16. For the purpose of clarity, I have left out the third conjunct in the figure. Multiple coordination will be discussed in Section 4.6.

17. [Spec,CP] can be filled by a wh-phrase in, e.g., relative clauses:

(i) [CP Hvem [C′ som sa   det]] er ikke kjent
     who   who said it is not known
    'Who said it is not known.'

(ii) Jeg vet   ikke [CP hva [C′ som   ble spist]]
    I   know not   what   which was eaten
    I don't know what was eaten.'

18. The overcorrection in (c) is explained in the section on overcorrection in English above.

19. Later in this section, we shall see that there are various kinds of lexical entries for conjunctions, and the extent to which the different ones are distributed in one speech community may vary.

20. The bracketed [α features] must be taken to mean 'morphosyntactic feature(s)' (specified for each language), not including semantic features or major category features.

21. I follow general practice in referring to these words by the term "initial", although they are final in some languages (e.g., Latin and Japanese).

22. They do not have a complete overlap with adverbs, since they cannot sit in a clause-final position.

23. The theory cannot explain why enumeration with non-empty conjunctions is also disallowed in these variants. However, native (British) English speakers of these variants have informed me that the CoP modifiers are less unacceptable in such examples, i.e., enumerations cases in which the conjunctions are realized.

(i) %either whimpered or shouted or screamed

(Gazdar et al. 1985:174)

24. Since the arguments of Ross are, then, still in use I would like to point out that his major syntactic evidence, from German, is not very convincing. Ross claims that *aber* 'but' is a conjunction associated with the second conjunct in (i). However, there is very little evidence that *aber* is really a conjunction here; as seen in (ii), it patterns with an adverb rather than a conjunction in that position. What looks like a conjunction *aber* is more like a homophonous adverb.

(i) a. Sie will tanzen, ich will aber nach Hause gehen
      she will dance I   will but to   house go
      'She wants to dance, but I want to go home.'

b. *Sie will aber tanzen, ich will nach Hause gehen
   she will but dance   I   will to   house go
   'She wants to dance, but I want to go home.'

                                            (Ross 1967/86:100)

(ii) a. *Sie will tanzen, ich will und nach Hause gehen
     she will dance I   will and to   house go
     'She wants to dance, and I want to go home.'

   b. Sie will tanzen, ich will auch nach Hause gehen
      she will dance I   will also to   house go
      'She wants to dance, and I also want to go home.'

25. Munn (1987a) actually suggests a BP which is similar to the CoP suggested in this thesis. However, since he assumes that the top node inherits the intersection of the features of both conjuncts, the BP actually ends up without features in the case where one conjunct is an AP and one is a PP. It might be this problem which has led to the theory discussed above.

5

Coordinate-Alpha

5.1. Introduction

Having seen the structural representation of conjunction phrases in Chapter 4, we are ready to consider how the conjuncts become attached to the CoP. It will be shown how a generalized transformation, coordinate-alpha, takes two fully projected CP structures and attaches them to the two positions in the CoP. Any two categories can in principle be coordinated, but the result—after possible deletion—must not violate the most general principles of X-bar structure (Section 5.2). Since the input components to coordinate-alpha are full CPs, we need a way that can reduce these components to smaller conjuncts such as DPs or Ps. A deletion approach is suggested, and other approaches in the literature are discussed (Section 5.3). Finally, evidence is presented in support of the idea that the coordinate-alpha components must be full CPs rather than smaller conjuncts. Some theories that do not share this assumption are also discussed (Section 5.4). A summary is given in 5.5.

5.2. The coordinate-alpha transformation

In this section, we shall examine how conjuncts are attached to CoP by a transformation: coordinate-alpha. This part of the theory is as important as that in the previous chapter: the structure of CoP. It should be noted, however, that the two components are in principle independent of each other. It would be possible to imagine coordinate-alpha attaching conjuncts to a different kind of CoP, just as it would be possible to maintain the structure of CoP in an approach without coordinate-alpha.

The transformation that attaches the CoP to its conjuncts, coordinate-alpha, is a very general one. While move-alpha "can move anything any-where" coordinate-alpha can coordinate any category with any other category at any stage in the syntactic derivation.

In fact, the general character of the transformation is maybe closer to what Chomsky (1955, 1957, 1965, 1992) calls generalized transformations: rather than being a singular substitution operation like move-alpha, coordinate-alpha is binary. In the terminology of Chomsky (1992:8), it takes a phrase-marker K (any phrase-marker to become a conjunct), inserts it in a designated empty position ø (a specifier or complement position) in a phrase-marker K′ (a conjunction phrase), in such a way as to satisfy X-bar theory.

The input structures on which coordinate-alpha operates are fully projected CPs (the importance of this will be clarified later). Coordinate-alpha may, however, attach to any category within either of the CPs. The idea of fully projected input structures which are since reduced is not new. Chomsky (1957:35–6) suggests that coordination happens by a rule which takes two grammatical sentences S1 and S2, which differ in that X appears in S1 where Y appears in S2, and X and Y are constituents of the same type. S3 is a sentence which results by replacing X by X + and + Y in S1. The description is too crude, but the basic idea is the same as in the present theory. Other linguists have suggested similar solutions, some of which are Gleitman (1965), Ross (1967/86:101), Goodall (1987), and van Oirsouw (1987), Wesche (1995), and Wilder (1994, 1995).

Some examples are in order. In (1), a conjunction phrase has been attached, by coordinate-alpha, to two CP structures. Whether they were attached to the CoP before or after their separate derivations is impossible to tell; either is possible. I.e., the two CPs might have been underived or derived at the point where CoP attached to them. (Strictly speaking, the CoP is now a CoP[CP]. Here and in the rest of this chapter, structures will be simplified for reasons of exposition and clarity.) The resulting sentence is shown in (2).

(1)

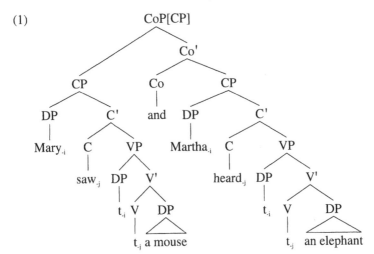

(2) Mary saw a mouse and Martha heard an elephant

When CoP attaches to the topmost nodes in the input structure, as above, the resulting extended structure is always generated by the grammar.[1] In all other cases, well-formedness depends on whether the extended (resulting) structure is accepted by X-bar theory, and principles of deletion (which will be discussed below).

5.3. Reduction

Any approach to coordination that assumes the input to coordinated structures to be full CPs must have some way of accounting for the fact that not all CoPs seem to have CP conjuncts. Sometimes the conjuncts are categories such as V or PP, and sometimes the conjuncts seem to consist of non-constituents, such as verbless clauses ("gapping"), subject + verb combinations ("right node raising"), etc.

In this section, we shall present a deletion account of this problem, but also discuss other ways that have been suggested in the literature. We shall see how coordinate-alpha can attach the CoP specifier and complement to categories that are further down in the component trees. Deletion makes it possible for the conjuncts to share identical structures. It has a very desirable consequence; it makes superfluous the need to have to

state explicitly which categories can be coordinated with which; as long
as they occur in the same position in their respective trees, they can be
coordinated and the rest can be deleted.

5.3.1. DELETION

Deletion has been suggested at various times in the literature, from
Gleitman (1965) to the more recent van Oirsouw (1987) (to be presented
in the next section), Kayne (1994) and Wilder (1994, 1995). The latter is
the most explicit and theoretically well-founded approach, and will be the
one upon which the present account is based. We shall, however, depart
from Wilder in important ways. First, we shall be much more liberal with
respect to what count as possible conjunct categories and second, we
shall suggest an additional operation, which will make it clear how we
can get other conjuncts than CP ones. We shall also assume, without
developing this point, that the deletion rules that are formulated here are
really constraints on LF, rather than rules operating in the syntax as such.
This assumption is partly theoretically motivated, aimed at keeping
within standard assumptions of the minimalist program (e.g., Chomsky
1995), but is also believed to be due to considerations such as recover-
ability of deleted items.

Wilder, like van Oirsouw, makes use of two deletion accounts—
Forward Deletion (FWD) and Backward Deletion (BWD), which both
work on a CoP with the structure suggested in the previous chapter. FWD
deletes in the second conjunct, hence is the one used for gapping (3), and
some types of coordination that looks like "small conjunct" coordination
(coordination in which the conjuncts are not CPs) (4):

(3) [CoP [John drinks beer]
     [Co' [Co and] [CP [C *e* [IP [DP Mary] [I *e* [VP [V ~~drinks~~ [DP
     wine]]]]]]]]]

(4) [John came in [and [~~John~~ sat down]]]   (Wilder 1995:10–12)

Elided material should be visible for LF interpretation and be semantically interpreted. Wilder (1995: §3, §6) gives two types of conditions on
ellipsis: content identification and formal licencing. The first type includes content-identity (5) (the contents of the elided material must be
identical—but not with respect to phonological and morphosyntactic
make-up—to that of the antecedent), context-identity (6) (the antecedent

of ellipsis site E stands in the same hierarchical relation to its conjunct (root CP) as E), and locality (7) (the antecedent of an ellipsis site must be identified by the most local conjunct).

(5) a. [John came in [and [~~John~~ / *~~Mary~~ sat down]]]

   b. [John drinks wine [and [his kids ~~drink~~ / *~~drinks~~ coca cola]]]

(6) *[The book pleased John [and [~~John~~ bought it]]]

(7) *[John came in [and [Mary sat down [and [~~Mary~~ / *~~John~~ read a book]]]]]   (Adapted from Wilder 1995:11–13)

The second type (formal licencing) consists of the head condition on FWD (an ellipsis site may not be c-commanded by an overt head in its domain (= conjunct)) (8), and the major constituent condition (a deletion site may not span a string which extends to a subpart of a major constituent) (9).

(8) *[John bought the book [and [Mary read ~~the book~~]]]

(9) *[Three blue cars arrived [and [~~three~~ red cars departed]]]
                         (Adapted from Wilder 1995:13–15)

BWD accounts for structures that look like right node raising and head-coordination:

(10) [John looked at ~~today's copy of the Times~~]
      and [Mary read today's copy of the Times

(11) Can ~~you do it~~ and will you do it?   (Wilder 1995:22–8)

BWD has two conditions which take care of the right-peripherality: an ellipsis site must be right-peripheral in its conjunct, and the licencing string must be right-peripheral in its conjunct. Wilder also notes that there must be form-identity between ellipsis site and antecedent in BWD.

(12) John said that I _
      and Mary said that we love jazz /she loved jazz /*she loves jazz
                                     (Wilder 1995:26)

5.3.1.1. *Small conjunct coordination*

While Wilder argues against "small conjunct" coordination, i.e., the possibility of conjuncts being other categories than CP (and also DP), I shall argue for a less restrictive approach here. There are empirical reasons to accept "small conjunct" coordination generally. To be fair, Wilder (1995:§2.2.2, 2.3) mentions agreement and pronoun-binding as two arguments in favor of nominal conjuncts (DPs) as an addition to CP conjuncts.

(13) a.   There were [DP a man and a cat] in the kitchen

    b.   [There was [DP a man] ~~in the kitchen~~] [and ~~there was~~ [DP a cat] in the kitchen]

(14) a.   [every dog] and [its̲ owner]

    b.   *[his̲ dog] and [every owner]   (Wilder 1995:5–6)

The two different analyzes in (13) account for the two possible agreement facts—singular as well as plural (both of which are found), Wilder says. He then refers to Aoun, Benmamoun and Sportiche (1994), who discuss some types of coordination in Arabic that look like DP coordination while they are probably better analyzed as clausal coordination.[2]

There are no other categories than DPs and CPs that can occur as conjuncts in Wilder's theory. This means that all other heads and categories can only take part in clausal coordination with deletion. This, however, does not seem to be right. Consider the German example (15) of unbalanced coordination (repeated from Chapter 2). *Begrüssen* normally assigns Accusative and *helfen* Dative.

(15) Maria [begrüsste und half]   dem   / *den   Mann
     Mary   greeted   and helped the.DAT the.ACC man
     'Mary greeted and helped the man'

As clausal coordination, it would have to be analyzed either as (16a) or as (16b), in Wilder's theory.

(16) a. [Maria begrüsste ~~den Mann~~ [und [~~Maria~~ half dem̲   Mann̲]]]
                  ACC   DAT

b. [Maria begrüsste ~~dem Mann~~ [und [~~Maria~~ half dem Mann]]]
         DAT   DAT

If (16a), in which each verb assigns its right case, were chosen, one of the conditions of BWD would be violated, viz. that of PF identity (the two object DPs have different case). If (16b) were chosen, the verb would have to check the wrong case, the problem this time being similar to that of nominal unbalanced coordination above.

There are other examples from German for other categories, too, such as prepositions. Consider an example with prepositions (repeated from Chapter 2) (*mit* normally assigns Dative, and *ohne* Accusative):

(17) Die Kinder kommen [mit und ohne] Mäntel
     the children come   with and without raincoats.ACC
     /*Mänteln
     / raincoats.DAT
     'The children come with and without raincoats.'

Again, there are two possible clausal analyses; the first one violates the PF condition on BWD, and the second contains a preposition assigning the wrong case:

(18) a. [Die Kinder kommen mit ~~Mänteln~~ [und [~~die Kinder~~
                                 DAT
     ~~kommen~~ ohne Mäntel]]]
           ACC

     b. [Die Kinder kommen mit ~~Mäntel~~ [und [~~die Kinder~~
                                 ACC
     ~~kommen~~ ohne Mäntel]]]
           ACC

The sentences find a neat solution if we accept V and P head coordination, respectively:

(19) a. Maria [[[begrüsste] und Co'] [half] CoP] dem Mann

     b. Die Kinder kommen [[[mit] und Co'] [ohne] CoP] Mäntel

The conjunct that is the actual case assigner in these instances is the specifier of CoP, which, by spec-head agreement, gives its case to CoP itself. The "wrong" case assigner is buried deep down in the complement position of CoP, and does not count.

A second argument for "small conjunct" coordination comes from Norwegian CoP adverbs (CoP initial particles). When these adverbs (*både* 'both', *enten* 'either', *hverken* 'neither') modify CPs, they trigger V2, just like other fronted constituents would do. When other categories are coordinated, they do not trigger V2 in their clauses. This is illustrated below. (20a) has CP coordination with verb-subject inversion in the first conjunct, (20b) has DP coordination without V2, and (20c) shows that V2 would be impossible with DP coordination.

(20) a. [Både gikk   Per   til jobben,   [og [Marit tok   trikken
         both walked Peter to.work,   and Mary took the.tram
         til skolen]]]
         to the.school
         'It is both the case that Peter walked to work, and that Mary
         went by tram to school.'   (Repeated from Chapter 4)

     b. Både [Per   og Marit] gikk   til jobben
        both   Peter and Mary walked to.the.work
        'Both Peter and Mary walked to work.'

     c. *Både gikk [Per og Marit] til jobben

If coordination is always CP coordination, (20b) ought to have resulted from (21).

(21) [Både ~~gikk~~ Per ~~til jobben~~ [og [Marit <u>gikk</u> <u>til jobben</u>]]]

However, (21) cannot be an acceptable deletion account, since the BWD of *gikk* in the first conjunct would violate both BWD conditions: an ellipsis site must be right-peripheral in its conjunct, and the licencing string must be right-peripheral in its conjunct. The fact that (20b) is perfectly acceptable, and much better than (20c), shows that at least DPs must be included among the categories that can be coordinated, and that a pure CP account does not give the right results.

The same point can be made for adverbs. (22a) shows CP coordination with inverted verb-subject in the first conjunct, contrasted with (22b), which has AdvP coordination and no V2. (22c) shows V2 order with AdvP coordination.

(22) a. [Både kjører Per   fort, [og [Marit kjører uforsiktig]]]
     both drives Peter fast   and Mary drives recklessly
     'It is both the case that Peter drives fast and that Mary
     drives recklessly.'

   b. Både [fort og uforsiktig] kjører de
     both fast and recklessly drive they
     'They drive both fast and recklessly.'

   c. ?Både kjører de [fort og usikkert]

(The reason why (22c) seems better than (20c), is not quite clear to me,
but it does not affect the argument). If all coordination were CP coordination, (22b) should have been derived from a deletion analysis based
on (23).

(23) [Både fort kjører de [og [de kjører uforsiktig]]]

But there is no deletion that would arrive at either of the sentences
(22b,c). We must conclude that the Norwegian word-order facts would
be a mystery, unless we accept coordination of categories other than just
CP—the two examples show the necessity of small conjunct coordination, viz. of DPs and AdvPs.

A third, and different, kind of argument—but as important—for coordination of categories other than CP and DP comes from languages in
which different categories are coordinated by different conjunctions:
Sissala, for example, distinguishes between CP, VP, and non-verbal coordination with three different conjunctions (including an empty one).
Nguna distinguishes CP and VP coordination. (Both languages are discussed in Chapter 3.) If all cases of coordination other than of DPs were
CP-coordination, this division of different conjunctions would be inexplicable.

It should be mentioned that there are other suggestions in the literature
apart from Wilder's that also wish to restrict the types of categories that
can occur as conjuncts. Kayne (1994) and Wesche (1995) (the latter to
be discussed in Section 5.3.2.4) suggest that conjuncts must be maximal
projections. Kayne (1994:59–63) has both a theoretical and an empirical
motivation for this stand. The theoretical one is that it follows from his
antisymmetry requirement; a constituent such as [*and* X^0] would violate
it, since the conjunction and the complement would c-command each

other. The empirical one is based on French pronouns, where, Kayne claims, restrictions on the possibility of coordinating pronominal clitics can be accounted for if one accepts a general prohibition against heads as conjuncts:

(24) *Jean te   et   me voit souvent
     Jean you and me sees often
     'Jean sees you and me often.'   (Kayne 1994:59)

The fact that it has been shown in the literature (Benincà and Cinque 1990) that some pronouns actually can be coordinated (25) is explained thus by Kayne: what looks like clitic head coordination must be analyzed as right node raising (RNR), which requires that the empty category precedes its licencer. This would also explain the difference between the possible acceptability of preverbal clitics (25) and the impossibility of postverbal ones, (26).

(25) ?Je lui [e]$_1$ et vous [ferais   un plaisir]$_1$
     I   him   and you would.do a pleasure
     'I would do him and you a pleasure.'

(26) *[Donne]$_1$-moi et [e]$_1$ lui un livre
     give   me and   him a book
     'Give me and him a book.'   (Kayne 1994:60)

However, French pronouns do not conformly follow this pattern. My informants dismiss both (25) and (26), but judge (27) as acceptable (albeit a bit strange) and (28b) as fine. (27) differs from (26) only in the order in which the pronouns occur. Importantly, the empty category follows its licencer, contrary to what Kayne suggests is the rule for RNR.

(27) ?[Donne]$_1$-lui et [e]$_1$ moi un livre
     give   him and   me a book
     'Give him and me a book.'

The pronouns can also follow indicative verbs, both in an ordinary and in a right dislocated position. Both cases would violate Kayne's requirement for RNR, thus indicating again that this is not RNR.

(28) a. ?Ma soeur [voit souvent]ᵢ lui et [e]ᵢ moi
       my sister sees often   him and   me
       'My sister often sees him and me.'

    b. Ma soeur nous [voit souvent]ᵢ, [e]ᵢ lui et moi
       my sister us   sees often   him and me
       'My sister often sees us, him and me.'

Finally, unless Kayne's claim is only intended for French, there is counter-evidence in other languages. For example, in Norwegian, which has been argued to have pronouns that are heads rather than maximal phrases (they can be modified by relative clauses, prepositional phrases, etc., see Hestvik 1992), pronouns can be coordinated:

(29) a. [Han og hun I den omfavnelsen der] er de søteste
      he and she in that embracing   there are the sweetest
      'The male and the female (engaged) in that embracing over there are the sweetest ones.'

    b. Jeg så [han og hun som hadde sittet sammen på den
      I   saw he and her who had   sat   together on that
      benken I natt]
      bench in night
      'I saw the male and the female who had sat together on that bench last night.'

Kayne's account of RNR is a deletion one, but he says little about it. However, without a restructuring part, a deletion account probably means that the deleted items are retrievable and thus available at LF. For the Norwegian (29a,b), this would not give the right interpretations since it is crucial that the pronominal modification is the same for both pronouns. I conclude that Kayne's arguments are not convincing, and that the data here and previously in this chapter show the need to accept conjuncts of all categories.

How can we account for the possibility of coordinating categories other than CP when we want to keep the insight that the input structures for coordination are CPs? Wilder gives no clue as to how DP coordination (the only other coordination than CP coordination that he accepts) takes place. However, when we want CP structures to be the starting-point, and yet allow small conjunct coordination, there must be some operation at work that makes it possible for the conjuncts to share whatever is not conjoined, and for the CoP to be situated somewhere below the top CP nodes. Consider first the result of Forward and Backward Deletion. If CoP had attached its specifier and complement to the P positions, we would obviously have an X-bar violation with several mothers, as described above, and illustrated in (30)–(31):

(30) a. [CP ~~Die Kinder kommen~~ [CoP mit ~~Mäntel~~]
     b. [CP ~~die Kinder kommen~~ [und [ohne Mäntel]]

(31)

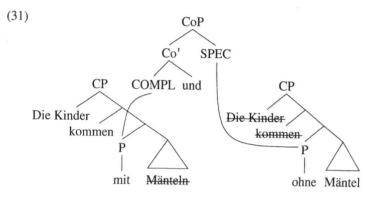

In order to avoid this X-bar violation, we must allow the conjuncts to share structures:

(32) *Operation Share*:
     If material above and/or below CoP attachment is deleted in one of the input CPs in accordance with FWD and BWD, the remaining material can be shared. The two CPs are rearranged into one CP by removing deleted material and inserting the CoP in the attachment position. The resulting structure must not violate X-bar theory.

The resulting structure will be:

(33) a.

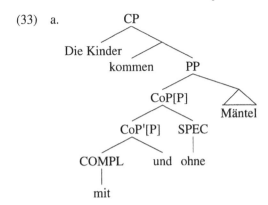

b. [CP Die Kinder kommen [CoP[P] mit und ohne] Mäntel

The tree in (33) is possibly not quite right. We recall that BWD requires phonetic identity. The deleted word in the first component tree must then have the accusative case form *Mäntel*, since both the deleted word and its antecedent must have the same form. In some sense, the dative-assigning preposition *mit* in this case must accept an accusative complement. In a minimalist theory, this is not a problem, however, since case and other features are not literally assigned at a certain point, but rather checked. If coordination and share take place before case checking, and the preposition responsible for dative case is in the CoP complement position, case checking of the accusative DP will be fulfilled by the accusative-assigning preposition in specifier position.

Deletion is optional. This means that like material can be coordinated, e.g. for emphasis, without being shared and without violating the grammar:

(34) a. [Mary saw a mouse] and [Martha saw a mouse]

b. [Mary saw] and [Martha saw] a mouse

Of course, this makes it possible to coordinate identical material without sharing, sometimes with pragmatically odd results, as in (35) (assuming that they denote the same referent, i.e., have the same indices). This should not be seen as a syntactic violation, however, since coordinating like material is sometimes used as a means of conveying a particular meaning, as in the Norwegian and English (36).

(35) a. (!)Mary saw a mouse and Mary saw a mouse

   b. (!)Mary and Mary saw a mouse

(36) a.   Karl ventet og ventet, men Mona kom ikke

   b.   Karl waited and waited, but Mona did not come

The fact that deletion is optional is also necessary for pairs such as (37) below. It is clear that the interpretation of *some boys* need not be the same; in (37a), we may have two sets of boys doing different things, in (37b), the same boys do both the walking and the talking.

(37) a.   Some boys walk and some boys talk

   b.   Some boys walk and talk

So-called right node raising involves the situation in which CoP has attached to the top of the component sentences while the shared material is at the bottom:

(38) [$_{CoP[CP]}$ Mary saw a̶ ̶m̶o̶u̶s̶e̶ and Martha heard <u>a mouse</u>]

Deletion has taken place according to the requirements of backward deletion; both the licencing string and the ellipsis site are right-peripheral. Since CoP has attached to the top of the input CPs, we cannot rearrange it. Neither can the non-deleted material be structurally shared by the two CPs, since this would violate X-bar theory—the DP *a mouse* having two mothers.

(39)

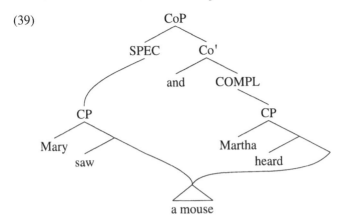

However, the possibility remains of actually leaving the tree as it stands. This violates nothing:

(40)

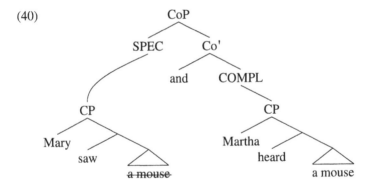

The coordination types that have traditionally been considered problematic in the literature represent no problem in this approach. Gapping is accounted for by the same means as coordination of "small conjuncts," as in (5b) in the beginning of this section, simply by applying FWD. Right node raising (10) is accounted for by BWD. Other non-constituent coordination is handled by FWD. No extra apparatus is needed.

5.3.2. OTHER APPROACHES TO REDUCTION

It is necessary for any theory of coordination that assumes full sentences as input for coordination to have some way of reducing identical material. If there were no such way all coordinated structures would have to have CP conjuncts. Below we shall take a look at some alternative ways to reduction that have been suggested in recent literature and discuss them with respect to several aspects of coordination. We shall discuss how they have tried to solve the reduction problem, and what constraints there are on the component structures. We shall see how they might handle the UC and EBC cases, but also look at some traditional problems like gapping and non-constituent coordination.

5.3.2.1. *Van Oirsouw's deletion approach*

Van Oirsouw (1987) proposes a theory which is very much like the one later suggested by Wilder. Crucial in the theory is the notion of *deletion sites*, based on a purely linear graphic representation (van Oirsouw 1987:123 ff). They are meant to suffice to account for most types of coordination, combined with Ross's (1970) directionality constraint: leftmost sites delete forward (i.e., subsequent occurrence of identical material disappears), rightmost sites delete backwards (i.e., the antecedent occurrence of identical material disappears). Van Oirsouw's peripherality constraint—the idea that a deletion target site is only accessible to deletion if it is peripheral (immediately left-adjacent or right-adjacent to its S-boundary)—is built into the representation.

(41) Leftmost sites:
      $_s[\ldots (XX) \ X] \ CONJ \ _s[\ldots (XX) \ X]$

(42) Rightmost sites:
      $_s[X \ (XX) \ldots] \ CONJ \ _s[X \ (XX) \ldots]$

The interpretation is: *X* is any constituent unlike one in the other conjunct, . . . is identical material, *CONJ* is the conjunction, *[ ]* are S-boundaries, *( )* indicate optionality. Left-peripheral sites delete forward, yielding (43), and rightward sites rightwards (44):

(43) a.   John ate a hamburger and Ø drank a beer

      b.   *Ø ate a hamburger and John drank beer

(44) a.   Peter ØØ and Harry drink red wine

      b.   *Peter drink red wine and Harry ØØ

The fact that the sites must be absolutely peripheral is shown in (45a), where, in the second conjunct, an unlike initial adverbial destroys the left-periphery of the possible deletion site, and in (46a), where the deletion site in the first conjunct is set firmly between the verb and the second object.

(45) a. *Yesterday John ate like a pig but the day before Ø was very modest[3]

   b. John ate like a pig yesterday but Ø was very modest the day before

   c. Yesterday John ate like a pig and Ø Ø got blind drunk

(46) a. *John gave Ø a book and Peter sold the girl in the red sweater a record

   b. John gave a book Ø and Peter sold a record to the girl in the red sweater

Traditionally problematic types such as gapping and non-constituent co-ordination do not represent a problem. Although there is a special gapping rule (47), the deletion account follows the general principles: verb sites (gapping) delete forward. Since the verb is part of the deletion site, other constituents being adjacent to the verb can be deleted with it, as in (48).

(47) Verb-sites:
   $_s[0 \ldots -V- \ldots (XX)]$ CONJ $_s[0 \ldots -V- \ldots (XX)]$
   (*0* is an ignored constituent, *-V-* is a verb which occurs somewhere in the deletion target site)

(48) John sometimes eats fish and Bill ØØ rice

Non-constituent coordination is no problem in the theory. Right node raising has been demonstrated in (46b), and an example of double object coordination, which follows ordinary forward deletion, is shown in (49a):

(49) a. John gave Mary a book and ØØ Sue a record

   b. *ØØ Mary a book and John gave Sue a record

However, the peripherality constraint in van Oirsouw's theory is too
strict: when a verb moves, e.g., in questions, and thus precedes the subject, the subject is no longer peripheral, and deletion is hence no longer
possible:

(50) a. I am ill and Ø must sleep

   b. *Am I ill and must Ø sleep?

This may work for English, but the peripherality requirement is too
strong for, e.g., Norwegian, where non-peripheral material can be deleted
both in questions and V2 related rearrangements:

(51) a. Er jeg syk og må   Ø sove?
         am I   ill and must sleep
         'Am I ill and must sleep?'

   b. I går   var Jon syk og Ø fikk ikke Ø sove
        yesterday was Jon ill and   could not   sleep
        'Yesterday, Jon was ill and couldn't get to sleep.'

More serious than this is the fact that van Oirsouw assumes all component sentences to be grammatical structures: "[It] derives well-formed
non-S coordinations from well-formed S-coordinations by means of deletion" (van Oirsouw 1987:123). Van Oirsouw's theory shares this feature
with many others, e.g., that of Chomsky 1957:36–7. This requirement
makes it very difficult to account for many of the examples of UC and
EBC presented here. Take, for example, the Czech UC case example
below (repeated from Chapter 2).

(52) Půjdu   tam [já a   ty]
      will.go-1SG there I and you
      'You and I will go there.'

If (52) were derived from well-formed sentences, then (53a,b) would
have to be considered well formed, which they are not:

(53) a. Půjdu   tam já
         will.go-1SG there I

b. *Půjdu   tam ty
   will.go-1 SG there you

Similarly, the English EBC example (54) would require (55a,b) to be well formed:

(54) [Them and us] are going to the game together

(55) a. *Them are going to the game together

   b. *Us are going to the game together

5.3.2.2. *Goodall's three-dimensional approach*

Goodall's (1987) extension of the GB theory assumes that coordinated structures exist as parallel structures (to be explained below). Each sentence has a Reduced Phrase Marker (RPM) (Lasnik and Kupin 1977)—at each level of representation—based on the relations of *precedence* and *dominance* between the terminals and non-terminals in that sentence. Coordination is seen as a union of two or more composite sentences' RPMs, which will only be possible if the RPMs are strictly parallel, as in (57), for the component sentences in (56).[4]

(56) a. Jane saw Bill

   b. Alice saw Bill

(57) {S, NP1 saw Bill, Jane VP, Jane V Bill, Jane saw NP, Jane saw Bill,
      NP2 saw Bill, Alice VP, Alice V Bill, Alice saw NP, Alice saw Bill}   (Goodall 1987:2.21)

In (57), each element, word or phrase, is in a relation of precedence or dominance to each of the other elements, except that NP1 and NP2 have no relation to each other. Given that the RPM for each of the component sentences (56a,b) is identical to the other (the first and the second line of (57)), NP1 and NP2 must be at exactly the same position in the resulting tree. The only way this can be realized is in a three-dimensional tree. (58) is the tree-representation and (59) the linearization, which has emerged through a specific Linearization Principle. The PF realization of (59) must of course insert a conjunction between the first (top) and the second (bottom) conjunct.

(58)

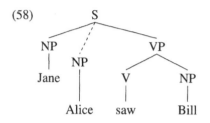

(59)

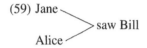

No deletion or other reduction is necessary: the fact that the component sentences are represented in one tree, with the conjuncts in different levels, means that the construction of the tree from the RPM reduction actually involves unifying the identical material in the two different components.

Non-constituent coordination generally, e.g. NP + PP, can be coordinated (60) as can right node raising (61)–(62):

(60) a. Elaine took [[$_{NP}$ Mary] [$_{PP}$ to the airport] and [$_{NP}$ Jane] [$_{PP}$ to the beach]]

   b. Elaine

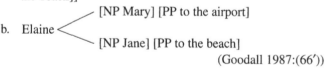

                                                          (Goodall 1987:(66′))

(61) Mary kissed and Jane hit that tall man in the black suit

(62) a. Mary kissed that tall man in the black suit
   b. Jane hit that tall man in the black suit

                                                       (Goodall 1987:96)

Gapping, (66) below, presents problems for a pure pattern-matching approach like Goodall's, but it is solved. Ordinary linearization would only give (64), then (65a,b), from (63a,b), but not (66), since it requires each element coordinated from the first string to precede the coordinated element from the second string.

(63) a. Mary eats apples

b. John eats oranges

(64)

(65) a. Mary eats apples and John eats oranges

b. Mary and John eat apples and oranges

(66) Mary eats apples, and John oranges

A linking operation must be added to link x and z—(68a) rather than the one used for ordinary coordination—(68b):

(67) In the union of the phrase markers for the sentences xyz and
vyw, link x and z.   (Goodall 1987:81)

(68)

There is an additional requirement for the well-formedness of the result of the linking operation, and that is that x, y, v, and w are constituents. This rules out sentences like (69a), while the constituent requirement is not needed for ordinary linearization, (69b).

(69) a. *[$_{NP}$ Simon] [$_{AdvP}$ quickly] dropped and [$_{NP}$ Jack] [$_{AdvP}$ suddenly] the gold and the diamonds

b. Simon quickly and Jack suddenly dropped the gold and the diamonds

Unlike category coordination is not a problem in Goodall's theory. As long as two categories are at the same place in the phrase-marker, they are conjoinable. The theory has many advantages, but also a few short-comings that are partly due to explicit requirements in the theory and partly to the fact that it is vague at critical points.

UC and EBC

Like that of van Oirsouw, Goodall's approach depends on the grammat-icality of the component sentences. This leads to the same difficulties in accounting for UC and EBC.

Conjunctions

The exact position of conjunctions in Goodall's theory is not clear. On the one hand, conjunctions are inserted at PF as linearization is taking place. They can be inserted in front of each conjunct or only in front of the last one (in English). On the other hand, since conjunctions obviously have some meaning, in that a construction of two conjuncts combined by *and* does not mean the same as one combined by *but*; they have to be represented in the syntax.

Goodall therefore introduces an extra layer of representation, in which the terminals in the phrase-marker are represented as an ordered set within the larger unordered set, and where the conjunction marks the set:

(70) { . . . and(John drank the poison, John died) . . . }

This structure is meant to be interpreted at PF by the linearization princi-ple. However, how this is possible, and how it interacts with the other requirements of the phrase-marker, is a mystery (this will also be dis-cussed below, in the section on linearity).

The status of the conjunction in this theory is vague and not compati-ble with the head properties that conjunctions are shown to have in this book. We shall not repeat those results, only mention some central prop-erties, such as the fact that different conjunctions subcategorize for dif-ferent categories (in English, *for* does only take full CPs; in Cayuga, only DPs can be coordinated by *hni'*), that different conjunctions lead to dif-ferent semantics (e.g., number of the CoP), and that conjunctions have predictive power with regard to word-order facts (UC). These properties, which are among those that show the head-status of conjunctions, are left unaccounted for in Goodall's theory. The lack of an account of conjunc-tions also makes it impossible to explain how coordinated structures with some conjunctions can have only a limited number of arguments com-pared with others, and how CoP adverbs are distributed and constrained.

Semantic interpretation

Since sentences are linearized at PF there is no predictable difference in interpretation between sentences like (71a) and (72b), which are two alternative linearizations of the same component sentences. It would have been desirable that the different interpretations were reflected in the syntax by there being different structures assigned to the two sentences. As the theory stands, it remains a mystery why only (71b) can have an interpretation where John bought (or Mary sold) less than ten cars.[5] (See also the discussion in Moltmann 1992.)

(71) a. [John bought a total of ten cars and Mary sold a total of ten cars]

b. [John bought and Mary sold] a total of ten cars

Similarly, two verbs that are coordinated can also lead to different interpretation of the construction, as in (72). Goodall's theory cannot account for the fact that only (72a) has an interpretation involving two different chickens.

(72) a. Judith [cooked a chicken and ate a chicken].

b. Judith [cooked and ate] a chicken.

Linear order

In Goodall's theory, linearization only happens at PF. Linear order is, however, important on many levels, both syntactic and interpretative. Goodall therefore offers an extension of the theory, in which terminal strings of two underlying sentences are given as an ordered pair marked by its conjunction type. The difference between sentences like (73) is represented as in (74).

(73) a. John drank the poison and died

b. John died and drank the poison   (Goodall 1987:31)

(74) a. { . . . and(John drank the poison, John died) . . . }

b. { . . . and(John died, John drank the poison) . . . }
(Goodall 1987:31)

There are two problems with this extension, however. First, the syntactic status of the ordered pair is not explained. The elements are not in a clear *precedence* or *dominance* relation with each other, as the reduced phrase- markers ought to be. In the three-dimensional tree the conjuncts occur at the same level, in fact, if the tree were two-dimensional, the conjuncts would be superimposed, one upon the other. And yet, the difference between the conjuncts must have a structural counterpart which is visible, not only at PF, in order to give a genuinely syntactic explanation for these facts. Another difficulty of this revised approach to phrase-markers, where ordered pairs are included, is the status of the conjunction preceding the ordered pair.

Linearity is not only necessary for the interpretation of temporality, as in Goodall's example. In UC constructions, it is essential that the direction of head and complement is like that of other head-complement structures in the language. Furthermore, pronominal reference shows that linear order (and not only c-command) is necessary for determining antecedence. In (75a), the pronoun in one conjunct can have an antecedent in the other conjunct, but not vice versa, as seen in (75b).

(75) a. Peter$_i$ and his$_{i/j}$ wife were watching the telly (DP & DP)

     b. His$_{*i/j}$ wife and Peter$_i$ were watching the telly (DP & DP)

Collective and respectively reading
The linearization principle, which states how linearization at PF occurs, does not state how the conjuncts should be linearized if the component sentences lead to more than one parallel structure, i.e., if there are more than one coordinated structure within one union of phrase-markers. It only states that elements from the first part of the ordered pair in the union should come before elements from the second part. E.g., if (76) is a linearized sentence the component sentences can be either as in (77) or as in (78), i.e., one *collective* and one *respectively* reading.

(76) [John and Mary] saw [the horse and the cow]

(77) a. John saw the horse

     b. John saw the cow

     c. Mary saw the horse

    d. Mary saw the cow

(78) a. John saw the horse

      b. Mary saw the cow

This leads to the sentence (79) being grammatical in Goodall's theory, although only in the *respectively* reading, the equivalent of (78), since the *collective* reading would violate agreement conditions (component sentences must be well formed).

(79) ??John and Mary saw himself and a cow (respectively)
                                        (Goodall 1987:60)

However, (79) is impossible for most speakers. A translation to Norwegian is interesting. In Norwegian, the 3rd person anaphor is ambiguous between singular and plural, and so the translation of (79) should at least give the *respectively* reading, but it ought also to be ambiguous. In fact it is not; the only interpretation of the anaphor is the plural, *collective*, one.

(80) Per og Kari så   seg selv og en ku
      Per and Kari saw 3P self and a cow
      'Per and Kari saw themselves/*himself and a cow'

The purely mechanical derivation of a *respectively* reading also seems wrong when the conjuncts have different thematic roles. The example (81) (also discussed in Chapter 7) shows how two structurally similar sentences that differ only with regard to their thematic roles cannot be coordinated, not even with a *respectively* reading.

(81) *[Marit og jeg] luktet [gass og parfyme]
      Marit and I   smelt gas and perfume
      (Experiencer&Theme Theme&Source)
      'Marit and I smell gas and (of) perfume.'

One might argue that even if there are certain problems with the *respectively* reading, i.e., for when it should apply, it is still an advantage that the theory accounts for it structurally. However, the *respectively* reading seems to be a purely pragmatic choice that does not only apply

to coordinated constructions, but to all (or most) plural DPs. In this
respect it belongs to the same category as the adverb *alternatingly*.
Consider the extract (82) from a postcard from a person who attended a
summer school in linguistics:

(82) . . . jeg nyter sommeren   og sitter ved guruenes føtter
        I   enjoy the.summer and sit   by   the.gurus' feet,
        vekselvis.
        alternatingly
        'I enjoy the summer and sit by the feet of the gurus, alternat-
        ingly.'

It is obvious that the person enjoys sitting at several gurus' feet, but not
by all at the same time, and not by one foot at the time, but by two—
given what we know about gurus and feet. The relevant DP above is not
a coordinated DP, and neither does it need to be for *respectively*: Furthermore, in (83), the object is a simplex plural DP, and yet the *respectively*
reading is perfectly legitimate, meaning that Mary kissed Mary's boyfriends, and Martha Martha's.

(83) Mary and Martha kissed all their boyfriends, respectively

5.3.2.3. *Johannessen's (1993c) approach*

Deletion presents some disadvantages. The most serious one is the fact
that coordination becomes subject to several rules or principles that are
more empirical than theoretical. This criticism hits the approach in the
present book. In Johannessen (1993c), I preferred merging (not unlike the
fusion approach suggested by McCawley 1988) to deletion. Thus, instead
of deleting one occurrence of material that was identical to another, the
two occurrences would be merged or fused.

The difference between merging and deletion is that in merging, no
structure has priority over the other. The component structures become
one structure, shared equally by both conjuncts. Conceptually, it can be
seen as unification (see, e.g., Shieber 1986) where compatible categories
can be unified. Two categories are compatible if they do not have conflicting contents. E.g., a [Spec, CP] filled with the lexical contents *Mary*
is compatible with an unfilled [Spec, CP], as well as another [Spec, CP]
filled with *Mary*. It can be merged with either. On the other hand, a
[Spec, CP] filled with *Martha* would have conflicting contents. Merging

can happen at all levels in syntax. Merging can be formulated simply as (84):

(84) Unifiable material in the same syntactic position can be merged

Merging has many advantages, since there need be no rules or principles like Forward and Backward Deletion, and the rules associated with these. However, there is one great disadvantage that accompanies merging—the fact that certain structures violate X-bar structure. Consider, e.g., (85), a RNR structure. The DP *mouse* has two mothers, thereby violating the usual requirement that every category should only be dominated by one category at the most local level.

(85)

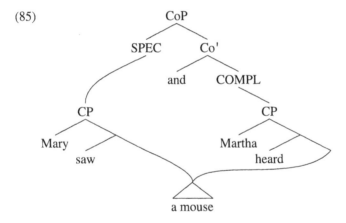

One might have included a rule to disallow this kind of structure, but then the question would remain how to analyze RNR sentences. If deletion is necessary for this kind of sentence, then it seems reasonable to include it for other kinds, too.

5.3.2.4. *Wesche's sharing approach*

Wesche's (1995) theory is based on two assumptions. The first one is that X-bar structure allows ordered lists as well as single items in the individual positions. She extends the usual X-bar schema to allow several items to appear in each rewritten category. These items are contained in an ordered list. There is a separate X-bar schema for coordinated structures:

(86) Coordinate X-bar-schema:

$X_{[Coord]} \rightarrow \langle X_1, \ldots, X_m \rangle$

$X'_{[Coord]} \rightarrow \langle X_{[Coord]} \langle Compl_1, \ldots, Compl_m]$

$X''_{[Coord]} \rightarrow \langle Spec_1, \ldots, Spec_m \rangle X'_{[Coord]}$

(Wesche 1995:103)

The conjuncts sit in the same tree (this is akin to Goodall 1987), except that Goodall suggests three-dimensional trees while Wesche's trees are two-dimensional—with the conjuncts sitting instead as ordered lists in the same positions in the tree. Conjunctions as such do not have a place in the tree. Rather, an abstract coordination lexeme (Wesche 1995:105) is adjoined to the maximal coordinate projection (the vertical lines indicate a shared element):

(87)

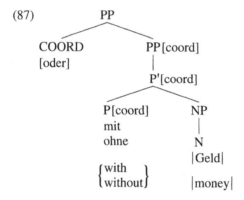

The prepositions in (87) are contrastive, while the shared noun is the same for both conjuncts. This is a result of the requirement that each coordination ranges over a maximal projection. It is somehow interpreted twice, and will, e.g., be assigned case twice. The PF (Phonetic Form) representation of coordinated structures arises after the application of two linearization rules: one for gapping and one for other kinds of coordination.

The second assumption is that a coordination structure always ranges over maximal phrases. Even if a coordinated structure seems to include only lexical heads, it is still considered to include maximal phrases. Thus, a phrase such as (88), which is seemingly just adjective (lexical head) coordination, is analyzed as DP (maximal phrase) coordination.

(88) sowohl [junge] als auch [alte] *Narren*
     both [young] and   [old] fools

From the assumption that only phrasal coordination is possible, it follows that there are two coordination types: Shared Constituent Coordination (SCC), in which one of the constituents in the coordination structure is shared, as in (88), in which *Narren* is shared by both contrastees, and Non-Shared Constituent Coordination (Non-SCC), in which every element of each conjunct contrasts with that of the other, as in the PP coordination below:

(89) (ein Papier) [PP auf einer interessanten Konferenz] oder
     (a paper) [at an   interesting   conference] or
     [PP in einer renommierten Zeitschrift]
     [in a   renowned   journal]

Wesche's theory is interesting in that the choice of phrase structure makes it possible to choose a solution which is neither deletion nor fusion. However, it also has a few problems.

UC and EBC
Since the shared element is to be interpreted as equally important for both conjuncts (e.g., a noun would be assigned case twice by two coordinated case-assigning verbs), it is hard to see that there is a way in which UC and EBC can be accounted for. To be fair, the theory does not intend to accommodate data other than symmetric ones, but in my opinion, it is a serious problem for this theory.

Conjunctions
The fact that the position of the conjunction is rather abstract with respect to the actual coordination tree makes it impossible for the theory to account for the facts that are related to the position and head-status of conjunctions. For example, the idea that conjunctions have predictive power with respect to word order cannot be accommodated in this theory.

Unlike categories
The theory says nothing about how to account for coordination of unlike categories. It is difficult to imagine how this could be done, given the fact that each contrastive pair—even at X^0 level—is dominated by the same syntactic category.
    There are problems and advantages in this theory, some of which are

discussed in Johannessen (forthcoming), but the most important is, in my opinion, that it is too simple to account for UC and EBC.

5.4. CoP components—full CPs or simplex categories?

There are different opinions in the literature as to what constitutes the input categories of coordinated phrases. Here, it is argued that the input categories for coordination are full CP structures rather than V, DP, PP, or other categories. There are a number of reasons for this.

First, there is simply no available level where syntactic categories are floating around either unattached to a syntactic host (for categories like DPs) or without argument positions (for categories like VPs). Second, coordinate-alpha is a syntactic transformation which does not have access to the lexicon, but only to syntactic structures (making X^0 categories unavailable).

Third, given free category coordination, a CP component analysis makes it possible to explain how so-called non-constituent coordination, i.e., coordination of sequences such as subject + verb (right node raising), object + adverbial, object1 + object2—all represented in (90)—can occur.

(90) a. [Mary likes] and [Jane would go anywhere to find] antique horse-brasses from the workshop of that genius in metal-work, Sam Small.   (Hudson 1976:535)

  b. Jack loves [his mother passionately] and [his brother affectionately].

  c. Dawn gave [Billy some milk] and [Edvard some squash].

Fourth, coordination of unlike categories can be accounted for. If we assume that the input structures are full CPs, then all elements in each CP have been licenced by the subcategorization requirements in that CP. Take the familiar example with a *that*-complementized object clause in English (91), or the French example (92):

(91) a. Pat was annoyed by [the children's noise and that their parents did nothing to stop it]

b. *Pat was annoyed by that their parents did nothing to stop it

(92) . . . qu'ils   soient [malades ou en bonne santé] . . .
       that they are   ill   or in good   health

(Haff 1987:216)

The *that*-clause is an acceptable object in (91a) because it is one of the realizations of the thematic role Proposition, for which the preposition subcategorizes. (As mentioned in Chapter 4, the reason it is not acceptable as an object in (91b) is that it gets case from the preposition—and it is acceptable in (91a) because it does not get case.) The adjective and PP coordination in (92) is likewise fine, since a copula verb subcategorizes for a Predicate. If conjuncts were just picked randomly in the lexicon by coordinate-alpha and put randomly into a conjunct, there would be no way of constraining complement-conjuncts. However, empirically, we know that there must be constraints. Take, for example, (93), where the verbs are semantically very similar, but still subcategorize differently.[6] Coordination of unlike categories that are not subcategorized for is impossible, as seen in (94).

(93) a. Kim turned out a success / political / to like anchovies / *doing all the work

     b. Kim ended up a success / political / *to like anchovies / doing all the work

(94) a. *Kim turned out [a success and doing all the work]

     b. *Kim ended up [a success and to like anchovies]

As long as we require the coordination components to be full CPs, unacceptable sentences like those in (94) would not be derived.

Fifth, we avoid having to make explicit statements as to what kinds of categories and sequences of categories can be coordinated. Furthermore, no explicit statement is needed to ensure the effect that only categories of the same bar-level can be coordinated.

5.4.1. OTHER APPROACHES TO INPUT CATEGORIES

Theories in which coordination is seen as a conjoining of simplex categories run into problems with respect to the points discussed in the previous section. We shall take a look at some approaches here, but evaluate them with respect to other traditional and untraditional problems, too, for the sake of completeness.

5.4.1.1. *Phrase-structure theory*

Phrase-structure approaches such as Jackendoff (1977) and Gazdar et al. (1985: ch.8) assume that there is a phrase-structure rule such as (95), which gives a tree such as (96).

(95) X → X [conj X]

(96)

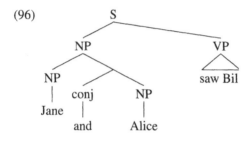

Phrase-structure based theories have certain advantages, such as simplicity (few, if any, deletion processes). Most, or all, of the phenomena from the problems list can be accounted for by rules. However, the rule schema in (95) must quickly be abandoned, as we shall see. The following problems also apply to Grootveld's (1992) theory (discussed in Chapter 4), which is also a phrase-structure approach.

Non-constituent coordination

Phrase-structure theories must resort to many specific rules in addition to the general schema above to account for non-constituent coordination. The general rule schema presupposes that the conjuncts consist of one constituent only. Therefore, the categories of conjuncts of non-constituent coordination must be stated explicitly. This is a major problem, since almost any kind of categories can be coordinated thus, and each combination will have to be explicitly stated. Thus, a sentence such as (97) can only be accepted by an additional rule such as S → NP V NP AdvP conj NP AdvP.

(97) Jack loves [his mother passionately and his brother affectionately]

Sometimes the categories to be coordinated are not of the same type, as in gapping: the unreduced conjunct is a full clause, while the reduced conjunct lacks a verb:

(98) Mary saw a mouse and Martha an elephant

Since the reduced clause is only allowed in a coordination context, its category is not that of an ordinary clause. Gapping, too, must therefore be expressed by a rule of its own, rather than by the rule schema above, e.g. by S → S conj NP NP.

Unlike categories
Phrase-structure theories also have problems accounting for unlike category coordination, given that the rule schema X → X [conj X] presupposes that the conjuncts have the same category. In order to account for a sentence such as (99), they must resort to a different, functional perspective.

(99) Zoe is [a woman, rich and in the lucky position of owning a castle] (NP&AP&PP)

The conjuncts are seen as having some sort of function, role, or relation in common, expressed in addition to the syntactic category. This suggestion can be found in GPSG, as in Gazdar et al. (1985:175), where the feature ⟨PRD, +⟩ (predicative) is introduced. Preuß (1989) introduces an extra level above the syntactic one where a category such as Pred embraces the syntactic categories involved. However, these additional categories are not defined, and it is not clear whether they are syntactic or semantic. Neither is it clear how many such additional categories are needed.

"Discontinous conjunctions"
"Discontinuous conjunctions", i.e., sets containing a CoP adverb plus a conjunction, such as *both . . . and, neither . . . nor*, are not considered to be a problem within a phrase-structure framework; the following schemata (among those given to take care of coordination) are taken from Gazdar et al. (1985:171–2):

(100) Binary coordination schema (CS^2)
       X → H[CONJ a0], H[CONJ a1]
       where a is in {⟨both, and⟩, ⟨either, or⟩, ⟨NIL, but⟩}

(101) Coordination LP schema (CS^{LP})
       [CONJ a0] < [CONJ a1]
       where a0 is in {both, either, neither, NIL}
       and a1 is in {and, but, nor, or}

However, as shown in (102), repeated from Chapter 4, the first part of a discontinuous pair is often found far away from the CoP. It is less clear how a phrase-structure rule would account for this kind of structure.

(102) Jeg sa   at   jeg *hverken* så   [Per eller Pål]
       I   said that I   neither saw Per or   Paul
       'I said that neither did I see Per nor Paul.'

The number of arguments of a particular conjunction is not a problem, however; it is given in the rules. E.g., in GPSG, a rule labeled CS^2 indicates there can be only two conjuncts. Multiple coordination, too, can be given simply by a rule label: CS$^+$ (Gazdar et al. 1985:171).

A serious objection to these schemata is the fact that the first part of the "discontinuous conjunctions" really should be analyzed as adverbs (see 4.7).

UC and EBC

Unbalanced and extraordinary balanced coordination have not, to my knowledge, been discussed in phrase-structure rule approaches, so the presentation here is my own suggestion. UC and EBC do not seem to be unaccountable for in phrase-structure rule theories, but hardly in a principled manner. For example, in the Czech example (52), the first conjunct alone determines verb agreement. This could plausibly be represented in a rule which encodes features in the conjuncts in terms of variables, so that the CoP could be represented as $NP_{[\alpha]} → NP_{[\alpha]}$ conj $NP_{[\beta]}$. The same type of rule could also account for receiving-type features such as case; the first conjunct gets the same case as the top-level category, while the second conjunct receives nothing (and must take default case, defined elsewhere).

The EBC example (54), where both subject NPs have deviant case, could likewise be accounted for by means of features in the phrase-structure rules: S → CoP[acc] VP, CoP[acc] → NP[acc] conj NP[acc].

It is possible, then, to account for UC and EBC constructions in these theories without serious problems. The difficulty, as I see it, is rather that any permutation of variable assignment is possible; it is hard to find a principled theory where the properties of unbalancedness or extraordinary balancedness follow from independent facts.

5.4.1.2. *Categorial grammar*

Before considering the problems and solutions in categorial grammar (CG), let us briefly take a look at its general theory of coordination. Steedman (1985) gives an account of coordination in categorial grammar based on Gazdar (1981) and Dougherty (1970):

(103) $X + \text{conj } X \rightarrow X$

X stands for any category, + for "one or more," *conj* for any conjunction. The definition could have based more directly within a categorial framework, along the lines of Lambek (1958), in which the conjunction would rather have been given a lexical entry X/X\X. (The forward slash has the meaning "Take the following category to your right," and the backslash "Take the following category to your left.") In Steedman's theory, two syntactic rules are, in principle, all that is needed in a linguistic description:

(104) a. Functional application: $X/Y \; Y \rightarrow X$
    b. Functional composition: $X/Y \; Y/Z \rightarrow X/Z$

Non-constituent coordination

CG uses the same mechanisms to derive non-constituent coordination (106), as ordinary constituent coordination (105). The former, right node raising, is an example of how CG employs unorthodox constituents: a category can be atomic, e.g. NP, or complex, as a functor, e.g. S/NP. A functor can be projected from the lexicon or it can emerge through syntactic combination with an adjacent category. In (106), the category of *Harry*, S/VP (a category type raised to appear as a category needing a VP to become a sentence), is combined with the category of *cooked*, VP/NP, by the rule of functional composition. The same has been done for the categories of *Mary* and *ate*, so that these two "non-constituents" can then be coordinated with each other.

(105) Peter ate apples and oranges

apples	and	oranges
NP	conj	NP

NP

(106) Harry cooked and Mary ate the beans

Harry	cooked	and	Mary	ate	the beans
S/VP	VP/NP	conj	S/VP	VP/NP	NP

S/NP		S/NP

S/NP

S

CG handles the above "non-constituent coordination" well because these particular conjuncts are regarded as constituents. A combination of object + adverb as in (107) does not have a simple solution in CG, though:

(107) Jane loved [Harry madly] and [John passionately]

There is no category combination which makes a constituent out of every conjunct. (Neither would it be desirable.) The solution therefore has to be to add a rule which allows constituents to be parallelly coordinated. This has been done by Barry and Pickering (1990):

(108) Parallel constituent coordination schema: Two (or more) strings may be coordinated to give a string of type X iff each has type X, and for some $n \geq 1$ and some types $X_1, \ldots, X_n$ each has a division into n maximal dependency constituents of type $X_1, \ldots, X_n$. (Barry and Pickering 1990)

Unlike categories
Coordination of unlike categories is solved the same way as in phrase-structure grammars: CG labels some categories by additional categories or features. This has been done by Barry and Pickering (1990) for adjective-phrases and noun-phrases, which are there regarded as PredPs.

Semantics
A very important feature in CG is the fact that its semantics builds up as the syntax builds up, compositionally. There is no additional interpreting

semantics elsewhere. It will therefore be a problem when the semantics of a coordinated structure is different from the one of its parts. This is, of course, the case whenever two singular NPs are coordinated into a plural category.

UC and EBC, and other problems
The points mentioned for phrase-structure rule theories above also apply to categorial grammar. There is nothing in principle which would make it impossible to have a CG description of UC, although there are practical problems. A first change would be for the coordination rules to no longer require the same syntactic categories or features of the conjuncts. The restrictions that would empirically be necessary would therefore have to be expressed differently, maybe as a list of prohibited category combinations. What seems more difficult is to give a principled account of the distribution of UC and EBC.

5.4.1.3. *Transformational theories*

Theories that take whole sentences as input to coordination avoid the problems that phrase-structure rule type theories face; those of having to specify all the various categories or category combinations that can be coordinated. Thus, as we have seen in a previous section, transformational theories such as that of Goodall, van Oirsouw, and the present theory do quite well with respect to non-constituent coordination and coordination of unlike categories. The fact that they are transformational makes it possible to "remove" what is superfluous when two full sentences (CPs) are coordinated.

5.5. Summary

This chapter has been devoted to the coming into existence of the CoP. The input to any CoP are full propositional structures that may since undergo deletion and sharing, which in turn result in head coordination and coordination of conjuncts smaller than CoP. The deletion and sharing are preferable to, for example, merging or fusion, since the result of such operations violates a basic feature of X-bar: the restriction that the number of mothers is only one for each node. Advantages and disadvantages of other approaches are discussed, with some emphasis on the problems presented in this book: those of unbalanced and extraordinary balanced coordination. The idea that there is only one kind of input category to CoP—full propositional structures or CPs—is contrasted with the other alternative: that of the input simplex categories (small conjuncts). There are several reasons for the CP approach, and these are pointed out.

Notes

1. This means that questions can be coordinated with declarative sentences, etc., contrary to, e.g., Gleitman (1965), who put an asterisk in the sentence below:

(i) *[What are you doing] [and [shut the door]]   (Gleitman 1965:262)

However, in spite of it obviously being odd for some speakers, there is no reason that it should be syntactically wrong. In some languages, this kind of structure is in fact quite common, such as Modern Greek:

(ii) [ti   bori   na tus   eftekse   i   ifijenia] [ke [thelun   tora
     what can.3SG to them harmed.3SG the Iphigenia and want.3PL now
     to   thanato tis]]?
     the death   hers
     'What harm can Iphigenia have done them for them now to desire her
     death?'   (Mackridge 1987:242)

2. Although I might agree with Aoun et al. in a clausal analysis there (Johannessen 1996), it is not the case that every instance of the kind of coordination they discuss should be analyzed as clausal. Basically, Aoun et al. claim that in the Arabic varieties they discuss, singular verb agreement co-occurring with a CoP DP must be due to the CoP actually being a disguised clausal CoP. This is supported by the fact that words like 'both' and 'together' cannot co-occur with the "clausal" coordination type.

In Johannessen (1996), it is shown that many languages can indeed have partial agreement co-occurring with words like 'both' and other words which force a group reading onto the conjunct, indicating that the conjuncts form a nominal CoP rather than a clausal one:

(i) . . . als sei   in ihren weiten Hindernissprüngen [Roß
        as were.3SG in their great   jumps   horse.NOM.SG
     und Reiter]   zusammengewachsen.
     and horseman.NOM.SG grown-together
     'as if horse and horseman were grown together in their great jumps'
                                      (F. Werfel, quoted in Findreng 1976:135)

Partial agreement of this kind (called "assigning-type of nominal unbalanced coordination" in this book) is only one kind out of many, of unbalanced coordination. And indeed, UC is a very important argument in favor of DP coordination. Another example is when two DPs have different case, as in Section 2.2.2.1. Without DP coordination, this would sometimes be classified as FWD and sometimes as BWD, which in itself would be somewhat suspicious. In addition, case checking would have to happen conjunct-internally, which would mean that a verb or preposition would have to check deviant case. If CP coordination were the only possible type, in the Eastern Mari example below, the verb of the first conjunct would have to check the deviant case of its object DP, and in the English example, a clause would have to be the complement of a preposition :

(ii) [CoP Mej agetan ~~murem~~   [den [~~mej~~ kukula   murem]]]
      I   cock   sing.ISG and I   cuckoo.COMP sing.ISG
     'I sing like a cock and a cuckoo.'

(iii) [CoP Pat was annoyed by the children's noise [and [~~Pat was annoyed by~~ that their parents did nothing to stop it]]]

Without DP coordination, the Eastern Mari example (ii) would contain a DP (that of the first conjunct) with no case-marking, which presumably would violate LF, since morphological case-features of the verbal head would not be checked against a DP. In (iii), a preposition would have to try to check its accusative case against a finite clause, which is not possible. Again, case-features would, wrongly, survive at LF.

With DP coordination, the deviance of the conjuncts would not matter, since the relevant conjuncts would be complements of the conjunction, and not available for case checking:

(iv) Mej [CoP agetan den kukula]   murem]]]
     I   cock   and cuckoo.COMP sing.ISG

(v) Pat was annoyed by [CoP the children's noise and that their parents did nothing to stop it]

3. There seem to be exceptions to this, however. This sentence is OK:

(i) Yesterday John ate like a pig and today ØØ like an ox

4. The category NP rather than DP will be used here and wherever it refers to work in which it has been used, in order to avoid anachronisms.
5. I am grateful to David Milward (p.c.) for pointing out this kind of problem.
6. I am grateful to Bob Borsley for pointing this out to me, and for the examples, based on examples in Pollard and Sag (1987:123).

6

Extraction out of CoP

6.1. Introduction

It has been widely accepted in the literature that linguistic theory ought to account for the contrast between the sentences in pairs such as (1) and (2).

(1) a. *What do you like [apples and t]?

   b. What do you like?

(2) a. *What do you [drink wine and eat t]?

   b. What do you [drink t and eat t]?

Since Ross (1967/86) the two types are assumed to violate the Coordination Structure Constraint with the Across the Board exception. In this chapter, we shall see that these two principles appear to be too strong, and that the desired results must be constrained on semantic rather than syntactic grounds.

In Section 6.2, we shall investigate the principles themselves, and see that there have in fact been several examples in the literature which seem to violate them. In Section 6.3, it will become clear that there are two kinds of extraction, the acceptability of which is determined by different factors. Section 6.3.1 contains an analysis of what appears to be extraction of whole conjuncts. It is inspired by facts from unbalanced coordination, and is basically what was presented in Johannessen (1993b). In this analysis, the position of the extracted element within the CoP is of prime importance. Section 6.3.2 contains a revised analysis of the data in 6.3.1, arrived at because of some serious problems in the first analysis. The revised analysis suggests that what goes on is CP coordination with merging rather than extraction. Section 6.3.3 discusses extraction of parts of conjuncts, which will be shown to be acceptable. Both the impossibility of extracting whole conjuncts and the possibility of extracting parts of conjuncts will be suggested to be semantically based. A summary is presented in Section 6.4.

6.2. The CSC–ATB principles and examples of violations

The Coordinate Structure Constraint (CSC) with the Across the Board exception (ATB) (Ross 1967/86), (3a,b) have received a lot of support in the linguistic literature.

(3) a. Coordinate Structure Constraint: In a coordinate structure, no conjunct may be moved, nor may any element contained in a conjunct be moved out of that conjunct.

(Ross 1967/86:98)

b. ... unless the same element is moved out of all the conjuncts.

Most theories of coordination (such as Schachter 1977; George 1980; Gazdar 1981; Gazdar et al. 1985; Steedman 1985; Goodall 1987) pride themselves of being able to derive them automatically, which enables them to avoid sentences like (1a) and (2a). In this chapter, we shall see that the CSC–ATB do not follow automatically by the theory of coordinate-alpha, but that neither should they, since the data show that some extractions must be allowed.

6.2.1. EXAMPLES OF VIOLATION OF THE FIRST PART OF THE CSC–ATB

The first part of the CSC says that no conjunct may be moved, unless all conjuncts are moved. There are a number of examples which seem to show that this rule must be too strict. Below, we shall see examples of topicalization and right dislocation, both types of which seem to show extraction of one conjunct only. All of them are examples of what can be descriptively called split coordination, which typically seems to violate the CSC by extracting a whole conjunct from the CoP. The extent to which this is possible varies in different languages; in Old Norse it is very common, and also in Swedish (according to Andersson 1982), while it is less common in English and Norwegian. However, the fact that the phenomenon exists, and is widely attested, shows that the CSC does not hold.

The Norwegian (4a) shows topicalization of one conjunct only.[1] The Swedish (4b) is an example of the same phenomenon. The result is a split direct object. (4c) shows "right dislocation", or rather, movement of one subject-conjunct only. So do the English (4d), from a novel, the Dutch (4e), the Old Norse (4f,g). The result is a split subject.

(4) a. Per så   jeg [t og Ola]
         Per saw I   and Ola
         'Per, I saw, and Ola.'

    b. [Kalle Jularbo] hörde jag [t och hans gamla
         K.J.   heard I   and his old
         dragspelsorkester]
         accordion band
         'K.J., I heard and his old accordion band.'
                                        (Andersson 1982:35)

    c. Per vasket klær   [t og Ola]
         Per washed clothes   and Ola.
         'Peter washed clothes, and Ola.'

    d. All the heaviness had gone [t and the height]
                                        (Morrison 1988:148)

    e. Jan gaat   naar huis, [t en Peter]
         Jan goes.SG to   home   and Peter
         'Jan goes home, and Peter.'
                                        (de Vries 1992:109)

    f. þa   klocc   hann mæð myklum harmi [t oc allr
         then was.moved.SG he   with much   grief   and all
         hæRr hans]
         army his
         'Then he and his men were moved by much grief.'
                                        (Lødrup 1977:30)

g. [Skegg-Ávaldi]   átti   búð saman   [t ok Hermundr] [. . .]
   Beard-Avald.sg had.sg hut together   and Hermund.sg
   'Beard-Avald and Hermund lived together.'

(Nygaard 1917:13)

To sum up, what these examples have in common is that they seem to be violations of the CSC; a whole conjunct is extracted out of the CoP.

6.2.2. EXAMPLES OF VIOLATION OF THE SECOND PART OF THE CSC–ATB

In addition to split coordination, it is also possible to extract part of a conjunct. Consider the sentences from English (5)–(6), Lakhota (7), German (8), and Dutch (9).

(5) a.   How many courses can you [take t for credit, and still remain sane]?

   b.   What kind of cancer can you [eat herbs and not get t]?

   c.   What kind of herbs can you [eat t and not get cancer]?

(Lakoff 1986)

(6) a.   Here's the whisky which I [went to the store and bought t]

   b.   Which dress has she [gone and ruined t] now

   c.   The screw which I've got to [try and find t] . . .

(Ross 1967/86:103–5)

(7) ixʔé-thaka ki wichásha ki nuwá-he   k'éyash wa-yáke-shni
    rock-big the man   the swim-CONT but   STEM-see-neg
    'The big rock, the man was swimming but didn't see.'

(Van Valin 1985)

(8) a.   Die Briefmarken hat Claus gekauft und will   sie   jetzt
         the stamps   has Claus bought and wants them now
         wieder verkaufen
         again sell
         'The stamps, Claus bought, and now (he) wants to sell them again.'

b. Das Gepäck liess er fallen und rannte zum   Hinterausgang
   the baggage let   he fall   and ran   to.the rear.exit
   'The baggage, he let fall, and ran to the rear exit.'

(Heycock and Kroch 1992:1–2)

(9) ?Na   Zwolle rijdt deze trein verder als intercity naar Groningen
    after Zwolle goes this train on   as intercity to   Groningen
    en   zal   alleen stoppen te Assen
    and will only   stop   in Assen
    'After Zwolle, this train goes on as an intercity to Groningen
    and will only stop in Assen.'

(Zwart 1991, quoted in Heycock and Kroch 1992:4)

In the examples (5)–(6), an "element contained in a conjunct" is moved out of one conjunct of the CoP without having moved out of the other.[2] Their oddity is explained in Section 6.3.3; they require a relevant semantic context in order to sound unmarked. In (7), there is a topicalised object, extracted out of the second conjunct only. The sentences in (8) are examples of what is often called SLF-coordination (*Subjekt-Lücke*, subject-gap, in a clause where the verb is *Finite/Frontal*, finite and fronted) (Heycock and Kroch 1992:1). In both cases, a topicalised object is extracted from the first conjunct. (9) is plausibly an extracted adverbial from the first conjunct. (The question mark is from the original paper from which the example is taken (Zwart 1991) and contrasts there with a different example marked by an asterisk.)

6.3. The analysis of CSC–ATB violations

The theory accounts for two very different ways of accounting for the two types of what seems to be violations of the CSC–ATB. First, we shall consider an analysis of split coordination in terms of extraction (of whole conjuncts). This analysis is inspired by the analysis of unbalanced coordination (Chapter 4). It was presented in Johannessen (1993b), but some otherwise unanswerable questions have led to a revision of the analysis. In the second section, we shall, therefore, reconsider the extraction analysis of split coordination, and present one based on the coordination of CPs plus deletion, rather than extraction. Third, we shall consider extraction out of parts of conjuncts, which will be shown to be acceptable.

6.3.1. THE ANALYSIS OF SPLIT COORDINATION AS EXTRACTION OF WHOLE CONJUNCTS

Let us analyze (4c), repeated below, as an example of split coordination. We will take the analysis step by step.

(10) Per vasket klær   [t og Ola]
     Per washed clothes   and Ola.
     'Peter washed clothes, and Ola.'

We assume the starting-point to be two underived propositions prior to coordinate-alpha.

(11) a. [VP Per [vasket klær]]
     b. [VP Ola [vasket klær]]

Coordinate-alpha attaches the subject of (11a) to [Spec,CoP] and the subject of (11b) to the CoP complement:

(12)

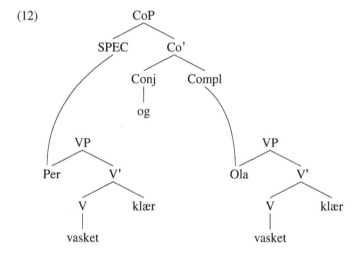

Forward deletion deletes the like material *vasket klær* from the first conjunct in accordance with the conditions on content identity and formal licencing (Chapter 5, Section 5.3.1):

(13) Per ~~vasket klær~~ og Ola <u>vasket klær</u>

The tree in (12) is an X-bar violation and is as such unacceptable. Operation Share (Chapter 5) therefore helps out, by removing the deleted material and inserting CoP in the attachment position, here: [Spec, VP]:

(14)

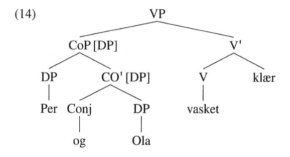

In order for the propositional structure above to be turned into an interpretable structure for PF and LF (by providing appropriate positions for checking morphological features), the introduction of functional categories into the tree is necessary. We assume that there are two Agr-projections; one for the subject and one for the object. The Agr-projections are triggers for obligatory movement: the verb moves to both Agr-positions, but in each case needs something to agree with, therefore something has to move to the specifier positions—something which has nominal features and is a maximal projection. The first conjunct in the CoP is a possible candidate, so it moves from its base position in [Spec, VP] to the [Spec, Agr-S″], i.e., the subject position, and then further to [Spec, CP].

(15)

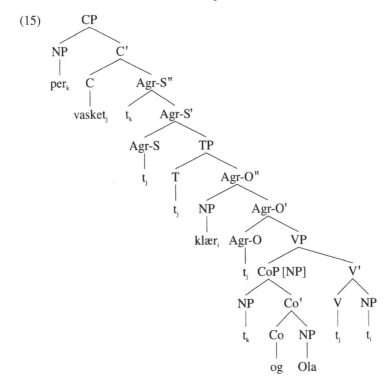

The analysis is supported by languages that have subject-verb agreement. Consider the Dutch and Old Norse sentences above. In all of (4e,f,g), the subject DP is obviously a CoP rather than a simplex DP. Nonetheless, only one conjunct has moved from the base position, and, crucially, that one is the only one agreeing with the finite verb. In all three cases, the conjunct is singular, and the verb is singular, in spite of the fact that verbs in these languages usually agree with the whole subject, i.e., the whole CoP, by semantic resolution rules. The agreement facts follow from the analysis in figure (15); the conjunct in the appropriate position in Agr-S″ determines agreement, while the the rest of the CoP is left in the base position, thereby being unable to influence the agreement features of the verb.

Notice that it is impossible to extract the other conjunct. This is emphasized in Andersson (1982:n1), and exemplified in the Norwegian (16). (16a) is not a possible topicalization (or split object), and (16b) not a possible right dislocation (split subject).

(16) a. *Ola så   jeg [Per og t]
         Ola saw I   Per and
         'Ola, I saw, Peter and.'

b. *Per vasket   klær   [Ola og t]
    Per washed clothes Ola and
    'Peter washed clothes, Ola and.'

This follows from the analysis in (15), and is due to case. In (16a), the first conjunct stays in the canonical object position, and gets case in the ordinary way. The second conjunct, however, is not in a case position. Neither has it been case-marked before movement to [Spec,CP], since the complement position in a CoP is never case-marked. (The case licencing is linked to that position only. Once an element leaves it, it has to be assigned case from somewhere.) The converse remarks can be made for (16b); here, the complement conjunct has moved to a case position, but the specifier conjunct is not assigned case, as a violation of the case filter. A complement conjunct, therefore, has to stay in its base position; as a sister of the head of CoP.

6.3.2. A REVISED ANALYSIS OF SPLIT COORDINATION

If the constructions in Section 6.3.1 are analyzed as extraction of whole conjuncts, several questions need to be answered. First, we need to know why it is that the part of the CoP that remains *in situ* in the extraction analysis above must be sentence final.[3]

(17) a. *Per så   jeg [t og Ola] i går
         Per saw I   and Ola yesterday
         'Per, I saw, and Ola yesterday.'
     b. *Per vasket   klær   [t og Ola] i går
         Per washed clothes   and Ola yesterday
         'Peter washed clothes, and Ola yesterday.'

This also entails that the main verb must move in order for the rest of the CoP to be sentence final, to avoid cases like (18).[4]

(18) *All the heaviness had [t and the height] gone

Second, there are some unresolved facts that have to do with case. In the extraction analysis, the explanation for the possibility of the DP staying *in situ* is that as a complement conjunct, it does not need to have case. However, there is reason to question this claim. Indeed, the Oslo dialect of Norwegian, which does have split coordination, does not allow unbalanced coordination of nominal constituents. This is quite surprising, given that the first analysis is based on the same explanation as unbalanced co-ordination; that of a conjunction licencing the lack of certain otherwise obligatory features, such as case. In fact, it also turns out that the Oslo dialect of Norwegian does require the complement conjuncts in split co-ordination to be case-marked (19) (the asterisks are for the split subject/object interpretation), a fact which is incompatible with the extraction analysis in Section 3.1.

(19) a. Per$_i$ vasket klær   [t$_i$ og jeg]   / *meg
     Per washed clothes   and I.NOM / me.ACC
     'Peter washed clothes, and I.'

    b. Per$_i$ så jeg [t$_i$ og dem]   / *de
     Per saw I   and them.ACC / they.NOM
     'Per, I saw, and them.'

Third, extraction of categories other than DPs does not behave in the expected manner. Given the analysis of VPs in unbalanced coordination, we should expect that in extraction of verbs, only the specifier conjunct could move, and that, parallel to what is the case with extraction of DPs, the specifier conjunct is the one which has the normal and expected features while the complement conjunct might be deviant. In the case of verbs, we should expect, then, that if only one conjunct has tense features, it ought to be the specifier one, which can move to a tense position. In topicalization of verbs (or rather VPs), however, we see that it is the verb of the complement conjunct—not of the specifier conjunct—which must have finite features, contrary to expectations. (In Norwegian, a topicalized verb can also inherit the features of the dummy verb, so that, here, it is optionally finite, see Lødrup 1990, and the example below.)

(20) a. Spise / spiser gjør   Ola og drikker
     eat.INF / PRES do.PRES Ola and drink.PRES
     'Eat, Ola does, and drinks.'

b. Spise   / *spiser gjør   Ola og drikke
   eat.INF / PRES do.PRES Ola and drink.INF
   'Eat, Ola does, and drink.'

An extraction analysis of (20a) would be something like (21).

(21)

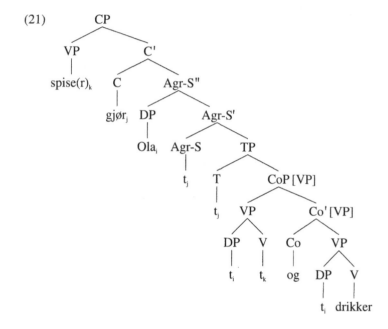

It is clear that this analysis has defects. An acute mystery is how it is that
the verb of the second conjunct has tense features when it is not in a tense
position. There is usually only one way for a verb to get tense features,
and that is to go to the tense position. Since there are two verbs with tense
features in (20a), there should have been two tense positions.

Coordination must, then, happen at least as high up as TP. There is,
however, reason to believe that CoP attaches as high as CP. The reason
is that when a sentential adverb, such as *ikke* 'not', is adjoined, it has
scope only over the last conjunct, and not over the whole sentence. Had
the conjuncts been TPs rather than CPs, and the sentential adverb had
been adjoined above CoP[TP]—as it should do, being sentential—the
adverbial would have been expected to have scope over all the sentence,
contrary to fact.

(22) Spise(r)   gjør   Ola og drikker   ikke
eat.INF(PRES) do.PRES Ola and drink.PRES not
'Eat, Ola does, and doesn't drink.'
(NOT: 'Ola doesn't eat and drink.')

We have to conclude, then, that the structure of (20a) is something like (23)—in which both conjuncts are CPs—and with the component sentences (24), yielding the tree in (25).

(23) [_CoP[_CP Spise(r) gjør Ola] [og [_CP drikke(r) t]]]

(24) a.   [CP Spise(r) gjør Ola]
     b.   [CP Drikke(r) gjør Ola]

(25)

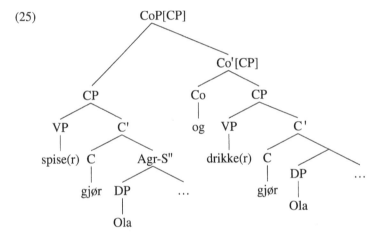

The fact that there is only one subject and one auxiliary verb in (20a) means that the subject and the auxiliary verb of the second conjunct will be deleted. This is done via FWD, in accordance with the conditions on content identification (content identity, context identity and locality) and formal licencing (the head condition and the major constituent condition).

(26) [CP Spise(r) ~~gjør Ola~~] [og [CP drikke(r) ~~gjør Ola~~]]

Notice that the major constituent ("a deletion site may not span a string which extends to a subpart of a major constituent") is not violated here in spite of the fact that only the head of CP, and not the specifier of CP, is deleted in the second conjunct. This is as it should be, since CP is the whole conjunct. The major constituent condition therefore has to be understood "downwards": a deletion site may not span part of a constituent below itself in the tree.

The sentence (27a), analyzed by extraction in the previous section, is easily analyzed as deletion (27b). The danger of extracting the wrong conjunct out of a CoP[DP] is not a problem here, since there is no extraction. (28) and (29) would therefore not be possible derivations.

(27) a. Per vasket klær og Ola.

   b. [CP Per vasket klær] [og [CP Ola ~~vasket klær~~]]

(28) *Per$_i$ vasket klær [Ola og t$_i$]

(29) *Ola$_i$ så jeg [Per og t$_i$]

An analysis of split coordination as CoP[CP] with deletion rather than as extraction (Section 6.3.1), then, accounts for the difficulties we started out with in this section.[5] First, the reason that there can be no shared element after the (remains of) the second conjunct, is that the second conjunct is simply the whole rest of the clause. There is thus no position in which a clause-final adverbial shared by both conjuncts could sit. Notice, however, that it is possible for an adverbial to follow in the second conjunct, but this will always only be interpreted as part of the second conjunct, as discussed for the negator *ikke* above. Thus, while we have seen that (30a) is impossible with the sentence-final shared adverbial, (30b), with an adverbial belonging only to the second conjunct, would not be out:

(30) a. Per så   jeg [t og Ola] i går
        Per saw I   and Ola yesterday
        'Per, I saw, and Ola yesterday.'

   b. [Per så   jeg] [og [Ola ~~så jeg~~ i går]]
        Per saw I   and Ola   yesterday
        'Per, I saw, and Ola yesterday.'

The second problem, that of case on the second conjunct, is also solved. The fact that both conjuncts in subject position must have nominative case in Oslo Norwegian follows from the fact that both are subjects in their own clause:

(31) a. Per vasket klær, og jeg / *meg
          Per washed clothes and I / me

      b. [CP Per <u>vasket klær</u> [og [CP jeg ~~vasket klær~~]]

The third problem of the extraction analysis, that of tense in coordinated verbs, has been given a deletion analysis above. What, however, determines the fact that (32c) is out?

(32) a. Spiser (PRES) gjør Ola, og drikker (PRES)

      b. Spise (INF) gjør Ola, og drikker (PRES)

      c. *Spiser (PRES) gjør Ola, og drikke (INF)

      d. Spise (INF) gjør Ola, og drikke (INF)
          'Eat does Ola, and drink.'

It is usually assumed (Lødrup 1990) that in the cases in which the topicalized verb is tensed, it has inherited its tense from the auxiliary verb. In minimalist terms, we will assume that there is spec-head agreement between the topicalized verb and the auxiliary head. It is often assumed that the type of a clause is determined by the element in C. We can assume that when there is a dummy verb in C it is not strong enough to determine the clause-type on its own, and gets help from whatever is in [Spec,CP]. Rather than inheritance of features, we can imagine that there is a straightforward checking of features between the two.

On the other hand, when the topicalized verb is non-finite, we may assume that the grammar accepts the features of the dummy verb as strong enough to determine the clause-type on its own, without the help of the specifier. We then have two different kinds of C—one requiring feature checking with the specifier, and being self-contented.

Coordinating clauses of the same type with each other is unproblematic (in the examples below, the topicalized verb is taken to sit in [Spec,CP] and the dummy verb in C):

(33) a. [CP Spiser (PRES) gjør Ola, [og [CP drikker (PRES) ~~gjør Ola~~]]

b. [CP Spise (INF) gjør Ola, [og [CP drikke (INF) ~~gjør Ola~~]]

Coordinating the two types with each other is possible in principle. However, as we know, only (34b) is possible.

(34) a. *[CP Spiser (PRES) gjør Ola, [og [CP drikke (INF) ~~gjør Ola~~]]

b. [CP Spise (INF) gjør Ola, [og [CP drikker (PRES) ~~gjør Ola~~]]

It is not quite clear why this should be. Presumably it has something to do with the fact that the second conjunct in (34b) still contains a finite verb after deletion, while this is not the case in (34a).

To sum up, in this section we have seen examples that look like violations of the first part of the CSC–ATB principle. However, since an analysis in terms of extraction leaves certain problems unanswered, it was suggested that they should be analyzed not by means of extraction, but by deletion.[6]

6.3.3. THE ANALYSIS OF EXTRACTION OF PART OF CONJUNCTS

The first point to establish when considering extraction of parts of conjuncts is that there is no unbalancedness, as was the case with (what seemed to be) "extraction of whole conjuncts." E.g., in (5)–(9) above, there are examples of extraction out of either conjunct. Extraction out of parts of conjuncts is constrained, however, but it will be shown that the constraints are semantic rather than syntactic.

The fact that extraction can happen out of either conjunct can be easily accounted for in the theory presented here. Let us see how extraction out of the first conjunct can happen. The component sentences of (5c), repeated in (35), can be assumed to be the ones in (36). (I have to stress that at pre-LF level, the sentences do not have an interpretation. The components are therefore simply syntactic construals generated by the transformational component.)

(35) What kind of herbs can you eat and not get cancer?

(36) [CP What kind of herbs can you eat] [and [CP Can you not get cancer]]

(37)

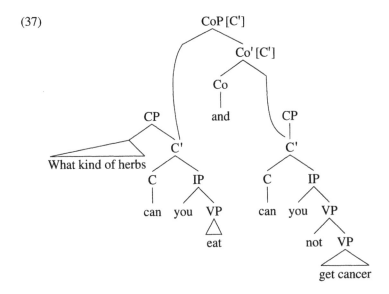

Deletion in accordance with the conditions for FWD gives us:

(38) [CP What kind of herbs can you eat] [and [CP Can you not get cancer]]

However, since the structure violates X-bar theory, Operation Share restructures the whole thing:

(39)

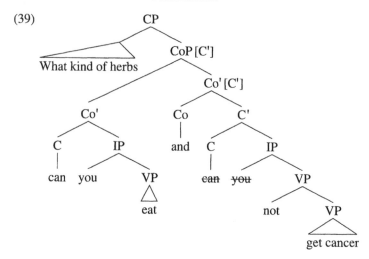

Extraction out of the second conjunct has the same analysis. Take sentence (40). It must have the components in (41):

(40)   What kind of cancer can you eat herbs and not get ?

(41)   [CP Can you eat herbs] [and [CP What kind of cancer can you not get]]

We first look at the point at which coordinate-alpha has operated:

(42)

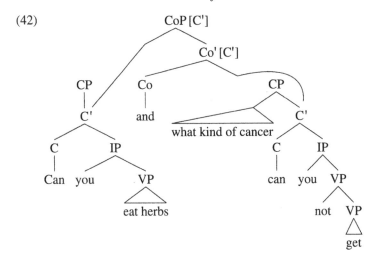

As before, since the structure is a violation of X-bar structure, we resort to Operation Share:

(43)

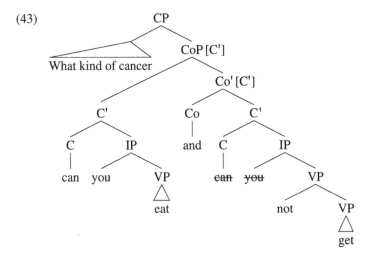

We can conclude, so far, that there is no syntactic restriction against extracting from any of the conjuncts. Deletion and sharing will always be possible. However, there are some constraints against extraction: the sentences in (44) seem to be completely unacceptable.

(44) a. *What kind of herbs can you eat and Mary see a mouse?

b. *What kind of mouse can you eat herbs and Mary not see?

c. *How big a meal did he eat and feel satisfied?

(Lakoff 1986:154)

Given the well-formedness of the sentences in (5–9), it is clear that the constraints must be semantic rather than syntactic. I shall not attempt to give a full semantic account, but let us start by suggesting a model-theoretic approach with operator-variable binding.

Assume, e.g., that part of the role of the conjunction is to force an operator to bind a variable in each conjunct. This does not happen in (45), but we could assume that a purpose predicate was inserted into the formula, giving (46), in which there is now a variable in each conjunct bound by the same operator. (Other possible predicates might be e.g. cause, time, and "despiteness.")

(45) For which x [x: cancer]
([Eat(you, herbs)] $\&_{[Co]}$ [-Get(you, x)])

(46) For which x [x: cancer]
([Purpose(Eat(you, herbs), -Get(you, x))] $\&_{[Co]}$ [-Get(you, x)])[7]

This explanation, unfortunately, cannot be right, since another suitable predicate to interpret (5b) might be "consequence," i.e., that something follows from something else. In (47), an extended formula for such a coordination is given. It is immediately clear that here, the operator binds only one variable in one conjunct, and none in the other.

(47) For which x [x: cancer]
([Eat(you, herbs)] $\&_{[Co]}$ [Consequence [-Get(you, x)], [Eat(you, herbs)]]])

A model-theoretic account is, therefore, not feasible. Instead, I believe that the constraints are based on facts to do with context and the interpretable relationship between the conjuncts. Lakoff (1986) has made an attempt to find the solution within a cognitive semantics framework. He has divided the sentences above into two main types, Scenario A and Scenario B, which have different extraction constraints (Lakoff 1986:153 ff).

Type A is coordination "in which the sequence of events fits normal conventionalized expectations" (sentence (6)). Type B is coordination "in
which a conventionalized expectation is violated" (sentence (5a)). Only
Type B permits there to be no extraction from the final conjunct. I do not
think the types and constraints which Lakoff puts forward are the ultimate
ones. E.g., a sentence such as (48) seems fine, even though it violates
Lakoff's Type B constraint:

(48) What kind of car can you drink vodka and still drive?

There are, therefore, many loose ends, but I do think the constraints for
possible extraction of parts of conjuncts are to be found within semantic
generalizations; i.e., those where the relationship between the conjuncts
determines possible extractions. To see that it is the context that is the
sole determinant of acceptable extraction out of parts of conjuncts, we can
try to find a suitable context for the sentences in (44), repeated here:

(49) a. *What kind of herbs can you eat and Mary see a mouse?

      b. *What kind of mouse can you eat herbs and Mary not see?

      c. *How big a meal did he eat and feel satisfied?
                                                    (Lakoff 1986:154)

To make (49a) acceptable, we can consider a situation in which Mary,
who has a slight mental defect, always sees an animal when someone eats
herbs. A friend of hers tells you that Mary actually sees different animals;
each herb triggers its own animal. In this context, you could ask her
friend the question in (49a). She does not see every kind of mouse,
though, so that (49b) is a possible question to find out which one is impossible for her to see. (49c) is felicitous to ask in a situation in which
you have just heard about a giant who for the first time has eaten enough
food to feel satisfied, and you wonder how big that meal was.

To sum up, extraction out of parts of conjuncts is possible when a link
can be established between the conjuncts which can be described in terms
of cause, consequence, despiteness, or time (there may be other relationships, too). Ordinary model-theoretic semantics will not capture this generalization, since there is nothing formally wrong with a representation
in which an operator binds only one or even no variable in the conjuncts.
Inserting a predicate into the formula to achieve bound variables in

each conjunct does not help, since only some predicates have this effect.

We have to answer the important question, however, of how it is that the conjunction forces the above interpretations only in extraction constructions where the CoP is within the scope of the extracted element. The answer must have to do with LF interpretation. The extracted element has scope over the CoP, and therefore over both conjuncts. The conjunction has as part of its meaning the function of joining two propositions together by predicates such as the mentioned cause, etc. The extracted element, which has scope over both conjuncts, triggers one of these functions, which is a way for both conjuncts to be influenced by the extracted element. The reason the same functions do not necessarily come out in ordinary unextracted coordination of propositions, is that there is nothing to trigger them. Each proposition is a self-contained unit, which is not influenced by the conjunction in other ways than maybe time-wise.

The analysis is supported by extraction from verbal coordination. We have already seen that serial verb constructions in which only the verb of the specifier conjunct has normal inflection can be analyzed as extraction. The example from Fulfulde (Chapter 2) is repeated here:

(50) Janngo   mi yahay,   mi foonda   ki, mi ndaara. . .
     Tomorrow I go.SG.HAB I investigate.SG.SI it I see.SI
     'Tomorrow I shall go and investigate it and see . . .'

(51)

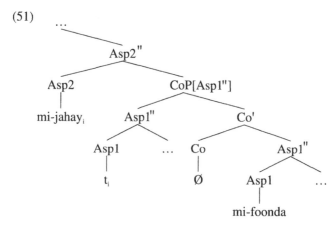

Since the verb has moved out and now has scope over both conjuncts it should trigger a special relationship betwen the conjuncts. This is exactly what happens: the conjuncts in serial verb constructions are closely knit together (see the brief description of serial verbs in Chapter 2) semantically.

Notice that in order to get the special readings mentioned, both conjuncts have to be within the scope of the extracted element. If the CoP had attached to the very top of the component conjuncts, there would have been no way to obtain this special kind of interpretation.

We can assume that the semantic constraints on extraction of parts of conjuncts also help constrain extraction of whole conjuncts. When something is extracted a special relationship is triggered between two elements. However, when a whole conjunct is extracted, there are no longer two available elements between which such a relationship could exist, and extraction must be ruled out. Thus, the semantic factors not only constrain extraction of parts of conjuncts, but constrains extraction of whole conjuncts—to such an extent that the latter is not possible. This conclusion is in accordance with what was said about split coordination earlier in this chapter—it is deletion, not extraction.

6.4. Summary

To sum up, I have shown that there are two kinds of constructions that seem to be violations of the CSC–ATB. The first kind looks like extraction of whole conjuncts, "split coordination," i.e., violation of the first part of the CSC–ATB. The second type is extraction out of part of a conjunct, i.e., violation of the second part of the CSC–ATB.

I have presented two alternative analyzes of split coordination, one which is constrained by syntax, in very much the vain of unbalanced coordination, in which the position within the conjunction phrase is crucial, and a second one based on coordination of full CPs to which deletion applies. Only the second analysis avoids a series of problems, such as having to explain why the CoP *in situ* is always sentence-final, why case is necessary in both DP conjuncts, and why it is the verb of the second conjunct which has to have tense features. Violations of the second part of CSC–ATB, in which the extracted element is only part of a conjunct, are shown to be acceptable. In these constructions, extraction can happen from either conjunct. They are semantically constrained, though. The same semantic constraints also would make it impossible to allow extraction of whole conjuncts. We can conclude that the first part of the CSC–ATB cannot be violated, since what looks like extraction is rather deletion, but the second part can.

Notes

1. The brackets are put around what is taken to be the coordination phrase from which the conjunct has been extracted.

2. Paul Postal (p.c.) takes the view that the sentences in (6) are not CSC violations; rather than having an extraction site in one conjunct only, he claims that there is an empty resumptive pronoun in the position in which I have indicated a trace. The reason for this point of view is that according to Postal, it is not possible to "extract" a phrase which cannot leave a pronoun, such as a color:

(i) What did you go and paint your house?

However, many (British) English-speaking informants have opposed his judgements, claiming instead that there is nothing wrong with "color-extraction."

3. I am grateful to Eric Hoekstra for pointing this out to me.

4. I am grateful to Bob Borsley for this point.

5. Avoiding (13) is a problem. An analysis is possible and in accordance with all the FWD and BWD principles, as shown in (i). However, it ought to have been ruled out.

(i) [All the heaviness <u>had</u> ~~gone~~] [and [the height ~~had~~ <u>gone</u>]]

FWD has deleted *had* from the second conjunct, while BWD has deleted *gone* from the first conjunct. Notice that if either the head condition on FWD or the major constituent condition on FWD also had applied at BWD, then (i) would have been correctly ruled out, since either *gone* of the first conjunct would have been c-commanded by an overt head, or since *had* of the second conjunct had been deleted without the rest of its constituent. However, both these conditions have been left out for BWD, in order to accept right node raising sentences. It remains a question for future research whether right node raising should be accounted for in a different way, thus extending these two conditions to BWD, or whether there might be some other reason for (i). Maybe there is a general constraint against switched antecedents and deletions next to each other.

6. A third possible analysis, suggested to me by Steve Harlow, is one in which the afterthought bit is just an added category adjoined somehow to the "first conjunct." I do not see this as a possible alternative within the present theory, however. First, why should adjunction happen only sentence-finally? Second, how would the adjoined category get its morphosyntactic features? Third, what would cause the conjunction to be inserted before it?

7. I am grateful to Kjell Johan Sæbø for suggesting this way of formalizing the semantic idea.

7

Semantic and Thematic Issues

7.1. Introduction

In this chapter, we shall take a look at some semantic and thematic issues. The first part, Section 7.2, deals with semantic issues. We shall discuss the difference between coordination and subordination, and show that the difference may not be as marked as one might have thought. Evidence is taken from a number of languages, in which the distinction between coordination and subordination is drawn at different places. Also, coordinating conjunctions have often developed from subordinating ones. We shall also discuss issues that have been viewed as problematic for some theories of coordination. These issues are to a large extent not a problem for the present theory (or for other modern approaches), but they are still interesting, and well worth looking at.

The second part of the chapter, Section 7.3, deals with thematic aspects of coordination. It seems clear that there are some constraints on coordination that have to do with thematic roles or properties. We shall investigate what these might be and how they might affect coordination with special reference to the theories of Grimshaw (1990) and Dowty (1991).

7.2. Semantics

Section 7.2, on semantics, is organized in the following way. In Section 7.2.1, it will be shown that the maybe disturbing similarity between subordinated structures and the structure of the CoP developed in this book is supported by semantic facts. In Section 7.2.1.1, it seems that, rather than there being a sharp universal distinction between coordination and subordination semantically there is a gradation from one extreme to the

other. This can be seen from the fact that the extent to which languages
uses coordinating conjunctions rather than subordinating ones varies. In
Section 7.2.2, support for the close relationship can be seen from the fact
that coordinating conjunctions often have developed from subordinating
ones.

In Section 7.2.3, we shall have a brief look at some problems raised by
semanticists concerning coordinated structures. The problems will not be
discussed to any great depth; it will merely be pointed out that the syntactic structures created by coordinate-alpha are a good starting point for
doing semantic analysis. The asset of the theory in this respect (as in
other theories in which syntax is interpreted by semantics) is the fact that
there is no semantic interpretation until coordinate-alpha has applied;
there is a CoP which at its top-level has the features of the conjunction,
including semantic specifications and constraints from its lexical entry,
and defined positions for the conjuncts, which means that there is easy
access to the components of the CoP too, when that is desirable, e.g. for
the analysis of entailment relations. Section 7.2.4 concludes the first part
of this Chapter.

7.2.1. COORDINATION AND SUBORDINATION

The conjuncts in conjunction phrases are usually considered to have the
same semantic status. The definition in Dik (1968) is a representative
example:

> (1) A coordination is a construction consisting of two or more mem-
>   bers which are equivalent as to grammatical function, and bound
>   together at the same level of structural hierarchy by means of a
>   linking device.   (Dik 1968:25)

Subordination is taken to be a completely different matter, in which the
elements surrounding the subordinator are not semantically equivalent.
Thus, a coordination [M1 co M2] is (most often) semantically equivalent
with [M2 co M1], while a subordination [M1 sub M2] is never semantically equivalent to [M2 sub M1] (Dik 1968:37).

However, I have shown that there are good reasons to analyze CoP as
a basically asymmetric structure, in which the two conjuncts have different positions in the phrase, leading them to have different syntactic behavior in some languages. There is no principled difference between a
coordinated and a subordinated structure in the theory presented here.

This ought not to be seen as a defect, but rather as a virtue: although there are cases which are clear-cut coordination and others which are clear-cut subordination, there are also cases which semantically fall in between.

7.2.1.1. *Cross-linguistic variation in the distribution of conjunctions*

In Endresen (1992a), the semantic distinction between coordination and subordination (infinitive) is not one between two main groups, but is rather one of degree, where several semantic steps lead from one extreme to the other. The hypothesis of a semantic scale is further supported by the fact that not all languages draw the division line at the same point. Endresen's hypothesis is that there is a polysemous relationship between the Norwegian coordinating conjunction *og* /o/, and the infinitival marker *å* /o/. The scale is given below; number I is the most coordinative, and IX the most subordinative (from Endresen 1992a:29–35).[1]

Number I: Mental parataxis of two equivalent things to one gestalt:

(2) Ho kjøpte mjølk /o/ brød
    she bought milk   and bread
    'She bought milk and bread.'

Number II: Mental parataxis of two equivalent atemporal relations to one gestalt—the relations have the same subject.

(3) Strømpene   er blå /o/ gule
    the.stockings are blue and yellow
    'The stockings are blue and yellow.'

Number III: Mental parataxis of two equivalent processes to one gestalt—the processes have the same subject.

(4) Han røyker sigar og drikk raudvin
    he   smokes cigar and drinks red.wine
    'He smokes cigar and drinks red wine.'

Number IV: Mental parataxis of two sequential processes to one gestalt—the processes have the same subject—the two processes do not have the same flow of energy.

(5) Han tok av seg   kleda   /o/ hoppa ut i elva
    he   took off himself the.clothes and jumped out in the.river
    'He took his clothes off and jumped into the river.'

Number V: Mental parataxis of two sequential processes to one
gestalt—the processes have the same subject—the two processes have the
same flow of energy—the second process describes the aim of the first
one, which describes a movement—the second process extends the first
one. (This kind of construction is discussed in Chapter 2 as pseudocoordination.)

(6) Han sprang /o/ kjøpte billettar
    he   ran   and bought tickets
    'He ran and bought tickets.'

Number VI: Mental parataxis of two processes to one gestalt—the
processes have the same subject—the two processes have the same flow
of energy—the second process extends the first one.

(7) Han prøvde /o/ reparere motoren
    he   tried to mend   the.motor

Number VII: Mental parataxis of two processes to one gestalt—the
processes have the same subject—the two processes have the same flow
of energy—the second process extends the first one—the first process
assigns a potential flow of energy from the subject to the second process.

(8) Han greier   /o/ sykle
    he   manages to cycle
    'He manages to cycle.'

Number VIII: Mental parataxis of a process and a complex atemporal
relation to one gestalt—the processes have the same subject—the two
relations have the same flow of energy—the process assigns a psycholo-
gical relation between the subject and the complex atemporal relation—
the complex atemporal relation extends the process.

(9) Han foretrekker /o/ stå
    he   prefers   to stand
    'He prefers to be standing.'

Number IX: A complex atemporal relation which is not the sink of any flow of energy.

(10) /o/ sitte på brygga med ein pils, det er livet
      to sit at the.pier with a lager, that is the.life
      'To sit at the pier with a lager, that is life.'

Although I agree with Endresen's point that semantically there may be cases that are not clear-cut, I do not agree that this can simply be represented as a scale. This is because the scale reproduced above does not reflect other cases where coordination is used for subordinate meaning. While it may be possible to describe English and Norwegian on a scale that goes from coordination to infinitive, this is not all the story. For example, in Greek, some of the meanings of the conjunction fit into the first part of the scale, but then there are other meanings that do not fit into it at all. Consider (11)–(15).

(11) vlepo ke hamojelas
      I.see and you.smile
      'I see you're smiling'

(12) ton akusa ke fonaze
      him I.heard and he.shouted
      'I heard him shouting.'

(13) m'ekanes ke se pistepsa
      me.you.made and you I.believed
      'You made me believe you.'

(14) ti epathes ke dhe milas
      what you.suffered and not you.speak
      'What's the matter with you since you don't speak?'

(15) bori na mi vriski erghates ke dhen erhete
      it.may.be to not he.finds workmen and not he.comes
      'Maybe he doesn't come if he doesn't find workmen.'
                                   (Mackridge 1987:242)

(11)–(13) contain conjuncts with one subject each. On the scale, this should mean that they denote two equivalent events, like I, but in fact, the constructions have more of a subordinate meaning; where one event depends on or is part of the other. The causality and consequence meanings of (14) and (15) also seem difficult to fit into the scale.

However, whether the semantics of coordination and subordination are analyzed in terms of scale or not, it is clear that different languages draw the line at different points:

(16)

Constr. Number	Fulfulde	Kanuri	Japanese	Standard English	Written Norwegian	Informal English	Greek	Spoken Norwegian
I	bee	-a	to	and	og	and	ke	/o/
II	Ø	(ye)	si	and	og	and	ke	/o/
III	Ø	(ye)	si	and	og	and	ke	/o/
IV				and	og	and	ke	/o/
V					og	and	ke	/o/
VI						(and)	ke	/o/
VII							ke	/o/
VIII								/o/
IX								/o/

(Endresen 1992b)

The fact that coordination and subordination are both relations between two arguments, is, of course, clear. However, the fact that the relations between the arguments are of different types is also clear, as is commonly recognized. What the table does, is show us that, although empirically, the same semantic relations are categorized differently in different languages. There is, therefore, no construction about which it is possible to claim that it is semantically coordinated or subordinated, and this is reflected in the syntax.

Interestingly, the lack of a clear semantic fence is accompanied by lack of a clear syntactic fence. E.g., one characteristic property of coordination is that the presence of a conjunction and its complement is not required by the first conjunct, as in (17). This contrasts with the conjunction and its complement following verbs that subcategorize for subordinate structures, as in (18).

(17) a.   Peter sang and danced

     b.   Peter sang

(18) a.   Peter prefers to sing

     b.   *Peter prefers

Interestingly, the English constructions that can have either *and* or *to*, i.e., that are both coordinating and subordinating, are also those in which the conjunction plus complement can be dropped, i.e., a characteristic of coordinations: [2]

(19) a.   Peter will try and/to sing

     b.   Peter will try

(20) a.   Can you manage and cycle over there?

     b.   Can you manage?

However, the same constructions are subordinating in that they require an infinitival verb-form in the second conjunct (21), as well as in the fact that conjunction and its complement can be moved out of the construction (22):

(21) a.   *Peter tried and sang

     b.   *Peter managed and cycled over there

(22) a.   To sing is what Peter will try

     b.   *And sing is what Peter will try

     c.   To cycle is what Peter can manage

     d.   *And cycle is what Peter can manage

7.2.2. THE ORIGIN OF CONJUNCTIONS

While probably all languages have ways of expressing semantic co-ordination, the way they do it varies considerably. Some languages have conjunctions, and some have not, some have different ones for different syntactic categories, and some use various kinds of different syntactic structures. In this section, it will be pointed out that many conjunctions have originated as subordinating elements. The fact that this is possible is a supporting factor for the "subordinate" coordinate structure suggested in this book; it makes the transition possible. Many of these languages have had coordination without conjunctions until very recently.

In Sarcee, DPs are usually coordinated asyndetically, as in (23a), but they can also be coordinated by means of a comitative/instrumental postposition *ih* + *ila* (23b). In spite of the choice of "conjunction," the latter construction probably is coordination rather than subordination, since the verbal suffix used is *-là* 'to handle plural objects'. This clearly suggests that the object DP is plural, which it would not have been, had the construction been one of subordination.

(23) a. [dítòo   dóó-ʔĩ]   iná áání-là
        own.father own.mother.DET she.told
        'She told her father and mother.'
                        (Cook 1984:87, cited in Mithun 1988:339)

    b. [tcágúá k'ìyìdjí ìstlá   ká-àhílà] kàdīlá-là
       weasel coat   legging shoe-with he.brought.out
       'He brought out weasel coats, leggings, and shoes.'
                        (Cook 1984:96, cited in Mithun 1988:339)

The Gã conjunction *kè* (in (24), repeated from Chapter 2) originated as a comitative verb. Mithun (1988:340) in fact assumes that the reason for the unbalancedness of coordinated subject noun-phrases, where only the first conjunct determines verb agreement, is a reflection of the fact that the first conjunct alone was a subject of the comitative verb.

(24) mì kè lè tà   / *trà
     I   and he sit.SG / sit.PL
     'I and he sit.'

In Cayuga an adverb *hni'* meaning 'also' or 'too' is often used as a co-ordinating conjunction. The difference can be seen in (25a,b); in the first instance, the particle has retained its original meaning; in the latter it has a pure coordinating meaning.

(25) a. A:yẽ   akwé:, onẽhẽ' osahe'tá' ohõn'atá'õ   hni'
      it.seems all   corn bean   potato.guess also
      'Oh, I guess everything, corn, beans, potatoes, and squash.'
                                  (Mithun 1988:341)

    b. Ne:' tshō: ne' onẽhẽ' sahe'tá' hni' õkwayẽthwẽ hne:'
      it   only the corn   beans   also we.planted   CONTR
      'No, we only planted corn and beans.'
                                  (Mithun 1988:342)

7.2.3. PROBLEM AREAS DEFINED BY SEMANTICISTS

Semanticists have noticed several areas in which simplex sentences differ from coordinated sentences. In each of the cases in (26) below, two simplex component sentences have a different semantic interpretation from the coordinated one.

(26) a. [John and Mary] were carrying four baskets
    a.′ John was carrying four baskets and Mary was carrying four baskets

    b. The glass is [red and blue]
    b.′ The glass is red and the glass is blue

    c. [John and Mary] are married
    c.′ John is married and Mary is married

    d. The old man left all his money to [Bill and Tom]
    d.′ The old man left all his money to Bill and he left all his money to Tom
                                  (Dik 1968:88)

First, this would constitute a problem if the properties of the coordinated sentence were believed to derived from a Boolean operator *and*. The Boolean operator has at least the two properties commutativity and associativity, which are exemplified in (27a,b), respectively.[3]

(27) a. walk and talk ≡ talk and walk

    b. (eat and drink) and be merry ≡ eat and (drink and be merry)
                                                    (Hoeksema 1987)

Natural language coordination cannot be reduced to Boolean coordination, some examples of which will be shown below.

Second, sentences such as (26) are a problem if coordination is assumed to consist of component sentences that are already fully interpreted semantically—as was the case in early generative grammar. If the levels are kept apart, as they have been since Chomsky (1981), so that there is a computational level distinct from the interpretational levels, the apparently unexplainable differences between the simplex and coordinated sentences is no problem.

A. *Entailment relations*
Hoeksema (1983,1987) shows how coordination in natural language is not always Boolean, as in (28) (in which the conjuncts are proper names), where (28a) does not entail the proposition in (28b), in contrast to the VP coordination in (29), in which there is such entailment. (The examples are taken from Hoeksema 1987.)

(28) a. [Henry and Lynne] drank all my liquor

    b. NOT → Henry drank all my liquor

(29) a. Henry [ate and drank]

    b. → Henry ate

B. *Singularity and plurality*
Coordination of singular terms counts as a plural term, as in (30a), but there are exceptions to this with certain singular quantifiers (e.g. *each* and *every*), as seen in (30b):

(30) a. [A man and a woman] were / *was arrested

    b. [Every day and every night] were / was spent in bed
                                                     (Hoeksema 1987)

C. *Multiple coordination*

A different problem is discussed by Link (1984) and Lønning (1989: §6). Associativity in multiple coordination is not free; e.g., strings of DPs grouped in different ways give different interpretations. This is illustrated in (31).

(31) a. [George and Martha] and [Nick and Honey] hate each other

b. [George and Martha and Nick] and [Honey] hate each other

c. [George and Martha and Nick and Honey] hate each other

d. [George] and [Martha and Nick and Honey] hate each other
(Link 1984:246)

D. *Pair-wise association*

Link (1984:246) also mentions conjunction phrases which must be interpreted as ordered pairs:

(32) [George and Martha] are [husband and wife]
(Link 1984:246)

E. *Anaphoric relations*

Heim, Lasnik, and May (1991) discuss the multiple ambiguity caused by, on the one hand, the fact that the subject is a CoP, and on the other, the fact that the object is a reciprocal pronoun. Their example is (33), which has at least the readings in (34):

(33) [John and Mary] told each other that they should leave

(34) a. John told Mary that *he* should leave & Mary told John that *she* should leave

b. John told Mary that *she* should leave & Mary told John that *he* should leave

c. John told Mary & Mary told John: *we* should leave
(Heim, Lasnik, and May 1991:63–4)

I shall not attempt to give an analysis of these or other semantic issues here. They have been treated by, among others, Hoeksema (1983), Partee and Rooth (1983), Link (1984), Hoeksema (1987), Lønning (1989), Heim, Lasnik, and May (1991), Lang (1991), and Lasersohn (1995), to which the reader is referred. However, it is important that there is a place for the semantic analysis, i.e., that the theory of coordination and the syntactic structures can provide an analysis in principle.

A crucial characteristic in the theory is that coordinate-alpha works on structures *which are not yet interpreted semantically*. Coordinate-alpha works, as explained in Chapter 5, in the syntactic component ("the computational system," Chomsky 1992:4), in which the structures are nothing more than formal, non-interpreted units. They do not get an interpretation until the interface levels LF and PF. This means that the theory avoids paradoxical situations in which the component sentences have one interpretation that is later altered as a result of them partaking in a coordinated structure. Let us first assume that the conjunction *and* has the lexical entry below.[4]

(35) *and*. Conjunction, arg1, arg2.
        Semantically conjunctive:
        $[X_{[-N]}$ and $Y_{[-N]}]$: $[X_{[-N]} \wedge Y_{[-N]}]$
        $[X_{[+N]}$ and $Y_{[+N]}]$: $[X_{[+N]} \wedge Y_{[+N]}]_{[pl]}$
        $[X_{[+N, \text{sg.quantifier}]}$ and $Y_{[+N, \text{sg.quantifier}]}]$: $[X_{[+N]} \wedge Y_{[+N]}]$

In relation to problem A, entailment, there is nothing in the lexical entry which gives a clue to why there should be the seeming asymmetry exemplified in (26)–(27). However, the entry does say that all ordinary [+N] categories that are coordinated form a semantically plural category. Taking this at face value, it means that there is in principle no difference between a CoP[+D] and a plural DP. The lack of entailment in (28) above therefore parallels that of (36). The task for semantics then is to describe the entailment differences between singular and plural subjects in general, not only coordinated ones.

(36) a.   My children drank all my liquor

      b.   NOT → My daughter drank all my liquor

Similarly, a verb that involves more than one action (the "equivalent" of a simplex plural DP) entails each of the actions, just as an overtly co-ordinated VP does. (37a) entails (37b), in the same way as (29a) above entails (29b). The task for semantics must then be to describe the entailment relations between actions in general, not overtly coordinated ones in particular.

(37) a.   Henry walked

    b.   → Henry moved his left leg

The singularity/plurality distinction in B is accounted for by the lexical entry of the conjunction. Singular quantifiers have an intrinsic singular value, which is inherited by the CoP. The task for semantics is to study the properties of the quantifier, not of CoP. The fact that singular quantifiers have a real semantic singularity which they let be inherited by CoP is supported by entailment relations. We have seen that all coordinated DPs are treated like semantically plural entities when it comes to entailment relations. Singularly quantified DPs do not fall under this generalization; the CoP keeps the singularity inherited by its conjuncts:

(38) a.   Every man and every woman solved the crossword puzzle

    b.   Every man solved the crossword puzzle

(Hoeksema 1987)

In relation to problem C, multiple coordination, the present theory allows for different associativity by a purely syntactic device only when the CoP is a left-hand group—as in (39a). It does not distinguish explicitly between CoPs that are right-hand grouped (in right-branching languages, and vice versa for left-branching languages), and those where the conjuncts are simply listed—when the conjunction is overtly expressed for each CoP. I.e., while the theory makes a distinction between (39a) and (39b), it does not structurally distinguish between (39b) and (39c).

(39) a.   [[A and B] and C and D and E]

    b.   [A and B and C and D and E]

    c.   [A and B and C and [D and E]]

However, explicit grouping can be made by the introduction of a Group projection. Multiple coordination is discussed in more detail in Section 4.6. Notice also that there are structural differences that reflect the semantics: while there is in general the possibility of deleting all but the last conjunctions in a multiple coordination structure, it is only possible as long as the next CoP is not a semantic group. Therefore, while it is possible to delete all the conjunctions but the last one in (39b), it is not possible to delete the one before the CoP group in (39c).

The paired reading between the CoPs in problem D is probably not easy to account for in a purely semantic analysis. However, the syntactic analysis makes the basis for such a reading available. The basic asymmetry of the conjuncts in CoP ensures the possibility of interpreting two CoPs parallelly. I.e., the members of the first CoP can be defined as having the same relationship with each other as the members of the second CoP, relationships which can then be used in semantics/pragmatics: pair the specifier of one CoP with the specifier of the other CoP and do the same with the complements.

The various interpretations in problem E also can be accounted for with the syntactic structures provided by the theory presented here. The CoP[DP] is basically the same as a plural DP. A reciprocal pronoun needs a plural DP as its antecedent. The reason it can force different readings onto the CoP[DP], is that it can pick out individual members from its antecedent. The members that are present in the CoP, i.e., the conjuncts, are of course available. An ordinary plural DP would also be available for picking out members to which the reciprocal could refer, though obviously with fewer ambiguities.[5]

Also, it should be noted that the distinction between syntactic strings and operations on these ("the computational system") on the one hand and different interpretational interfaces on the other (which is basically the conception of grammar since Chomsky 1981) is essential in order to avoid many problems having been put forward prior to the time that this distinction was introduced.

7.2.4. SUMMARY

The conjunction phrase suggested in this book shows that the conjuncts do not have equal status; only one is a complement of the conjunction (although both conjuncts are arguments). This makes coordinated structures more like subordinated structures. In this section, we have seen that there are several phenomena that support the similarity in structure between coordination and subordination. One factor is the variation between languages with respect to where the distinction between coordination and subordination is drawn. Another factor is that coordinating conjunctions often have started out as subordinating conjunctions. We have looked at various problems suggested for coordination in the literature, and concluded that most of them are not a problem in the present theory, because of the separation between the computational and the interpretational levels.

7.3. Thematic properties

We have seen that there is no explicit constraint against which categories can be coordinated with which. Any two categories are in principle conjoinable; only very general principles such as X-bar theory can prevent a CoP from being grammatical in a certain context. There is reason to think that there are constraints belonging to the thematic dimension. We shall see that two conjuncts must not be different with respect to thematic roles or features.

The section is organized in the following way. Section 7.3.1 contains a general outline of the relationship between the lexicon, thematic roles, and syntactic categories. Section 7.3.2 shows how, in general, conjuncts of the same CoP cannot be interpreted as having different thematic roles, but it also presents some cases where the conjuncts are best analyzed as being different in this respect. In Section 7.3.3, we shall see that employing Grimshaw's (1990) theory, which distinguishes between two types of dimensions—a thematic and an aspectual one, does not provide a solution to the problem. A solution using Dowty's (1991) thematic features is more promising. A summary is given in Section 7.3.4.

7.3.1. THEMATIC ROLES AND THE LEXICON

We have seen how sentences with UC constructions like (40) can be accounted for by appealing to two parts of the theory: the structure of CoP, and the fact that any two categories can be coordinated if the material outside CoP can be merged.

(40) Mary thought about [the mouse and that she wanted to buy an elephant]

However, we have not yet seen how it is that the *that*-clause is situated as the complement of a preposition in the component sentence. This will become clear now that we shall look at the way the lexicon is organized, and get an idea of how lexical elements are projected to the syntax.

The structure of the lexicon has been given a lot of discussion in recent years. Here, I take it that specification of argument structure is given in terms of thematic roles rather than specific syntactic categories. Following Grimshaw (1981), Pesetsky (1982), Chomsky (1986b: 86–92), and Rothstein (1992a), I assume that a certain category *s-selects* the thematic roles of its arguments. Each thematic role has a canonical structural representation (CSR) which indicates which syntactic categories realize it. Take as an example *about*:

(41) *about*, preposition {Theme, Proposition}

We can further suppose that the CSRs for Theme and Proposition are as below:

(42) Theme: DP
      Proposition: CP[that]
                   CP[wh]
                   VP[SC]
                   DP["with cognate noun"]

With this kind of general information we can get the following sentences (including the unacceptable (43b)):

(43) a. Mary thought about the mouse

      b. *Mary thought about that she wanted to buy an elephant

      c. Mary thought about what she wanted to buy

      d. Mary thought about the mouse eating

      e. Mary thought about the fact/point/idea/question that the
          mouse was eating a lot

The idea of the lexicon subcategorizing for thematic roles rather than syntactic categories makes it more general than it would otherwise have been. In addition, it makes it possible to account more intuitively for the fact that some categories are obviously subcategorized for and yet do not show up in simplex contexts. An example is the difference between (40) and (43b).

7.3.2. THEMATIC PROBLEMS

In the previous chapters, we have seen that any two syntactic categories, whether the same or different, can be coordinated if only the rest of the structure is unifiable, i.e., like in some sense.

However, it has been known for a long time that there are constraints on the acceptability of some of these structures. E.g., Chomsky (1965), Fillmore (1968), Schachter (1977), Sag et al. (1985), Gazdar et al. (1985), and Goodall (1987) all have stressed that it is important that the conjuncts must have some thematic or semantic properties in common, whether it is deep case, semantic features, archecategories, semantic function, or something else. In the following sections we shall see some examples that support this general point, but also some counter-examples, which should be accounted for.

7.3.2.1. *Conjuncts with unacceptable different thematic roles*

In this section, we shall see some examples which seem to show that it is impossible for conjuncts to have different thematic roles. Thematic roles have been discussed by a variety of linguists, and different roles have been suggested by most. Some of the more influential ones are Gruber (1976), Williams (1981b), Marantz (1984), Andrews (1985), di Sciullo and Williams (1987), as well as Rappaport and Levin (1988), Zubizarreta (1987), and Grimshaw (1990). Most of the thematic roles to be used in the examples in this section are quite uncontroversial, I believe, at least as far as the typical argument roles like Agent, Theme, Source, and maybe Instrument, are concerned. I have included roles for non-arguments, i.e., adjuncts, some of which may be less common, the point of which is simply to label all kinds of participants in the sentence. These are Instrument, Manner, Comitative, Time, Direction.

Some examples of unacceptable coordination are given in (44). Notice that, apart from (44b), all conjuncts belonging to the same CoP have the same syntactic category features. Most of them also sit in the same syntactic position. The intuitive thematic role labels given for each structure suggest that there must indeed be some kind of thematic principle constraining such structures.

(44) a. *[John and the hammer] broke the window
                    (Agent & Instrument)   (Fillmore 1968)

   b. *John ate [quickly and a grilled sandwich]
                    (Manner & Theme)   (Schachter 1977:87)

   c. *John [probably and unwillingly] went to bed
                    (Attitude & Manner)   (Schachter 1977:89)

   d. *John ate [with his mother and with good appetite]
                    (Comitative & Manner)   (Schachter 1977:89)

   e. *[June 6 and 7 and the theatre group] repeated the show for
      orphans from the Barcley Home and patients at Dover
      Hospital   (Time & Agent)
                    (Adapted from Rohdenburgh 1974)

   f. *[Water and Peter] filled the tank
                    (Theme & Agent)   (Adapted from Dowty 1991)

   g. *Carol ran [to the stadium and at five o'clock]
                    (Direction & Time)

   h. *Jane walked [slowly and there]   (Manner & Direction)

   I. *[The baker and the bread] baked   (Agent & Theme)

   j. *The man and the ski competition] started at six
                    (Agent & Theme)

The fully acceptable examples in (45) contrast with the ones above, not
only in that the conjuncts have different syntactic categories, but also in
that they seem to have the same thematic roles.

(45) a. Mrs. Samson plays [beautifully and with great empathy]
                    (AdvP & PP)

   b. They have resided [in the palace and everywhere else too]
                    (PP & AdvP)

c. Peter visits his friend [every second week and on Christ-
mas Eve] (DP & PP)

The Norwegian examples in (46) show the same kind of unacceptability
as the English ones in (44).

(46) a. *Jeg luktet [gass og parfyme] (Theme & Source)
I smelt gas and perfume
'I smelt gas and (of) perfume.'

b. *Kyllingen smaker [fisk og øl] (Source & Theme)
the.chicken tastes fish and beer
'The chicken tastes (of) fish and beer.'

Notice that there is no problem when the arguments have the same thematic roles:

(47) a. Jeg luktet [gass og røyk] (Theme & Theme)
I smelt gas and smoke
'I smelt gas and smoke.'

b. Jeg luktet [hårspray og parfyme] (Source & Source)
I smelt hair.spray and perfume
'I smelt (of) hair spray and (of) perfume.'

The Norwegian examples are composed of syntactically simplex, and
perfectly acceptable, sentences. The ones for (47a) are illustrated below.

(48) a. Jeg luktet gass (Experiencer, Theme)
I smelt gas
'I smelt gas.'

b. Jeg luktet parfyme (Theme, Source)
I smelt perfume
'I smelt of perfume.'

The problem is not that the accompanying subject must alternate between
two different roles, since a CoP subject with different roles would solve
that problem, but the result is still unacceptable:

(49) a. *[Marit og jeg] luktet [gass og parfyme]
(Experiencer & Theme, Theme & Source)
'Marit and I smell gas and (of) perfume.'

b. *[Høna og kyllingen] smaker [fisk og øl]
(Experiencer & Theme, Source & Theme)
'The hen and the chicken taste (of) fish and beer.'

On the basis of the examples, we can conclude so far that the grammar has a principle such as (50), which constrains possible interpretations of coordinations.

(50) *Thematic coordination principle*: Conjuncts of the same CoP must not have different thematic roles.

7.3.2.2. *Conjuncts with acceptable different thematic roles*

There seems to be a complication with respect to the previous generalization. The examples in (51) show that it is not only *like* thematic roles that can be coordinated; also *unlike* roles can be conjuncts in the same CoP, such as Agent and Causer:

(51) a. [The evil man and the thunder] frightened the child
(Agent & Causer)

b. [Guy (who rubbed her with a towel) and the sun] dried her quickly
(Agent & Causer)

c. I was saved by [good luck and my strong friend]
(Causer & Agent)

With Andrews (1985:70), I use the role Causer as distinct from Agent. The reason for distinguishing the two roles is that they lead to different syntactic possibilities. Consider the facts in (52)–(55) noticed by Lødrup (1989:207).

(52) a. The sun burnt me
(Causer)

b. The man burnt the evidence
(Agent)

(53) a.   A burning sun

    b.   *A burning man

(54) a.   The rain damaged the ice sculptures   (Causer)

    b.   The man (with the hammer) damaged the ice sculptures
                                                        (Agent)

(55) a.   The damaging rain

    b.   *The damaging man

The examples show how present participles cannot be interpreted as agentive: a verb with an Agent subject cannot be paraphrased by a present participle modifying an Agent noun. Consider, e.g., the difference between the subject-roles in (52)–(54). Only the Causer-role leads to an acceptable construction with the verb being a present participle modifying the original subject.

Other different roles can also be coordinated. (56) shows a CoP with Theme and Proposition conjuncts. (I use the role Proposition, with Chomsky (1986b), as distinct from Theme, to account for the fact that verbs like *push, kiss* do not take a propositional object.)

(56) a.   Fido thought about [the bone and that he wanted to eat it]
                                                (Theme & Proposition)

    b.   [The death of his wife and that he is in prison now] worry me
                                                (Proposition & Theme)

Now that we see that different (although intuitively also similar in some sense) roles can be coordinated, we seem to have to leave the simple Thematic coordination principle and look for a slightly more complex generalization.

7.3.3. GRIMSHAW'S ARGUMENT STRUCTURE

Let us see if Grimshaw's (1990) theory can help us. Her theory is based on a binary prominence hierarchy along an aspectual dimension in addition to the thematic one. This enrichment may be what we need. We shall look at each dimension in turn.

7.3.3.1. *The thematic dimension*

Grimshaw (1990:2.6), referring to work by Zubizaretta, Rappaport and Levin, argues for a theory where it is not the roles themselves that are important, but their place in a thematic hierarchy. A lexical entry consists of a list of arguments, with no thematic information; the thematic roles can be deduced from the lexical meaning of the head (via its lexical semantic structure). The labeling of roles does not, in fact, play a role at any stage, rather it is their place in the thematic role hierarchy which is important. The hierarchical ordering of thematic roles is one part of what she calls argument structure, the other part being the aspectual structure which divides an event into parts. (We shall return to the aspectual structure later.) Her hierarchy is presented in (57). I have extended it to the one in (58), for reasons that will become clear below.[6]

(57) Agent → Experiencer → Goal / Source / Location → Theme
                                        (Grimshaw 1990:8)

(58) Agent → Causer → Experiencer → Goal / Source / Instrument
     / Benefactive/ Malefactive / Location → Theme

Let us see how part of the lexical entries for some of our verbs would look. I include adjuncts as well as strictly subcategorized-for arguments in order to show how thematic roles constrain coordination in general. This is not a departure from Grimshaw, given that she assumes thematic roles to be predicted from the lexical meaning of the head: just as the thematic roles of *arguments* are predicted by the heads, so are the roles of *adjuncts*. (I do not claim, by doing it in this way, that there is no difference between adjuncts and arguments in other respects.) Following Grimshaw, the order of arguments in the lexical entry reflects the ordering of roles in the hierarchy.

(59) a. break (Agent (Instrument (Theme)))
     b. bake (Agent (Theme))

(60) a. save (Agent (Theme))
             (Causer (Theme))

b. worry (Experiencer (Theme))
      (Experiencer (Proposition))

There is a clear difference between (59) and (60) in that all the roles of a verb in (59) can co-occur in an uncoordinated structure, as in (61) below, in contrast to those in (60). (The asterisks in the examples in (62) below are for the given interpretation. Of course, there might readily be a different interpretation for the PP, such as, e.g., Instrument.)

(61) a. John broke the window with the hammer
                                  (Agent, Theme, Instrument)

     b. The baker baked bread   (Agent, Theme)

(62) a. *My friend saved me by/of/with/in/etc. good luck
                                    (Agent, Theme, Causer)

     b. *That he is in prison by/for/from/etc. her death worries me
                         (Proposition, Theme, Experiencer)

I have represented roles that cannot co-occur, except when coordinated, under each other in the lexical entry. It is a notational choice, to make it clear that the roles do not co-occur in the same type of event.

The semantics of the verb *break* makes it possible (among other things) that an agentive event happens with the help of an instrument. Instrument is, therefore, a possible role for the agentive event. However, it is not possible for the causative event to have an additional instrument participant. As long as the description of the event is neutral with respect to the Instrument part, it is actually possible to coordinate the two different roles, as in (63). However, when the description of the event includes Instrument, which is not compatible with Causer (probably because the Causer is in itself the instrument for the event), coordination is no longer allowed:

(63) a. John and the storm broke the window

     b. *John and the storm broke the window with the hammer
        and its heavy hail.

(64)   break (Agent (Instrument (Theme)))
       (Causer (Comitative (Theme)))

The fact that there is actually a difference between Instrument and
Comitative in (63b) can be seen in the two PPs in (65); the position of the
PP in (65a) is crucial for the interpretation of the PP as being Instrument
rather than Comitative.

(65)   a.   The boy broke the window with the hammer (Instrument)

       b.   The boy with the hammer broke the window (Comitative?)

We are now in a position to state the thematic constraints in a way compatible with Grimshaw's thematic prominence hierarchy:

(66)   *Hierarchical Coordination Principle*: Conjuncts of the same
       CoP must not have thematic roles of different thematic promi-
       nence.

(67)   *Thematic Prominence*
       Two constituents have the same thematic prominence iff
       a.   their coarguments have the same thematic roles, and

       b.   they sit in the same position relative to their coarguments

Now, however, we get a complication with the Norwegian *lukte* 'smell',
smake 'taste' and similar verbs. We have seen that the two possible
argument-structures (given in (68)) are realized in the same way.

(68)   lukte (Experiencer (Theme))
       (Source (Theme))

According to the new principle, we should now be able to coordinate
Experiencer and Source, since they sit in the same position in the lexical
entry, but that would yield the wrong result:

(69)   *[Marit og parfymen] luktet [gass og meg]
                         (Experiencer & Source, Theme & Theme)
          'Marit and the perfume smelt gas and me.'

7.3.3.2. *The aspectual dimension*

We might have explained the reason that the sentences in (46) are unacceptable with the interplay between thematic roles and syntactic position. It is common in the literature (from Fillmore 1968 to Dowty 1991) to link thematic roles to certain syntactic positions. That alone would not work very well for (46), however, where the wrong roles have the same thematic prominence.

We might look for a solution in Grimshaw's aspectual dimension. She assumes, as mentioned above, that in addition to the thematic dimension there is an aspectual dimension. It originates in an analysis of events in terms of accomplishment and resulting state. Aspectual prominence is linked to the first subpart of any event, where the initiating process is. Let us try this solution here: We assume that the roles in (46), which have the *same thematic* prominence, have *different aspectual* prominence, as illustrated below:

(70)

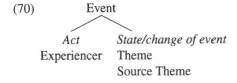

In an event-structure of the event of somebody smelling something, the smeller is in the first sub-event—experiencing the smell of the second part of the event. On the other hand, somebody or something having a certain smell—i.e., being the source of the smell—as in the bottom line of the figure above, clearly involves a state, so that both participants are involved in the second part of the event. Different place in event-structure is difference in prominence, and we therefore extend the Thematic Prominence principle above into the Relative Prominence principle:

(71) *Relative Prominence*
Two constituents have the same relative prominence iff
a. their coarguments have the same thematic roles, and

b. they sit in the same position relative to their coarguments, and

c. they and their coarguments have the same aspectual prominence

We might then have concluded that the reason that the sentences in (46) are not possible, is that the two members that have equal thematic prominence in each CoP have different aspectual prominence, thereby violating the suggested Hierarchical Coordination Principle.

7.3.3.3. *Problems with the aspectual dimension*

However, we cannot just adopt the aspectual dimension for this one reason. We would also have to adopt the rest of the aspectual theory. Central in Grimshaw's discussion is the verb *frighten*. Since the Causer role is not included in her theory, the role which is given to the subject of *frighten*-verbs is Theme. However, if the Causer role is not distinguished from the Theme role, the principle in (66) would not be able to give us the perfectly acceptable (73), since the entry (72) could not give rise to a coordination of thematic roles with different thematic prominence.

(72) frighten (Experiencer (Theme))
      (Agent (Experiencer))

(73) [The evil man and the thunder] frightened the child
                                                (Agent & Theme)

In order for the correct (73) to be generated, it is important to distinguish Causer from Theme: the Causer role would occur with the same prominence as the Agent in the hierarchy, and the result would be fine:

(74) frighten (Causer (Experiencer))
      (Agent (Experiencer))

(75) [The evil man and the thunder] frightened the child
                                                (Agent & Causer)

In Grimshaw's analysis the *aspectual* dimension instead has a value Cause. The idea is defended by the fact that in event-terms, a Cause is the very first part of any activity or event. In order to maintain the thematic coordination principle, however, we would have to see the aspectual dimension as stronger than the thematic dimension, for it to work on the *frighten*-coordination above. In other words, the aspectual Cause would have to somehow override the thematic Theme.

However, there is nothing in the theory to suggest such difference in power between the two dimensions. On the contrary, the two dimensions are equally strong. Consider, e.g., one of the major arguments for the two-tiered analysis; that argument-head compounding is sensitive to both dimensions independently.

Grimshaw (1990:15) explains (76) and (77a,c) by *thematic* prominence: the least prominent participant must be inside the compound—closest to the head:

(76) a. Man fears god   (Experiencer, Theme)

    b. A god-fearing man   (Theme-head)

    c. *A man-fearing god   (Experiencer-head)

However, the *aspectual* dimension plays a part, too, in order to explain why (77b) is not possible (1990:25), in spite of it having (in her analysis) the least prominent member as part of the compound.

(77) a. God frightens man   (Theme (for Grimshaw), Experiencer)
    b. *A god-frightening man   (Theme-head)
    c. *A man-frightening god   (Experiencer-head)

It is here that Cause from the aspectual dimension enters the picture. Since *god*, the least prominent member in the thematic dimension, is Cause, it is the most prominent member in the aspectual dimension. This conflict makes it impossible for any of the two members to join in the compound. We see, then, that both dimensions are equally important.

Grimshaw's analysis of compounds looks convincing, but it turns out to yield some unanswered questions. What are the thematic roles in the examples below? On the basis of the roles she gives *frighten*, we can assume that they are as indicated:

(78) a. The rain destroyed the crop   (Theme (for Grimshaw), Malefactive

    b. Crop-destroying rain   (Malefactive-head)

    c. *Rain-destroying crop   (Theme-head)

(79) a. The soap irritated the skin   (Theme (for Grim.),
                                                     Malefactive)

    b. Skin-irritating soap   (Malefactive-head)

    c. *Soap-irritating skin   (Theme-head)

In (78c) and (79c), predictably, the Theme subject (least prominent thematically) is also Cause (most prominent aspectually), and these participants can therefore not enter a compound with the participle. However, in (78b) and (79b), it is actually fine to compound the thematically most (presumably) prominent participant with the head. It seems, therefore, that the two-tiered prominence hierarchy cannot account for compounds, generally.

Since the prominence hierarchy cannot account for compounds generally, and not for the impossible coordination examples in (46), there seems little point in keeping Cause in a different dimension from the other roles. In the thematic hierarchy Causer would be next to Agent, and is thus of very high prominence. This would predict the unexplained compounds in (78)–(79) above with Grimshaw's own generalizations: Malefactive is less prominent than Causer, and therefore participates in the compounds.

We could then retain the *thematic* version of the hierarchical coordination principle (66). We still have one problem that remains, however, and that is the case of *lukte*. The two argument structures of *lukte* have Experiencer and Source as their most prominent roles, respectively. They should therefore be able to be coordinated, but they are not (see above).

It seems clear that generalizations that are grounded in thematic properties do constrain possible coordinations. It seems, further, that thematic roles as categories are too coarse. Either there must be many more distinct roles, or the roles are themselves not primitives, but can be analyzed into smaller elements. The last possibility is explored by Dowty (1991), who analyzes thematic roles in terms of features. It is plausible that, rather than absolute identity of conjoinable thematic roles, what is needed is thematic features from the same role-type. Let us first look at Dowty's features:[7]

(80) *Agent features*:
- Volition alone
  (*John* is being polite to Bill)
- Sentience/perception alone
  (*John* knows the statement)

- Causation alone
  (*His loneliness* causes his unhappiness)
- Movement alone

  (*The rolling tumbleweed* passed the rock)
- Independent existence

  (*John* needs a new car)

Patient features:
- Change of state
  (John made *a mistake*)
- Incremental theme
  (John filled *the glass* with water)
- Causally affected
  (Smoking causes *cancer*)

- Stationary relative to another participant
  (The bullet entered *the target*)

- Existence not independent of event
  (John built *a house*)
  (Dowty 1991:572–3)

Applying the features to the acceptable examples with different thematic roles above (repeated in (81)–(82)), we find that a thematic generalization can be made.

(81) a. [The evil man and the thunder] frightened the child
  (Agent & Causer)

b. [Guy (who rubbed her with a towel) and the sun] dried her quickly
  (Agent & Causer)

c. I was saved by [good luck and my strong friend]
  (Causer & Agent)

(82) a. Fido thought about [the bone and that he wanted to eat it]
  (Theme & Proposition)

b. [The death of his wife and that he is in prison now] worry me
  (Proposition & Theme)

The examples of Agent and Causer roles in (81) can be described in terms of Dowty's Agent features (volition, causation), while those of

Theme and Proposition cannot. It seems, therefore, that a thematic principle could be formulated along the lines of (83).

> (83) *Thematic Feature Coordination principle*: For two conjuncts A and B of the same CoP, if A has thematic features from a thematic type T, then B has also got features from the same type.

If we now consider the unacceptable coordination with examples like *lukte* (repeated below), we find that, here too, Dowty's features are helpful.

> (84) *Jeg luktet [gass og parfyme]   (Theme & Source)
>   I   smelt gas and perfume
>   'I smelt gas and (of) perfume.'

Neither element of what has been given Theme and Source roles is typical of Dowty's feature types. The Theme role can be described by the feature (stationary), but the Source type does not seem to fit in. The coordination is therefore not valid according to the principle in (83).

It is not possible to pursue the topic further in this book, but it seems clear that coordination is constrained by thematic properties of some sort, possibly of the feature type proposed in Dowty (1991). However, since Dowty's features do not cover the roles of adverbials. There is thus more to be worked out here.

7.3.4. SUMMARY

In this section, we have first looked at the relationship between the lexicon, thematic roles and syntactic categories. We have then considered coordination of categories having different thematic roles, and concluded that this is not acceptable in principle. However, we have seen some examples where different thematic roles could actually be interpreted in conjuncts of the same CoP. In order to account for them within the present framework, we have considered and rejected the theory of Grimshaw (1990), while we still keep the door open for the idea that the relevant generalizations can be found in a theory of thematic features, such as that of Dowty (1991), rather than roles.

7.4. Summary

We have looked at the semantic and thematic properties of conjunction phrases. We have seen that there are several phenomena that support the similarity in structure between coordination and subordination. One factor is cross-linguistic—there is variation between languages with respect to where the distinction between coordination and subordination is drawn. Another factor is the origin of conjunction—they have often have started out as subjunctions. We have further looked at various problems suggested for coordination in the literature, and concluded that most of them are not a problem in the present theory.

We have then considered coordination of categories having different thematic roles, and concluded that thematic properties are important in constraining coordination, although it is not clear what kind of properties or how it happens.

Notes

1. The characterizations as they are presented here must be understood as approximate descriptions, since first, they are my own translations from Norwegian, and second, the terminology is partly invented by Endresen to fit the framework of Cognitive Grammar, and is partly adapted from work by linguists such as George Lakoff and Ronald W. Langacker.

2. The generalization does have its limits; in German, it is possible to have (i), but the coordinating conjunction *und* 'and' can never be used instead of *zu* 'to'.

  (i)   Ich versuche
       I   try

  (ii) Ich versuche dir zu helfen
       I   try   you to help
      'I try to help you.'

  (iii) *Ich versuche dir und helfen
       I   try   you and help
      'I try and help you.'

3. The third characteristic of Boolean coordination is the fact that the CoP is true only if both its conjuncts are true. An interesting puzzle (from Smullyan 1978: puzzle 33) comes out of this strict requirement, which has to do with the relationship between the the truth-values of the conjuncts and the requirements for use:

> On the island of knights and knaves, all the inhabitants are divided into two groups; knights, who always tell the truth, and knaves, who always lie. What are A and B if A says: 'I am a knave, but B isn't'? The answer, of course, is that A is a knave. (Had the statement been uttered by a knight,

then both the conjuncts would have had to be true. The first couldn't be true, however, in the case that A were a knight.)

The interesting point for the present purpose is that the two conjuncts could not have been uttered separately by A, although they could be uttered jointly as a coordination by the same person. Uttered separately, the first statement, 'I am a knave', would have been true, which would have been a violation of a knave's personality. Although the problem follows from rules for truth-conditional logic, these rules coincide with those for natural language, and is therefore relevant in the current discussion. The situation is summarized below.

(i) Impossible for a knave:
    a. I am a knave (true)
    b. B isn't (false)

(ii) Possible for a knave:
    I am a knave, but B isn't (false)

4. The lexical entries for the other conjunctions in English or Norwegian could be the following ones:

(i) *or/eller*. Conjunction, arg1, arg2.
Semantically disjunctive:
[X or 'Y]: $[X \lor Y]$
Semantically uniting:
[X or 'Y]: $[X \land Y]$

In questions with a rising intonation, the Norwegian disjunctive conjunction loses its disjunctive power, and the question turns into a yes/no question:

(ii) Vil du ha   kaffe eller tè? Kaffe, takk.
    will you have coffee or   tee coffee please
    'Do you want coffee or tea? Coffee, please.'

(iii) Vil du ha   kaffe eller té? Ja, takk.
    will you have coffee or   tee Yes please
    'Do you want coffee or tea? Yes, please.'

but/men: Conjunction, arg1, arg2.
Semantically adversative:
[X but Y]: $[X \land Y]$

for/for: Conjunction, arg1, arg2.
Semantically causative:
$[X_{[+CP]} \text{ for } Y_{[+CP]}]: [Y_{[+CP]} \rightarrow X_{[+CP]}]$

5. Many words have the semantic characteristic of being able to pick out members of a set. Besides *respectively, alternatingly* is such a word, and (i) shows that members can be picked out even pair-wise from an ordinary, not co-ordinated, plural NP. (More is said about *respectively* in Chapter 5.)

(i) ... jeg nyter sommeren   og   sitter ved guruenes   føtter, vekselvis.
    I   enjoy the-summer and sit   by   the-gurus' feet,   alternatingly

6. The hierarchies differ from others in certain respects. E.g., in Bresnan and Kanerva (1989:23), the suggested hierarchy has Location following Theme, and Benefactive preceding Instrument. These differences, however, are not relevant for any of the discussions here. The main discussions will depend on the more uncontroversial order of Agent, Experiencer, Malefactive, and Source all preceding Theme.

7. It deserves to be mentioned that Dowty's features are actually proto-features, that may have different weight. I shall not go into this problem complex here.

8

Conclusion

In this book, I have presented a theory of coordination that is based on two independent components: an X-bar theoretic conjunction phrase (CoP) and a generalized transformation (coordinate-alpha). In addition to accounting for more well-known kinds of coordination, these two components together also cater for two very interesting types—unbalanced and extraordinary balanced coordination (UC and EBC).

UC can be schematically represented as *[X&Y] vs. *[Y&X]*, i.e., the order of the conjuncts is essential for the acceptability of the whole construction. An illustrative example is the widely known phenomenon in English in which the second conjunct of an object CoP will not have accusative case: *Mary told it to him and I*. EBC would be $[X_{[\phi]}\&Y_{[\phi]}]/Z$ or $[Y_{[\phi]}\&X_{[\phi]}]/Z$, vs. $*X_{[\phi]}/Z$ or $*Y_{[\phi]}/Z$—in other words, a situation in which a CoP occurs in a position in which a simplex phrase cannot occur. Again English can illustrate this, in the commonly used accusative pronouns in CoP subjects: *Him and me went to the cinema yesterday*.

Both phenomena are more common in the languages of the world than has possibly been previously acknowledged: I have found 32 languages (from closely related to unrelated) in which UC occurs regularly. The direction of the unbalancedness correlates with the general direction of head-complement: out of 12 OV languages, 11 have the deviant UC conjunct in the first position; out of 14 VO languages, all have the deviant UC conjunct in the second position. Six languages have a word order which is mixed or unclear, and cannot be made subject to these generalizations. The deviant conjunct of UC constructions often has features which seem to be unmarked. Similarly, both conjuncts of EBC constructions seem to have the default or unmarked form. These facts show that UC and EBC follow the same regular patterns.

The CoP is very well suited to account for the above facts: the conjuncts naturally sit in different positions, and interact in different ways with the rest of the clause. The specifier conjunct agrees by spec-head agreement with the conjunction (the head). This way, it can give features to the top CoP (such as agreement features) or receive features from CoP (such as case). The complement conjunct has no direct link to the outside, which is the reason for its unmarked nature. In EBC constructions, neither conjunct has direct links with the outside: the specifier conjunct still agrees with the conjunction, but the CoP is not able to neither give nor receive features to the rest of the clause. This happens in speakers or languages that are "CoP sensitive."

The transformation coordinate-alpha is able to coordinate anything. It is not in any way constrained. It can attach the positions of CoP to any category in a CP structure. The result is constrained by X-bar theory, and by thematic properties. Non-constituent coordination is assumed to be repeated binary CoP coordination. Particles such as *both* or *neither* are often called "discontinous conjunctions" or "initial conjunctions" in the literature. In this book they are cross-linguistically argued to be adverbs on the basis of facts relating to word order, and phonological and semantic facts.

It has been generally accepted in the literature that the CSC–ATB constraint counts almost without exception. I have shown that it is actually possible to extract parts of conjuncts, while it is not possible to extract whole conjuncts. The constraint on both is semantic; extraction, i.e. when something from a CoP gets scope over that CoP, triggers a predicate to operate between the conjuncts. This is not always possible; in general, it is always impossible when a whole conjunct is extracted, since a relationship between one thing with nothing is impossible. If a semantic context can be found which makes likely a relationship between the conjuncts, then extraction out of either is fine.

References

Abbott, B. (1976) "Right Node Raising as a test for constituenthood," *Linguistic Inquiry* 7, 639–42.

Abney, S. P. (1987) *The English noun phrase in its sentential aspect*, Ph.D. dissertation, MIT, Cambridge, Mass.

Åfarli, T. A. (1991) "On sentence structure," *Lingua* 84, 239–58.

Åfarli, T., and C. Creider (1987) "Nonsubject pro-drop in Norwegian," *Linguistic Inquiry* 18: 2, 339–45.

Alhoniemi, A. (1985) *Marin kielioppi. Hilfsmittel für das Studium der Finnisch-Ugrishcen Sprachen X*, Suomalais-Ugrilainen Seura, Helsinki.

Andersson, L.-G. 1982 "What is Swedish an exception to? Extractions and island-constraints," in E. Engdahl and E. Ejerhed, eds., *Readings on unbounded dependencies in Scandinavian languages*, Umeå studies in the humanities 43, Umeå, 33–45.

Anderson, S. R. (1985) "Inflectional morphology," in T. Shopen, ed., iii. 150–201.

Andrews, A. (1982) "The representation of case in Modern Icelandic," in J. Bresnan, ed., *The mental representation of grammatical relations*, MIT Press, Cambridge, Mass., 427–503.

Andrews, A. (1985) "The major functions of the noun phrase," in T. Shopen, ed., i. 62–154.

Aoun, J., E. Benmamoun, and D. Sportiche (1994) "Agreement, word order, and Conjunction in some varieties of Arabic," *Linguistic Inquiry* 25: 2, 195–220.

Arden, A. H. (1954) *A progressive grammar of common Tamil*, Christian Literature Society, Madras, India.

Arnott, D. W. (1970) *The nominal and verbal system of Fula*, Oxford University Press, Oxford.

Barrs, A., and H. Lasnik (1986) "A note on anaphora and double objects," *Linguistic Inquiry* 17, 347–54.

Barry, G., and M. Pickering (1990) "Dependency and constituency in categorial grammar," MS, Edinburgh University, Centre for Cognitive Science, Edinburgh.

Bartlett, J. (1972) *Concordance to Shakespeare*, Macmillan St. Martin's Press, London.

Benincà, P., and G. Cinque (1990) "On certain difference between enclisis and proclisis," Paper presented at the University of Geneva.

Berntsen, M., and A. B. Larsen (1925) *Stavanger bymål*, Utgitt av Bymålslaget, I kommisjon hos H. Aschehoug & Co., Oslo.

Best, R. I., and O. Bergin (1929) *Lebor na huidre*, Royal Irish Academy, Dublin.

Blass, R. (1989) "Pragmatic effects of coordination: The case of 'and' in Sissala," *UCL Working Papers in Linguistics* 1, University College, University of London, 32–52.

Bleiler, E. F. (1978) *Basic Japanese grammar*, Charles E. Tuttle Company, Tokyo.

Bokamba, E. G. (1985) "Verbal agreement as a non-cyclic rule in Bantu," in D. L. Goyvaerts, ed., *African Linguistics: Essays in memory of M. W. K. Semikenke* (Studies in the Sciences of Language 6), Benjamins, Amsterdam, 9–54.

Borsley, R. D. (1994) "In defense of coordinate structures," *Linguistic Analysis* 24: 3–4, 218–46.

Borsley, R. D., and J. Stephens (1989) "Agreement and the position of subjects in Breton," *NLLT* 7, 407–27.

Botha, T. J. R., et al. (1989) eds. *Inleiding tot die Afrikaanse taalkunde*, Academica, Pretoria.

Bresnan, J., and J. M. Kanerva. (1989) "Locative inversion in Chichewa: a case study of factorization in grammar," *Linguistic Inquiry* 20: 1, 1–50.

Bright, W. (1992) (ed.) *International encyclopedia of linguistics*, Oxford University Press, Oxford.

Brody, M. (1990) "Some remarks on the focus field in Hungarian," *UCL Working Papers in Linguistics* 2, University College, London.

Burgers, M. P. O. (1963) *Teach yourself Afrikaans*, English Universities Press, London.

Burton, S., and J. Grimshaw (1992) "Coordination and VP-internal subjects," *Linguistic Inquiry* 23, 305–12.

Bussman, H. (1990) *Lexicon der Sprachwissenschaft*, Alfred Kröner Verlag, Stuttgart.

Chomsky, N. (1955) "The logical structure of linguistic theory," MS, Harvard, Cambridge, Mass.

Chomsky, N. (1957) *Syntactic structures*, Mouton, The Hague.

Chomsky, N. (1965) *Aspects of the theory of syntax*, MIT Press, Cambridge, Mass.

Chomsky, N. (1970) "'Remarks on nominalisation," in R. A. Jacobs and P. S. Rosenbaum, eds., *Readings in English transformational grammar*, Ginn, London, 184–221.

Chomsky, N. (1981) *Lectures on government and binding*, Foris, Dordrecht.

Chomsky, N. (1982) *Some concepts and consequences of the theory of government and binding*, MIT Press, Cambridge, Mass.

Chomsky, N. (1986a) *Barriers*, MIT Press, Cambridge, Mass.

Chomsky, N. (1986b) *Knowledge of language*, Praeger, New York.

Chomsky, N. (1988) "Some notes on the economy of derivation and representation," *MIT Working papers in linguistics* 10, 43–74.

Chomsky, N. (1994) "Bare phrase structure," *MIT Occasional Papers in Linguistics* 5, MIT, Cambridge, Mass.

Chomsky, N. (1995) *The minimalist program*, MIT Press, Cambridge, Mass.

Contreras, H. (1991) "On the position of subjects," in S. D. Rothstein, ed., *Syntax and Semantics 25: Perspectives on phrase structure: heads and licensing*, Academic Press, San Diego, 63–80.

Cook, E.-D. (1984) *A Sarcee grammar*, University of British Columbia Press, Vancouver.

Corbett, G. G. (1979) "The Agreement Hierarchy," *Journal of Linguistics* 15, 203–24.

Corbett, G. G. (1983) "Resolution rules: agreement in person, number, and gender," in G. Gazdar, E. Klein, and K. Pullum, eds., *Order, concord and constituency*, Foris, Dordrecht, 175–206.

Corbett, G. G. (1991) *Gender*, Cambridge University Press, Cambridge.

Corbett, G. G., and R. J. Hayward (1987) "Gender and number in Bayso," *Lingua* 73, 1–28.

Crystal, D. (1991) *A Dictionary of linguistics and phonetics*, Basil Blackwell, Oxford.

Diderichsen, P. (1968) *Elementaer Dansk Grammatik*, Gyldendal, Copenhagen.

Dik, S. C. (1968) "Coordination: its implications for the theory of general linguistics," North-Holland Publishing, Amsterdam.

Dixon, R. M. W. (1972) *The Dyirbal language of North Queensland*, Cambridge University Press, Cambridge.

Dougherty, R. C. (1970) "A grammar of coordinate conjoined structures," *Language* 46, 850–98.

Dover, K. J. (1960) *Greek Word Order*, Cambridge University Press, Cambridge.

Dowty, D. (1991) "Thematic proto-roles and argument selection," *Language* 67: 3, 547–619.

Dyvik, H. (1980) *Grammatikk og empiri*, Doctoral dissertation, University of Bergen, Bergen.

Eftichidou, E., I. Manolessou, and M. Vassiliou (1995) *Greek proper names and the nature of R*, Paper given at The Second International Conference of Greek Linguistics, Salzburg.

Eitrem, S. (1966) *Latinsk grammatikk*, Aschehoug, Oslo.

Emonds, E. (1972) "A reformulation of certain syntactic transformations," in S. Peters, ed., *Goals of Linguistic theory*, Prentice-Hall, Englewood Cliffs, NJ.

Emonds, J. (1986) "Grammatically Deviant Prestige Constructions," in M. Brame, H. Contreras, and F. Newmeyer, eds., *A festschrift for Sol Saporta*, Noit Amrofer, Seattle, 93–129.

Endresen, R. T. (1992a) "Og og å—homonymi eller polysemi?" MS Department of Linguistics, University of Oslo, Oslo.

Endresen, R. T. (1992b) "Synkront og diakront om og og å," Talk presented at the seminar Lingvistikk med någå attåt, Department of Linguistics, University of Oslo, Oslo.

Fillmore, C. J. (1968) "The case for case," in E. Bach and R. T. Harms, eds., *Universals in linguistic theory*, Holt, Rinehart and Winston, New York.

Findreng, Å. (1976) *Zur Kongruenz in Person und Numerus zwischen Subjekt und finitem Verb im modernen Deutsch*, Universitetsforlaget, Oslo.

Fukui, N., and M. Speas (1986) "Specifiers and projection" in N. Fukui, T. Rapoport, and E. Sagey, eds., *MIT Working Papers in Linguistics* 8, MIT, Cambridge, Mass., 129–72.

Gazdar, G. (1981) "Unbounded dependencies and coordinate structure," *Linguistic Inquiry* 12, 155–84.

Gazdar, G., E. Klein, G. Pullum, and I. Sag (1985) *Generalized phrase structure grammar*, Basil Blackwell, Oxford.

George, L. (1980) *Analogical generalisations of natural language syntax*, Ph.D. dissertation, MIT, Cambridge, Mass.

Georgopoulos, C. (1991) "Canonical government and the specifier parameter," *Natural Language and Linguistic Theory* 9, 1–46.

Gil, D. (1982) "Case-marking, phonological size, and linear order," in P. J. Hopper and S. A. Thompson, eds., *Syntax and Semantics 15: Studies in transitivity*, Academic Press, New York, 117–42.

Givón, T. (1970) "The resolution of gender conflicts in Bantu conjunction: when syntax and semantics clash," in *Papers from the sixth regional meeting, Chicago Linguistic Society*, Chicago, 250–61.

Givón, T. (1976) "Topic, pronoun and grammatical agreement," in C. Li, ed., *Subject and topic*, Academic Press, New York.

Givón, T. (1979) "Grammar as a processing strategy," in T. Givón, ed., *Syntax and semantics 12: Discourse and syntax*, Academic Press, New York.

Gleitman, L. R. (1965) "Coordinating conjunctions in English," *Language* 41, 260–93.

Goldsmith, J. (1985) "A principled exception to the Coordinate Structure Constraint," *CLS* 21, part 1, Chicago Linguistic Society, Chicago, 133–43.

Goodall, G. (1987) *Parallel structures in syntax. Coordination, causatives and restructuring*, Cambridge University Press, Cambridge.

Greenberg, J. H. (1963) "Some universals of grammar with particular reference to the order of meaningful elements," in J. H. Greenberg, ed., *Universals of language*, MIT Press, Cambridge, Mass., 73–113.

Grimshaw, J. (1981) "Form, function and the language acquisition device," in C. L. Baker and John McCarthy, eds., *The logical problem of language acquisition*, MIT Press, Cambridge, Mass., 165–82.

Grimshaw, J. (1990) *Argument structure*, MIT Press, Cambridge, Mass.

Grønbeck, K. (1979) *The structure of the Turkic languages*, Indiana University Research Institute for Inner Asian Studies, Bloomington, Ind.

Grootveld, M. (1992) "On the representation of coordination," in R. Bok-Bennema and R. van Hout, eds., *Linguistics in the Netherlands 1992*, 61–73. John Benjamin's Publishing Company, Amsterdam.

Gruber, G. (1976) *Lexical Structure in Syntax and Semantics*, North Holland, Amsterdam.

Haegeman, L. (1991) *Introduction to government & binding theory*, Basil Blackwell, Oxford.

Haff, M. H. (1987) *Coordonnants et éléments coordonnés*, Solum Forlag, Didier Érudition, Oslo and Paris.

Haman, A. (1962) *Lärobok i estniska*, Bokförlaget Medborgarskolan, Uppsala.

Harlow, S. (1989) "The syntax of Welsh soft mutation," *NLLT* 7, 289–316.

Hartmann, K. (1991) *Koordination —"Lücken" in der Forschung?* Mag. art. thesis, Köln.

Hayward, R. J., and G. G. Corbett (1988) "Resolution rules in Qafar," *Linguistics* 26, 259–79.

Heim, I., H. Lasnik and R. May (1991) "Reciprocity and plurality," *Linguistic Inquiry* 22, 63–101.

Hellan, L. (1988) *Anaphora in Norwegian and the theory of grammar*, Foris, Dordrecht.

Hestvik, A. (1992) "LF movement of pronouns and antisubject orientation," *Linguistic Inquiry* 23, 557–94.

Heycock, C., and A. Kroch (1992) "Verb movement and coordination in the Germanic languages: evidence for a relational perspective on licensing," MS and Paper presented at the 8th Workshop on Comparative Germanic Syntax, Tromsø, 20–2 Nov.

Hoeksema, J. (1983) "Plurality and conjunction," in A. G. B. ter Meulen, ed., *Studies in modeltheoretic semantics*, Foris, Dordrecht, 63–106.

Hoeksema, J. (1987) "The semantics of non-Boolean 'and'," Paper presented at the LSA/ASL meeting, Stanford, Calif., July.

Hoekstra, E. (1992) "On the nature of expletive heads," Paper presented at the 8th Workshop on Comparative Germanic Syntax, Tromsø, 20–2 Nov.

Hoem, I., E. Hovdhaugen, and A. M. Vonen (1992) *Kupu Mai Te Tuutolu. Tokelau oral literature*, Institute for Comparative Research in Human Culture, Serie B: Skrifter, LXXXIV, Scandinavian University Press, Oslo.

Höhle, T. N. (1989) "Assumptions about asymmetric coordination in German," J. Mascaro and M. Nespor, eds., *Grammar in Progress. GLOW essays for Henk van Riemsdijk*, Foris, Dordrecht.

Holmberg, A. (1986) *Word order and syntactic features*, Doctoral dissertation, University of Stockholm.

Hudson, R. A. (1976) "Conjunction reduction, gapping, and right-node raising," *Language* 52, 535–62.

Hudson, R. A. (1987) "Zwicky on heads," *Journal of Linguistics* 23, 109–32.

Hudson, R. A. (1988) "Coordination and grammatical relations," *Journal of linguistics* 24, 303–42.

Iversen, R. (1918) *Syntaksen i Tromsø bymaal*, Følgeskrift til "Maal og minne," I kommisjon hos H. Aschehoug & Co., Kristiania (Oslo).

Jackendoff, R. (1977) *X′ syntax*, MIT Press, Cambridge, Mass.

Jackendoff, R. (1990) "On Larson's treatment of the double object construction," *Linguistic Inquiry*, 21: 3, 427–56.

Jakobson, R. (1936) "Beitrag zur allgemeinen Kasuslehre," *Travaux du Cercle Linguistique de Prague*, 240–99. Reprinted in E. P. Hamp, F. W. Householder, and R. Austerlitz, eds., *Readings in Linguistics II*, University of Chicago Press, Chicago, 1966.

Johannessen, J. B. (1989) "Klitika—en avgrensning," *Norsk lingvistisk tidsskrift* 2, 117–47.

Johannessen, J. B. (1990) *Unbalanced coordination—barriers, binding and thematic relations*, Research Paper No. 44, Centre for Cognitive Science, Edinburgh University, Edinburgh.

Johannessen, J. B. (1992) "Prominence constraints on coordination?" Paper presented at the autumn meeting of the Linguistic Association of Great Britain, University of Surrey, Guildford.

Johannessen, J. B. (1993a) "A configurational theory of coordination," in D. Adger and C. S. Rhys, eds., *Working papers* 8, Centre for Cognitive Science, Edinburgh University, Edinburgh.

Johannessen, J. B. (1993b) "Coordination and extraction," Paper presented at the spring meeting of the Linguistic Association of Great Britain, University of Birmingham.

Johannessen, J. B. (1993c) *Coordination. A minimalist approach*, D. Phil. thesis, University of Oslo.

Johannessen, J. B. (1993d) "Coordinate-alpha and unbalanced coordination," in A. Kathol and M. Bernstein, eds., *ESCOL'93, Proceedings of the Tenth Eastern States Conference on Linguistics*, Cornell University, Dept. of Modern Languages and Linguistics, Ithaca, NY, 153–62.

Johannessen, J. B. (1994) "Coordinate-alpha," in P. Ackemaa and M. Schoorlemmer, eds., *Console 1 Proceedings*, Holland Academic Graphics, The Hague, 99–114.

Johannessen, J. B. (1996) "Partial agreement and coordination," *Linguistic Inquiry* 27: 4, 661–76.

Johannessen, J. B. (forthcoming) Review of Birgit Wesche (1995) *Symmetric Coordination*, to appear in *Linguistische Berichte*, Frankfurt.

Johnsen, A. (1942) *Kristiansands bymål*, Utgitt av Bymålslaget, H. Aschehoug & Co., Oslo.

Johnsen, L. (1988) "A note on subcoordination," *University of Trondheim Working Papers in Linguistics* 6, 195–202.

Josefsson, G. (1991) "Pseudocoordination—A VP + VP coordination," *Working Papers in Scandinavian Syntax* 47, 130–56.

Joseph, D. D., and I. Philippaki-Warburton (1987) *Modern Greek*, Routledge, London.

Kayne, R. (1984) *Connectedness and binary branching*, Foris, Dordrecht.

Kayne, R. (1994) *The Antisymmetry of Syntax*, MIT Press, Cambridge, Mass.

Kershaw, P. (1992) "Conjunction and case-assignment: a parameter," Handout and abstract from a talk given at the Second Language Research Forum, University of Minnesota, 4 Apr.

Kiparsky, P. (1968) "Tense and mood in Indo-European syntax," *Foundations of Language* 4, 30–57.

Lakoff, G. (1986) "Frame semantic control of the cordinated structure constraint," in A. M. Farley et al., eds., *CLS 22, Part 2: Papers from the parasession on pragmatics and grammatical theory*, CLS, Chicago, 152–67.

Lambek, J. (1958) "The mathematics of sentence structure," *American Mathematical Monthly* 65, 154–70.

Lang, E. (1984) *The semantics of coordination*, John Benjamins, Amsterdam.

Lang, E. (1991) "Koordinierende Konjuntionen," in A. von Stechow and D. Wunderlich, eds., *Semantik/Semantics*, Walter de Gruyter, Berlin, 597–623.

Langacker, R. W. (1969) "Pronominalization and the chain of command," in D. A. Reibel and S. Schane, eds, *Modern Studies in English, Readings in Transformational Grammar*, Prentice-Hall Inc., Englewood Cliffs, NJ, 160–86.

Larsen, A. B., and G. Stoltz (1912) *Bergens bymaal*, Bymålslaget / H. Aschehoug & Co., Kristiania (Oslo).

Larson, R. K. (1990) "Double objects revisited: Reply to Jackendoff," *Linguistic Inquiry* 21: 4, 589–632.

Lasersohn, P. (1995) *Plurality, conjunction and events*, Kluwer Academic Publishers, Dordrecht.

Lasnik, H., and J. J. Kupin (1977) "A restrictive theory of transformational grammar," *Theoretical Linguistics* 4, 173–96.

Lewis, G. L. (1967) *Turkish grammar*, Clarendon Press, Oxford.

Link, G. (1984) "Hydras. On the logic of relative constructions with multiple heads," in F. Landmann and F. Veltmann, eds., *Varieties of formal semantics*, Foris, Dordrecht, 245–57.

Lødrup, H. (1977) "Mikill maðr ok sterkr," Norskrift, Nordic Department, University of Oslo, 30–5.

Lødrup, H. (1989) *Norske hypotagmer*, Novus, Oslo.

Lødrup, H. (1990) "VP-topicalization and the verb gjøre in Norwegian," *Working Papers in Scandinavian Syntax* 45, 3–12, Lund, Sweden.

Longacre, R. E. (1985) "Sentences as combinations of clauses," in T. Shopen, ed., ii. 235–86,

Longobardi, G. (1994) "Reference and Proper names," *Linguistic Inquiry* 25: 4, 609–66.

Lønning, J. T. (1989) *Some aspects of the logic of plural noun phrases*, Ph.D. dissertation. Available as Cosmos report 11, Department of Mathematics, University of Oslo, Oslo.

Lorimer, D. L. R. (1935) *The Burushaski language*, Instituttet for sammenlignende kulturforskning, H. Aschehoug & Co., Oslo.

McCawley, J. (1988) *The syntactic phenomena of English*, i and ii, University of Chicago Press, Chicago.

Mackridge, P. (1987) *The modern Greek language*, Clarendon Press, Oxford.

McNally, L. (1992) "VP coordination and the VP-internal subject hypothesis," *Linguistic Inquiry* 23, 329–35.

Marantz, A. (1984) *On the nature of grammatical relations*, Linguistic Inquiry Monograph 10, MIT Press, Cambridge, Mass.

Martin, S. E. (1975) *A reference grammar of Japanese*, Yale University Press, New Haven.

Matthews, P. H. (1981) *Syntax*, Cambridge University Press, Cambridge.

May, R. (1991) "Indices and identity: a study of the theory of anaphora I, II, III," Talks and handouts from a national Norwegian seminar for research students, University of Tromsø, 23–5 May.

Mithun, M. (1988) "The grammaticization of coordination," in J. Haiman and S. A. Thompson, eds., *Clause combining in grammar and discourse*, John Benjamins Publishing Company, Amsterdam, 331–60.

Moltmann, F. (1992) "On the interpretation of three-dimensional syntactic trees," To appear in *Proceedings from SALT II*.

Morgenstierne, G. (1935) "Preface," In D. L. R. Lorimer.

Morrison, T. (1988) *Sula*, Triad Grafton Books, London.

Muadz, H. (1991) *A planar theory of coordination*, Ph.D. dissertation, University of Arizona, Tucson.

Munn, A. (1987a) "Coordinate structure and X-bar theory," *McGill Working Papers in Linguistics* 4, McGill University.

Munn, A. (1987b) "Coordinate structures, X-bar theory and parasitic gaps," Honours research paper, McGill University.

Munn, A. (1992) "A null operator analysis of ATB gaps," *Linguistic Review* 9, 1–26.

Muysken, P. C., and H. C. van Riemsdijk (1985) (eds.) *Features and projections*, Foris, Dordrecht.

Napoli, D. J. (1983) "Comparative ellipsis: a phrase structure analysis," *Linguistic Inquiry* 14, 675–94.

Nordgård, T., and T. A. Åfarli (1990) *Generativ syntaks. Ei innføring via norsk*, Novus forlag, Oslo.

Nygaard, M. (1917) *Bemerkninger, rettelser og supplementer til min Norrøn Syntax*, Videnskabsselskapets skrifter. Kristiania.

Nygaard, M. (1966) (1905). *Norrøn syntax*, Aschehoug, Oslo.

van Oirsouw, R. R. (1980) *Deletion processes in coordinate structures in English*, Ph.D. thesis, University of Cambridge.

van Oirsouw, R. R. (1987) *The syntax of coordination*, Croom Helm, London.

Ouhalla, J. (1991) *Functional Categories and Parametric Variation*, Routledge, London.

Partee, B., and M. Rooth (1983) "Generalized conjunction and type ambiguity," in R. Bäuerle, C. Schwarze, and A. von Stechow, eds., *Studies in discourse theory and interpretation of language*, Walter de Gruyter, Berlin, 361–83.

Payne, J. R. (1985) "Complex phrases and complex sentences," in T. Shopen, ed., ii. 3–41.

Pesetsky, D. (1982) *Paths and categories*, Ph.D. dissertation, MIT, Cambridge, Mass.

Platzack, C., and A. Holmberg (1989) "The role of Agr and finiteness in Germanic VO languages," *Working papers in Scandinavian syntax* 43, Department of Scandinavian Linguistics, Lund, 51–76.

Pollard, C. (1991) *Topics in constraint-based syntactic theory*, Lecture notes given in The Third European Summer School in Language, Logic and Information, Universität des Saarlandes, Saarbrücken, 12–23 Aug. Based on C. Pollard and I. A. Sag, "Agreement, Binding and Control: IBSS2," draft of 24 June 24.

Pollard, C., and I. A. Sag (1987) *Information-based syntax and semantics*, i. CSLI Lecture notes 13, CSLI, Stanford, Calif.

Pollard, C., and I. A. Sag (1988) "An information-based theory of agreement," MS, Carnegie Mellon University/Stanford University.

Pollard, C., and I. A. Sag (1990) "Anaphors in English and the scope of binding theory," to appear in *Linguistic Inquiry*.

Pollard, C., and I. A. Sag (1991a) "Ch 6: Binding theory," in C. Pollard (1991).

Pollard, C., and I. A. Sag (1991b) "Ch 2: Agreement," in C. Pollard (1991).

Pollard, C., and I. A. Sag (1994) *Head-driven Phrase-Structure Grammar*, University of Chicago Press, Chicago.

Pollock, J.-Y. (1989) "Verb movement, UG and the structure of IP," *Linguistic Inquiry* 20, 365–424.

Preuß, S. (1989) *Koordination und Kongruenz in einer Verallgemeinerten Phrasenstrukturgrammatik*, Magister thesis, Teknische Universität Berlin, Berlin.

Pullum, G., and A. M. Zwicky (1986) "Resolution of syntactic feature conflict," *Language* 62: 4, 751–73.

Quirk, R., S. Greenbaum, G. Leech, and J. Svartvik (1985) *A comprehensive grammar of the English language*, Longman, London.

Radford, A. (1988) *Transformational grammar*, Cambridge University Press, Cambridge.

Radford, A. (1990) *Syntactic Theory and the Acquisition of English Syntax*, Basil Blackwell, Oxford.

Rappaport, M., and B. Levin (1988) "What to do with theta roles," in W. Wilkins, ed., *Syntax and semantics 21, Thematic relations*, Academic Press, New York, 7–36.

Remes, H. (1982) *Viron kielioppi*, WSOY, Helsinki.

Renzi, L. (1988) (ed.) *Grande grammatica italiana di consultazione*, i, IL Mulino, Bologna.

Rizzi, L. (1990) *Relativized minimality*, MIT Press, Cambridge, Mass.

Rohdenburgh, G. (1974) *Sekundäre Subjektivierungen im Englishen und Deutschen*, Bielefeld.

Ross, J. R. (1967) *Constraints on variables in syntax*, Ph.D. dissertation, MIT, Cambridge, Mass.

Ross, J. R. (1970) "Gapping and the order of constituents," in M. Bierwisch and K. Heidolph, eds., *Progress in linguistics*, Mouton, The Hague, 249–59.

Ross, J. R. (1986) *Infinite Syntax!* Reprinted Ph.D. dissertation, Ablex Publishing Corporation, Norwood, NJ.

Rothstein, S. D. (1992a) "Case and NP licensing," *NLLT*, 119–40.

Rothstein, S. D. (1992b) "Heads, projections and category determination," in K. Leffel and D. Bouchard, eds., *Views on Phrase Structure*, Kluwer, Dordrecht, 97–112.

Roussou, A., and I. M. Tsimpli (1994) "On the interaction of case and definiteness in Modern Greek," in I. Philippaki-Warburton, K. Nicolaidis, and M. Sifianou, eds., *Themes in Greek linguistics : papers from the First International Conference on Greek Linguistics, Reading, September 1993*, Benjamins, Amsterdam, 69–76.

Rouveret, A. (1990) "X-bar theory, minimality, and barrierhood in Welsh," in Randall Hendrick, ed., *Syntax and semantics 23: The syntax of the modern celtic languages*, Academic Press, San Diego, 28–80.

Sadock, J. M. (1985) "Autolexical syntax: a proposal for the treatment of noun incorporation and similar phenomena," *NLLT* 3, 379–439.

Sadock, J. M. (1986) "Some notes on noun incorporation," *Language* 62, 19–31.

Sag, I., G. Gazdar, T. Wasow, and S. Weisler. (1985) "Coordination and how to distinguish categories," *NLLT* 3, 117–71.

Schachter, P. (1977) "Constraints on coordination," *Language* 53: 1, 86–102.

Schachter, P. (1985) "Parts-of-speech systems," in T. Schopen, ed., i. 3–61.

Schütz, A. J. (1969) "Nguna texts," *Oceanic Linguistics Special Publication No. 4*, University of Hawaii Press, Honolulu.

Schwartz, B. D. (1985) "Case and conjunction," *Southern California Occasional Papers in Linguistics* 10, 161–86.

di Sciullo, A. M., and E. Williams (1987) *On the definition of word*, Linguistic Inquiry Monograph 14, MIT Press, Cambridge, Mass.

Sebba, M. (1987) *The syntax of serial verbs*, John Benjamins Publishing Company, Amsterdam.

Shieber, S. (1986) *An introduction to the unification-based approaches to grammar*, CSLI Lecture Notes 4. CSLI, Stanford, Calif.

Shopen, T. (1985) (ed.) *Language typology and syntactic description*, i–iii. Cambridge University Press, Cambridge.

Sigurðsson, H.Á. (1988) *From OV to VO: Evidence from Old Icelandic*, Working Papers in Scandinavian Syntax, Department of Scandinavian Linguistics, Lund, Sweden.

Smullyan, R. M. (1978) *What is the name of this book?* Prentice-Hall, Englewood Cliffs, NJ.

Speas, M. J. (1990) *Phrase-structure in natural language*, Kluwer, Dordrecht.

Stahlke, H. (1984) "Independent and clitic pronouns in English," in *Papers from Chicago Linguistic Society*, Chicago, 358–64.

Steedman, M. (1985) "Dependency and coordination in the grammar of Dutch and English," *Language* 61: 3, 523–68.

Steedman, M. (1989) *Gapping as constituent coordination*, MS–CIS–89–76, LINC LAB 162, University of Pennsylvania, Philadelphia.

Stowell, T. (1981) *Origins of phrase structure*, Ph.D. dissertation, MIT, Cambridge, Mass.

Svenonius, P. (1992) "The extended projection of N: identifying the head of the noun phrase," *Working Papers in Scandinavian Syntax* 49, 95–121.

Szabolcsi, A. (1989) "Bound variables in syntax (are there any?)," in J. Bartsch et al., eds., *Proceedings of the Sixth Amsterdam Colloquium*, Grass, Foris, Dordrecht.

Tait, M. E. (1991) *The syntactic projection of morphological categories*, Ph.D. dissertation, University of Edinburgh.

Toporičič, J. (1972) *Slovenski knjižni jezik*, iii. *Založba Obzorja*, Maribor.

Trávníček, F. (1949) *Mluvnice spisovné cestiny*, ii. *Skladba*, Melantrich, Prague.

Tsimpli, I. A. (1990) "The clause structure and word order of Modern Greek," *UCL Working Papers in Linguistics* 2, University College, University of London, 226–55.

Van Valin jr., R. D. (1985) "Case marking and the structure of the Lakhota clause," in J. Nichols and A. C. Woodbury, eds., *Grammar inside and outside the clause*, Cambridge University Press, Cambridge, 363–416.

Van Valin jr., R. D. (1986) "An empty category as the subject of a tensed S in English," *Linguistic Inquiry* 17, 581–6.

Van Valin jr., R. D. (1990) "Semantic parameters of split transitivity," *Language* 66: 1, 221–96.

de Vries, G. (1992) *On coordination and ellipsis*, Doctoral dissertation, Catholic University of Brabant, Tilburg.

Watson, R. (1966) "Clause to sentence gradations in Pacoh," *Lingua* 16, 166–88.

Wesche, B. (1995) *Symmetric coordination. An alternative theory of phrase structure*, Max Niemeyer Verlag, Tübingen.

Westergaard, M. R. (1986) *Definite NP anaphora: a pragmatic approach*, Norwegian University Press, Oslo.

Wiklund, A.-L. (1996) "Pseudocoordination is subordination," Paper presented at the XVIth Scandinavian Conference of Linguistics, Turku.

Wilder, C. (1994) "Coordination, ATB and Ellipsis," in J.-W. Zwart, ed., *Minimalism and Kayne's Asymmetry Hypothesis*, Groninger Arbeiten zur Germanistischen Linguistik 37, Groningen, 291–329.

Wilder, C. (1995) "Some properties of ellipsis in coordination," *Geneva Generative Working Papers*, ii/2, 23–61. Also in A. Alexiadou and T. A. Hall, eds., *Studies on Universal Grammar and Typological Variation*, John Benjamins, Amsterdam, 1997.

Williams, E. (1978) "Across-the-board rule application," *Linguistic Inquiry* 9, 31–43.

Williams, E. (1981a) "Transformationless grammar," *Linguistic Inquiry* 12: 4, 645–53.

Williams, E. (1981b) "Argument structure and morphology," *Linguistic Review* 1, 81–114.

Williamson, K. (1989) "Niger-Congo overview," in J. Bendor-Samuel, ed., *The Niger–Congo languages*, University Press of America, Lanham, 3–46.

Xromov, A. L. (1972) *Jagnobskij jazyk*, Nauka, Moscow.

Zingarelli, N. (1990) *Il nuovo Zingarelli. Vocabolario della lingua italiana*, Zanichelli, Bologna.

van Zonneveld, R. (1992) "Ongelijke nevenschikking en SGF," *Tabu* 22: 3, 153–170.

Zribi-Hertz, A. (1989) "Anaphor binding and narrative point of view: English reflexive pronouns in sentence and discourse," *Language* 65: 4, 695–727.

Zubizaretta, M. L. (1987) *Levels of representation in the lexicon and in the syntax*, Foris, Dordrecht.

Zwart, J.-W. (1991) "Subject deletion in Dutch: a difference between subjects and topics," in M. Kas, E. Reuland, and C. Vet, eds., *Language and Cognition* 1, University of Groningen, Groningen, 333–49.

Zwart, J.-W. (1992) "SOV languages are head-initial," Paper presented at the 8th Workshop on Comparative Germanic Syntax, Tromsø, 20–2 Nov.

Zwart, J.-W. (1995) "Review of Johannessen, J. B.: Coordination. A minimalist approach," *GLOT International* 1, 11–3.

Zwicky, A. (1984) "Welsh soft mutation and the case of object NPs," in J. Drogo, V. Mishra, and D. Testen, eds., *Papers of the 20th Regional Meeting of the Chicago Linguistic Society*, Chicago, 287–402.

Zwicky, A. (1985) "Heads," *Journal of Linguistics* 21, 1–30.

Zwicky, A. (1987) "Suppressing the Zs," *Journal of Linguistics* 23, 133–48.

Zwicky, A. M. (1990) "What are we talking about when we are talking about serial verbs?" in B. D. Joseph and A. M. Zwicky, eds., *When verbs collide: papers from the 1990 Ohio State miniconference on serial verbs*, The Ohio State University, Columbus, 1–13.

Index

abessive 44
absolutive 20, 95, 120, 121, 136
accusative 120, 121–2, 123, 136
Across the Board Principle *see* CSC/ATB
adjacency factors 8
adjectives, verbal 20–1
adjuncts, thematic 253
adpositions 43–6
adverbs 244–5, 271
  initial conjunctions as 154–62, 168,
    170, 271
affixes 43–6, 98
Afrikaans 27–8, 56, 57
Agent 254, 256–7, 258, 259, 262, 265–6
agreement 46–7, 76–8, 96, 97, 99, 180
alternatingly 200, 269
Amharic 34–5, 55
anaphor 63, 247, 250
and 245–6
  lexical entry 120–1, 123, 124, 126,
    140, 141, 153, 248
answers, simple 121–2
aorist imperative, Greek 35
apposition 86, 89–90
Arabic:
  agreement 19, 31, 67
  Classical 31
  DP or clausal coordination 180
  UC in Palestinian 31–2, 56, 119
aspect 2, 49, 129–30, 146, 261–6
assigning-type coordination 8–9
  see also under EBC; UC
asyndetic coordination 84
avoidance strategies 25, 39

balanced coordination 119, 139–40
  see also EBC; OBC
Bantu languages 25
Bare Phrase Structure approach 112
barrier approach 114–15
behindance 166, 167
Benefactive 258
bilingualism 88
binary branching 144, 148
binary coordination 6, 8
  multiple coordination analyzed
    as 143–5, 154

Boolean operator *and* 245–6
both 91, 149, 151–2, 154–62, 167,
  182–3, 207–8, 271
Breton 42
Burushaski 9–10, 27, 55, 117, 120
BWD *see* Deletion (Backward)

Canonical Structural Representation 252
case:
  assignment 38–9, 113–27, 136, 138,
    153, 169
  checking, in deletion 187
  Chomsky's theory 120, 123
  conjunctions and 119–23, 136, 138,
    153, 154, 169
  lack of 121, 139, 143
  multiple coordination 147, 153, 154
  in OBC 139–40
  in UC 9–20, 21–5, 38–9, 113–27
  unmarked 121, 136–8, 270
  see also default case *and individual
    cases*
categorial grammar (CG) 209–11
category-specific assignment *see* EBC
CATE suffixes, Estonian 16, 44–5, 146
causality, Modern Greek 241, 242
Causer 256–7, 258, 259, 262, 263–4,
  265–6
Cayuga 85, 196, 244–5
Celtic languages *see* Breton; Irish
CG (categorial grammar) 209–11
child language 55, 88–9, 97, 142–3, 170
clausal coordination 80, 85, 87–8, 160
clitics 98, 99, 184–5
collective reading 198–200
Comitative 253, 254, 260
comitative case 16, 25, 44, 46–8, 244
command, infinitive of 35–6
comparative case 12
complement and functional elements 98–9, 105
complement position 2–3, 50, 112, 113,
  141
complementizer-sharing 39
compounds 72, 86, 263–4
computational system 4, 26, 246, 248,
  250, 251

conditional clauses 39–40, 41–2
Conjunction Phrase *see* CoP
conjunctions:
  agreement, determiners of 76–8, 96
  and case 119–23, 136, 138, 153, 154,
    169
  clitic 98, 99
  closed lexical class 97–8, 105
  and complement 98–9, 105
  dependence, phonological and
    morphological 98, 105
  descriptive contents, lack of 100–2,
    105
  -deviant conjunct order 55, 60
  discontinuous 207–8, 271
  disjunctive 268
  distributional equivalents 81–2, 96,
    100–2
  distributives not conjunctions 149–50
  D-structure projection 102–3, 105
  empty 21, 84–90, 98, 102–3, 107,
    129–30, 152–3
  head-hood 2, 3, 74–107, 167–8, 196;
    functional 2, 74, 96–105;
    pretheoretic criteria 2, 74–96
  initial *see separate entry*
  lexical entries, see under *and*
  morphosyntactic locus 78–9, 96
  Munn's theory and 166
  obligatoriness 82–90, 96, 102, 105
  one for each conjunct 91, 148–50
  origins 4, 88, 196, 244–5
  quasi-operators 95
  projection of features to CoP 93–6,
    105
  and reduction 183, 196, 203
  and semantics 95–6, 196, 239–43,
    244–5; as functors 75–6, 96, 100
  specifier position 103–4, 105
  subcategorization 79–80, 96, 196
  and subordination 4, 239–43, 244
  theta-marking 164, 166
  uniqueness 91–2, 96
  and word order 92–3, 96, 162, 196
  see also "initial conjunctions" *and
    under* multiple coordination
conjuncts, specifier and complement
  positions 2–3, 50, 112, 113, 141
consequence, Greek expression of 241,
  242
coordinate-alpha 1, 3, 4, 175–213, 248,
  270, 271
  input as full CPs 176, 204–11
  lexicon inaccessible to 5, 204

operation 175–7
  see also reduction of input
Coordinate Structure Constraint 3,
  112–13
Coordination Structure Constraint
  see CSC/ATB
CoP 8, 108–74
  alternative approaches 162–9
  asymmetry 238–9, 244, 250
  categories 111–12, 164–6
  conjunction projects features to 93–6
  distribution 93
  and EBC 136–9, 165, 169–70, 271
  input categories as full CPs 204–11
  in minimalist framework 110, 116–19
  in multiple coordination 143–54
  OBC 139–40
  position of conjuncts 108–10
  spec-head agreement 93, 110, 116–19,
    131, 133
  structure 1, 6, 108–13, 270–1
  and UG 140–3
  and X-bar theory 108, 270
  and UC 113–36, 169, 251, 270–1
  see also CoP adverbs; extraction
CoP adverbs 154–62, 165–6, 167, 168,
  170, 271
  in small conjunct coordination 182–3
copular predicate constructions 76–7
correction, over- 123–7, 138, 169
CP structures 85, 97, 176, 204–5
CSC/ATB (Coordination Structure
  Constraint/Across the Board
  exception) 3, 214, 215, 271
  violations 127, 130, 215–18, 218–35
CSR (Canonical Structural Representation) 252
Czech:
  agreement 31, 67, 164
  UC 8–9, 28, 30, 164, 208; CoP
    structure in 118–19, 192–3
  word order 31, 55

D-structure projection 102–3, 105
Danish; pseudocoordination 48, 49, 51
data collection 5–6
dative 9–10, 11–12
default case 121–3
  conjunction as licencer of 120–3
  in EBC 3, 65, 95, 136–8, 170, 270
  multiple coordination 146, 153
  specifier conjunct 143
  in UC 2, 120–3, 143, 164, 169, 270
default direction in branching 144

deletion 3, 178–89, 190–3
  Backward (BWD) 178–9, 181, 186–7, 188, 189
  in clausal coordination 80
  Forward (FWD) 178–9, 186, 219
  in multiple coordination 90
  in small conjunct coordination 180–9
  split coordination as 222–8
  and unlike categories 169, 196, 203
  Van Oirsouw's approach 190–3
  see also empty conjunctions
dependency grammar 74, 105
dependent marker, Turkish 36–7
determiners 64, 79, 101
Direction 253, 254
directionality parameter 110, 190
discontinuous conjunctions 207–8, 271
disjunction 100, 268
  exclusive 69
distributional equivalents 81–2, 96, 100–2
distributive words 149–50, 151–2
  see also individual words
dominance 193, 198
DP coordination 39, 69–70, 84, 85, 180
Dutch:
  distributive 'conjunctions' 149
  extraction of part of conjunct 217–18
  initial particles 161
  multiple coordination 145, 148
  split coordination 221
  UC 10–11, 39–40, 118, 120
  word order 56, 57–9
Dyirbal 86, 98, 102–3

each, every 246, 249
Eastern Mari 213
  UC 11–14, 118, 120, 123; word order and 54, 55, 92–3
EBC (Extraordinary Balanced Coordination) 1, 2, 60–6, 141
  assigning-type 8, 60–1
  and categorial grammar 211
  category-specific assignment 136, 137–8, 170, 271
  child language 142–3, 170
  conjunctions 3, 95–6
  CoP theory accounts for 136–9, 169–70, 270, 271
  CoP sensitive language 136, 137–8, 170, 271
  default 3, 65, 95, 136–8, 139, 170, 270
  Grootveld on 166–7
  OBC more marked than 140–1, 142

overcorrection 125, 126, 137–8
  and phrase-structure theory 208–9
  receiving-type 8, 14–15, 61–6
  and reduction 192, 196, 203
either 151, 154–62
elision 82–3, 107
empty conjunctions 21, 84–90, 98, 102–3, 107, 129–30, 152–3
empty determiner, Italian 64
empty object construction 73
empty operators, Norwegian 134, 135–6
English:
  adpositions/case-marking overlap 43–4
  agreement 76–7
  child language 142
  conjunctions 98, 102; see also individual entries
  CoP adverbs 154–5
  default case 121–2, 123, 136
  distributive 'conjunctions' 149
  EBC 1, 2, 14–15, 61–3, 142, 270
  extraction of part of conjunct 217–18
  gapping 56
  head as morphosyntactic locus 78
  multiple coordination 90, 104, 146
  OBC as marked 141
  overcorrection 120, 123–7, 169
  presentation constructions 146
  pronouns 63, 122
  split coordination 216
  subordination-coordination relationship 242, 243
  that-complementized clauses 120, 204–5, 251–2
  thematics 254–5
  UC 14–16, 55, 63, 270
  word order 55, 56
entailment relations 246, 248–9
essive case, Estonian 16, 44
Estonian 16, 56, 59, 118
  CATE suffixes 16, 44–5, 146
exclamations 122
Experiencer 255, 256, 258, 259, 260, 261, 262, 263, 264
extraction out of CoP 3, 49, 54, 214–36, 271
  CSC-ATB principles and violations 215–18, 218–35
  part of conjunct 54, 217–18, 228–35, 271
  semantic constraints 232–3, 271
  whole conjunct 54, 219–28, 235, 271
Extraordinary Balanced Coordination *see* EBC

Focus Phrases 97, 151
French:
  accusative case unmarked 136
  EBC, receiving-type 63–4
  initial particles 161–2
  multiple coordination 148
  pronouns 63–4, 184–5
  resolution rules 26
  that-complementized clauses 204–5
Fulfulde:
  aspect 129, 146
  serial verbs 86, 128–30, 146, 234
  subordination/coordination relation-
    ship 242
  UC, verbal receiving-type 35, 55, 88,
    128–30
functional categories 97, 162, 220
functional head-hood 2, 74, 96–105
FWD *see* deletion (Forward)

Gã 28–9, 56, 244
gapping 1, 8, 56–7, 166, 177, 178
  and reduction 189, 191, 194–5, 202
gender 25, 26–7, 30, 31–3, 78, 119
Generalized Phrase Structure Grammar 74, 207
generalized transformation 5, 176
  see also coordinate-alpha
German:
  CoP adverbs 155, 158
  extraction of part of conjunct 217–18
  head as morphosyntactic locus 78
  lack of empty operators 134, 135–6
  postpositions 59
  resolution rules 29, 39
  subordination/coordination relation-
    ship 267
  UC: clausal 39, 40–1, 131–6; nomi-
    nal 29, 180–2, 212–13; verbal 38–9,
    130–1
  word order 56, 57–9, 131, 155, 158
Germanic languages; functional
  categories 97
Goal 258
government 114, 115, 116, 118, 119, 193
GPSG 74, 207
Greek, Homeric 35–6, 56, 118
Greek, Modern 47–8, 64, 122, 148, 212,
  241–2
  and initial conjunctions 91, 161–2
Greenlandic, West 42–3
Group projection 249
group readings in multiple coordination
  148–9, 150–1, 152, 153–4

Habitual 129
head 4, 74
  agreement determinant 76–8, 96
  -complement relations 4, 98–9,
    105
  -coordination, BWD and 179
  D-structure projection 102–3, 105
  distributional equivalent 81–2, 96,
    100–2
  empty *see* empty conjunctions
  functional 2, 74, 96–105
  government, Rizzi's theory 115
  -head agreement 141, 148
  morphosyntactic locus 78–9, 96
  obligatoriness 82–90, 96, 102
  projection of features to CoP 93–6
  semantic functor 75–6, 96, 100
  subcategorization 79–80, 96, 196
  uniqueness 91–2, 96
  word order determinant 92–3, 96
  in X-bar theory 4, 5, 74, 92, 96
  see also conjunctions (head-hood)
Head-driven Phrase Structure Grammar
  74
Hebrew 67
  Biblical 19
  Old 18–19, 30, 31, 56, 118
  Samaritan 19
Hierarchical Coordination Principle 260,
  262
Hopi 29–30, 55, 119

Icelandic 122
imperatives, Homeric Greek 35–6
independent words shared syntactically
  by two conjuncts 43–4
inessive case, Eastern Mari 12, 14
infinitives
  of command, Homeric Greek 35–6
  in serial verb construction 37
INFL 138
"initial conjunctions" 154–62, 165–6,
  167, 168, 170, 271
  in small conjunct coordination 182–3
input categories as full CPs 204–11
  categorial grammar 209–11
  phrase-structure theory 206–9
Instrument 253, 254, 258, 259, 260
instrumental case, Sarcee 244
interpretational and computational levels
  separated 246, 248, 250, 251
inversion, subject-verb 155–8, 159
Irish 52–3
  Old 19–20, 52–3, 56, 118, 120, 146

Italian 16–17, 56, 64, 120, 121
iteration of specifiers 103–4

Japanese 56–7, 104, 161, 242
  UC: nominal 17–18, 118; verbal 36
  word order 55, 56–7, 88
juxtaposition 36–7

Kanuri 242
al-Kashgari 87
Kwa languages *see* Gã

Lakhota 217–18
Latin:
  conjunctions 91, 98, 161
  multiple coordination 148
  UC 30, 55, 119
lexicon 4, 5, 251–3
  categories 96–7
  entries 120–1, 140; see also *and*
  heads as closed class 97–8, 105
  projections 103–4
LF (Logical Form) 4, 234
licencing:
  of case, by conjunctions 120–3, 153,
    154, 169
  formal, in deletion theory 178, 179,
    219
likes, coordination of 47, 141, 187–8
Linear Correspondence Axiom 109
linearization 194, 195, 196, 197–8
lists, ordered, in X-bar theory 201–2
Location 258
logical form (LF) 4, 234

Malefactive 258, 263, 264
Manner 253, 254
Mari *see* Eastern Mari
merging 200–1, 251
minimalist program 4–5, 138–9, 178
  CoP in 110, 114, 116–19
Mood 97, 99
morphology:
  dependence 98, 105
  morphemes realized by allomorphs 101
morphosyntactic locus, head as 78–9, 96
movability 47
multiple coordination 6, 8, 143–54
  binary analysis 143–5, 154
  Borsley on 169
  case 146, 153, 154
  CoPs 104, 143–54
  conjunctions 91, 98, 148–50, 154; pho-
    nologically null 90, 98, 107, 152–3

group readings 148–9, 150–1, 152,
  153–4
semantic problems 247, 249–50
spec-head agreement 144–5, 153, 154
see also serial verb constructions

negation 27–8, 97, 99, 158, 159
neither 151, 154–62, 207–8
Nguna 86, 183
nominative case:
  in complement conjuncts 10, 120,
    123–7, 226–7
  by overcorrection 120, 123–7
  unmarked 121, 123, 136
non-constituent coordination 1, 3
  categorial grammar 209–10
  CP component analysis on 204
  Munn's theory 166
  phrase-structure theory 206–7
  and reduction 191, 194
  as repeated binary coordination 271
  transformational theories 211
Non-Shared Constituent Coordination
  203
Norse, Old:
  agreement with nearest conjunct 67
  empty object construction 73
  gender resolution 26–7, 78, 119
  resolution rules 26–7, 30
  split coordination 216–17, 221
  UC, nominal assigning-type 27, 30–1
  word order 31, 56
Norwegian:
  accusative as default case 121
  agreement 77
  avoids conflicts between conjuncts 25
  Bergen dialect 8, 18, 62–3, 65, 136
  child language 142
  compounds, coordination within 72
  conditional clauses 41–2
  conjunctions 79–80, 98, 102, 268
  CoP adverbs 155–7, 159, 182–3
  EBC 65, 142
  elision 83
  empty object construction 73
  empty operators 134, 135–6
  Kristiansand dialect 65
  multiple coordination 90
  Oslo dialect 139–40, 142, 223, 226–7
  peripherality constraint and 192
  presentation constructions 93
  pronouns 94, 136, 185
  pseudocoordination 48, 49–51
  respectively reading 199–200

Norwegian (*cont.*):
split coordination 216, 221–2, 221
Stavanger dialect 18
subject-verb inversion 155–7
subordination/coordination relationship 239–41, 242
thematic constraints on coordination 255–6
Tromsø dialect 18
UC 1–2; clausal 41–2; nominal 18
word order 56
not only . . . but also 158
nouns, verbal 37
number:
semantic resolution 20, 78
UC 9, 12, 20–1, 25, 29–32, 33, 118, 119, 123

OBC (Ordinary Balanced Coordination) 139–40, 140–3, 148, 170
object:
empty 73
that-complemetized clauses 120, 204–5, 254–5
Operation Share 186, 229–30, 231
operators:
Boolean, *and* 245–6
conjunctions as quasi- 95
empty 134, 135–6
operator-variable binding 232
optative 35–6
Ordinary Balanced Coordination *see* OBC
Ottoman 87
overcorrection 123–7, 138, 169

pair-wise association 247, 250
Palestinian Arabic *see under* Arabic
parallelism 157, 193
participles in Japanese UC 36
PC (pseudocoordination) 48–51
peripherality 179, 188, 190–1, 192
phonetic form (PF) 4
phonology:
dependence of functional categories 98, 105
null *see* empty conjunctions
soft mutation, Welsh 24–5, 118, 147
phrasal verbs 82–3
phrase-structure theory 74, 206–9
possessive 's 168
postpositions 12, 44–5, 59
precedence 193, 198
prepositions 14, 82–3, 101

presentation constructions 93, 146
principles and parameters framework 4–5
see also minimalist program
projection 110, 116
conjunctions 93–6
conjuncts 112, 169, 183–5
input to coordinate-alpha 176, 204–11
pronouns:
anaphoric 63
binding 180
emphatic 63–4
English 63, 122
French 63–4, 184–5
left dislocated (focused) 122
Norwegian 94, 136, 185
Spanish 66
Proposition 257, 259, 265–6
pseudocoordination 48–51
pure and impure categories 136, 138, 170

Qafar:
conjunctions 95, 99
default 65, 95, 120, 136
EBC, receiving-type 65–6
resolution rules 20, 32
UC 20, 32, 55, 119
quantifiers, singular 246, 249
questions 121–2, 212

Reduced Phrase Marker (RPM) 193
reduction of input to coordinate-alpha 177–204
merging approach 200–1
sharing approach (Wesche) 201–4
three-dimensional approach (Goodall) 193–200, 202
transformational theories and 211
see also deletion
Relative Prominence Principle 261
relativized minimality approach 114, 115–16
resolution rules, semantic 25–7, 76–7, 78
Arabic 31
German 29, 39
Old Norse 26–7, 30, 78, 119
Qafar 20, 32
respectively 82, 95–6, 198–200
right node raising (RNR) 177, 179, 184–5, 188, 189, 209
ruler concept in dependency theory 105
Russian 56

's, possessive 168
Samoan 21

Sarcee 84, 244
semantics 237–51
  adpositions/case-marking overlap 43
  anaphoric relations 247, 250
  and categorial grammar 210–11
  cognitive 232–3
  and comitative/coordination distinc-
    tion 47–8
  conjunctions and 95–6, 196, 239–43,
    244–5; as semantic functors 75–6,
    96, 100
  and entailment relations 246, 248–9
  and extraction from CoP 218, 232–3,
    271
  and multiple coordination 247, 249–50
  and pair-wise association 247, 250
  and pseudocoordination 49
  and reduction 197
  singularity and plurality 246, 249
  subordination-coordination relation-
    ship 4, 238–43
  see also resolution rules
Semitic languages 34–5
Serbo-Croat 31, 32–3, 56, 67, 119
serial verb constructions 34, 128–30, 146
  Amharic 34, 35
  aspect 129–30
  empty conjunctions 86, 129–30
  extraction of part of construct 234–5
  Fulfulde 35, 128–30, 146, 234
  Sidaamu Afo 37, 146–7
Shared Constituent Coordination
  (SCC) 203
Sidaamu Afo 37, 55, 146–7
singularity and plurality, semantic problems of 246, 249
Sissala 84, 85, 183
SLF-coordination 218
Slovene 33, 56, 119
small conjunct coordination 178, 180–9
smell (of) 260, 264, 266
sociolinguistic influence 123–7
soft mutation, Welsh 24–5, 118, 147
Source 255, 256, 258, 260, 261, 264
Spanish 66, 136
spec-head agreement 3, 143, 168, 271
  in clausal UC 133
  in minimalist interpretation 116–19
  in multiple coordination 144–5, 153,
    154
  in small conjunct coordination 182
  as unification 110–11
  in verbal assigned-type UC 131
  and X-bar theory 4, 5

specifier position 2–3, 50, 93, 112, 113,
    141
  of functional categories 103–4, 105
  iteration 103–4
split coordination 215–17, 222–8
stress 13, 45–6, 98, 162
subcategorizers, conjunctions as 79–80,
    96, 196
subcoordination 48–51
subordinate clauses 159
subordination/coordination relationship 4,
    46–8, 238–43, 244, 250–1
Swahili 33, 55, 119
Swedish 48, 49, 51, 216
symmetry 46
  CoP as asymmetric 238–9, 244, 250
  Kayne's antisymmetry thesis 89, 109,
    183–4
syntax 26–7, 248
  see also computational system

Tajikistan 38
Tamil:
  complement conjunct lacking case 120
  multiple coordination 104, 147
  resolution rules 26
  UC 20, 26, 55, 118
tense-affixes 101
terminative, Estonian 44
that-complementized clauses 120, 204–5,
    251–2
Thematic Coordination Principle 256,
    266
Thematic Prominence Principle 260, 261
thematics 251–66
  constraints on coordination 4, 253–7,
    271
  Dowty's analysis 264–6
  Grimshaw's argument structure 257–66
  and lexicon 251–3
Theme 254, 255, 256, 257, 258, 261,
    262, 263–4, 265–6, 259, 260
Time 253, 254
Tokelauan 20–1, 56
topicalization 122, 215, 216, 223–4,
    227–8
transformation, generalized 5, 176
  see also coordinate-alpha
Turkic languages 21–4
  conjunctions 21, 87, 88, 102–3
  symmetry in word structure 46
  UC 21–4, 118
  word order 55, 88
  see also individual languages

Turkish, Modern 54, 69–70, 120, 123
  conjunctions 36, 87
  UC 23–4, 36–7

UC (Unbalanced Coordination) 1–2,
  7–42
  assigning-type 8–9, 116, 118–19;
    see *also under* nominal *and* verbal
    below
  case 9–20, 21–5, 38–9, 113–27
  in child language 55, 142–3, 170
  choice of name 141
  clausal 39–42, 131–6
  CoP, role of 113–36
  CoP structure theory accounts for 169,
    251, 270–1
  delimiting 42–54
  gender 25, 30, 31–3, 119
  morpho-syntactic, delimiting of 42–51
  multiple *see* multiple coordination
  nominal 9–33, 113–27; assigning-
    type 25–33, 119; receiving-
    type 9–25, 30, 119, 117–18
  nominative case produced by over-
    correction 123–7
  number 9, 12, 20–1, 25, 29–30, 30–2,
    33, 119, 123
  person 9, 25
  receiving-type 8, 118; *see also under*
    nominal *above and* verbal *below*
  semantic-pragmatic, delimiting of 52–4
  theories not accounting for 168, 192–3,
    196, 198, 203
  and UG 54–60
  verbal 34–9, 127–31; assigning-type
    38–9, 130–1; receiving-type 34–8,
    116, 127–30; *see also* serial verb
    constructions
  word order of language correlates with
    direction of unbalancedness 2, 8, 39,
    54–60, 67, 88, 113, 270
UG 4–5, 54–60, 110, 140–3
Uighur, Old 21–3, 86, 87
Unbalanced Coordination *see* UC
unification 110–11, 200
Universal Grammar 4–5, 54–60, 110,
  140–3
unlike category coordination 1, 3, 111–12
  and categorial grammar 210
  CP component analysis 204–5

merging and deletion analysis 169
Munn's theory does not explain 166
phrase-structure theory 207
and reduction 169, 196, 203
transformational theories 211
unmarked case 121, 136–8, 270

variation, parametric 140–3
Vedic 24, 56, 59, 118
verbal adjectives 20–1
verbal nouns 37
verbs:
  assigning different case to shared
    complement 38–9
  comitative, origin of conjunction 244
  incorporation of conjunct into 42–3
  phrasal 82–3
  topicalization 223–4, 227–8
  see also aspect; serial verb construc-
    tions
vowel reduction, Eastern Mari 12–13
VPs 84, 85, 86, 223–4

Welsh 24–5, 37, 56, 147
  soft mutation 24–5, 118, 147
West Greenlandic 42–3
wh-phrases 135
word-internal coordination 72
word order:
  affects agreement 31
  conjunctions and 92–3, 96, 162, 196
  direction of unbalancedness correlates
    with 2, 8, 54–60, 67, 88, 92–3, 113,
    131, 270
  initial particles affect 155–8, 159, 162
  and lexical/functional distinction 97
  mixed 131, 133–4, 270
  and UC 39–41, 54–60

X-bar theory 2–3, 4, 5, 92, 201–2, 271
  CoP and 108, 270
  heads and 4, 5, 74, 92, 96
  specifier and complement posi-
    tions 2–3, 141
Xhosa 25

Yagnobi 38, 55, 127–8

zeugma 53–4
Zulu 25